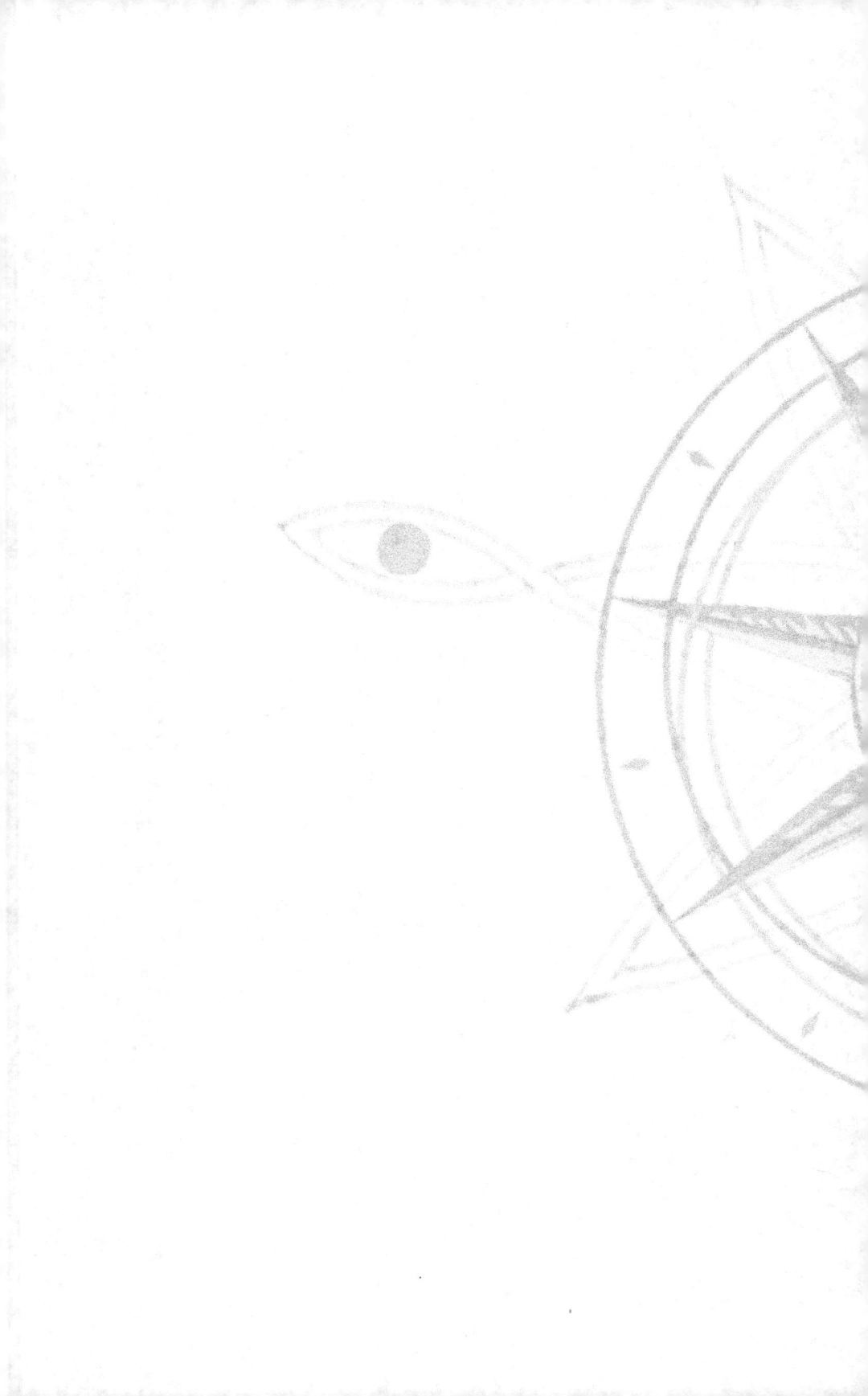

You know.®

How to Invite & Nourish a Relationship with Your Intuition

Jennifer L. Halls

Edited by: Michael Gordon
Copy edited by: Kathleen Miritello
Author photo taken by: Amy Hart, https://amyhartstudios.com
Book design, cover design and layout by: Elsa Safir,
https://www.elsasafirdesign.com

Author's Note

For the ease of reading this book, I have chosen to make the font larger than the customary typeface. Also, there are about 40 blank pages to give the book some space. So the book looks about 100 pages longer than it really is. Please don't be intimidated by its hefty length.

Everything written in this book is true and told as authentically as possible. The stories come from transcripts of recorded sessions with clients, meticulous notetaking, conversations with clients about their experiences, while some are strictly from my own remembrance and perspective.

I've changed most of the clients' names, as well as many identifying details, characteristics, times and places for privacy. To facilitate an efficient telling of the stories, some examples have been compressed, compiled and/or altered slightly.

The teachers and friends whose real names are used have given permission for me to use their full name.

Publishings

Reviews

In an age in which we are overwhelmed with choices and decisions, *You know.*® reminds us that our body has the answers we need. Using practical examples from her years of experience guiding people to listen to their own intuitive wisdom, Jennifer shows how the responses we feel can help us make decisions that lead to a fuller and more authentic life. She has done a beautiful job of making the book read easily and shows how a relationship with intuition is accessible to everyone. Even if you use only one of the many practices—one of my favorites being "Stand In the And"—your ability to access the guidance of your inner intuition will expand, and you will find yourself less overwhelmed and more able to hear the voice of your Soul.

-**Catherine Anderson**, author of *Meeting Your Soul on the Labyrinth*
CreativePilgrimage.com

~

Reading Jennifer's words is like watching intuitive connections happen in real time. If you have ever wondered what intuition is, how it works, and how it can help you in your life, you have only to open this book, pick a page, and start reading.

-**Jenni Field**, pastry chef, writer, instructor & founder of
PastryChefOnline.com

~

This book has opened me up in a completely new way. I have always called on spirit, but truly inviting spirit in has unlocked a part of my heart that needed deeper connection with my intuition. This book is more than just a guide. It is a true invitation to ground yourself in your own wisdom, to trust your knowing within and to deepen your relationship with the intuition that has always been there.

-**Susan Hough**, author of *Walking With Sobonfu: A Guide to Claiming Your Authenticity and Deepening Your Sense of Community*,
LivingYourGifts.com

~

Reading *You know.®* felt like sinking into a warm bubble bath for the soul—comforting, immersive and something I never wanted to end. Each chapter is filled with heartfelt stories that sparked memories of times my intuition was guiding me, even when I didn't realize it, and then offered a path to strengthen that connection to my own inner wisdom.

I especially loved the clues she provides for recognizing when we're disconnected from intuition—feelings of dread, obligation, or resistance—and how to use them as guideposts back to the wisest part of ourselves. And just when I thought the chapters couldn't offer more, each one ends with an Invitation—a poetic, prayer-like reflection that gently integrates each story's wisdom into everyday life.

This book has profoundly impacted me, rekindling and deepening my trust in my own inner knowing. Now that I've finished, I'm going to read it all over again. Some books aren't just meant to be read; they're meant to be lifelong companions, guiding us back to what we have always known to be true.
-**Catherine Rains**, artist, worldwide mixed media instructor & creator of **Collage Joy**, CatherinesRains.com

~

Reading Jennifer's vivid and captivating stories about her every day and profound encounters with her intuition, I came to realize that I actually can tune into my own intuitive signals. Have a highlighter ready because you'll find yourself pausing often over beautifully rendered insights and scenes. And the invitations at the end of each easily-accessible chapter, especially the one on how making art connects us to our Soul, give us a step-by-step guide for understanding and developing our inner wisdom.
-**Patrick Scott**, international travel writer & former editor with *The New York Times*

What People Say About Jennifer

"Jennifer Halls is a midwife for the Soul."
— **Sobonfu Somé**

"In one hour Jennifer helped our firm more than the two years we spent with a team of consultants that cost over ten grand."
— **Joe T.,** attorney/partner, **Raleigh, NC**

"She's the 'Mary Poppins' of Intuitive Consultants. Jennifer's magical, but she makes you work to learn it for yourself."
— **T. H.,** attorney, **Washington, DC**

"YOU'RE THE BEST!!! I love your strong, powerful spot-on advice! Just what I was needing... Wowza!"
— **M.V.,** business owner, **Sydney, Australia**

"...no matter what I say it will never do you or your work justice. You have helped me more than many business consultants I have hired with difficult business situations, as well as in generating creative ideas. Your questions are insightful and your guidance practical and useful. Working with you is a true collaboration at many levels."
— **M.W.,** foundation president, **NYC, NY**

"Jennifer you are an alchemist of the Spirit—a courageous teacher—a sculptor of invisible things..."
— **K. L.,** author, poet, **Charlotte, NC**

"Jennifer's ability to help (me) access parts of my own personal wisdom, has been an invaluable part of my decision making process. Piles of self-help books and hours of meditation cannot compare to the quality and amount of specific, personal, practical, and highly useful information gleaned from a session with Jennifer Halls."
— **E.H.,** university student, **Durham, NC**

Dedication

To my Mom, who got excited a few days before any of us knew big changes were about to happen in our lives. "I'm so excited!" *Why mom?* "I don't know, I just know something good is about to happen." She made intuition normal because she was always right. Mom, I miss you more than I can ever express with words.

To my Dad, for calling to ask if this book was finished, once a week (and more), for many, many years.

And to my husband, Michael, for always believing in me. I love you. XO

CONTENTS

PART 1
How I Learned to Embrace My Intuition

PART 2
Intuition Building Blocks

PART 3
How to Navigate Intuitive Blocks

PART 4
Connecting With Guidance

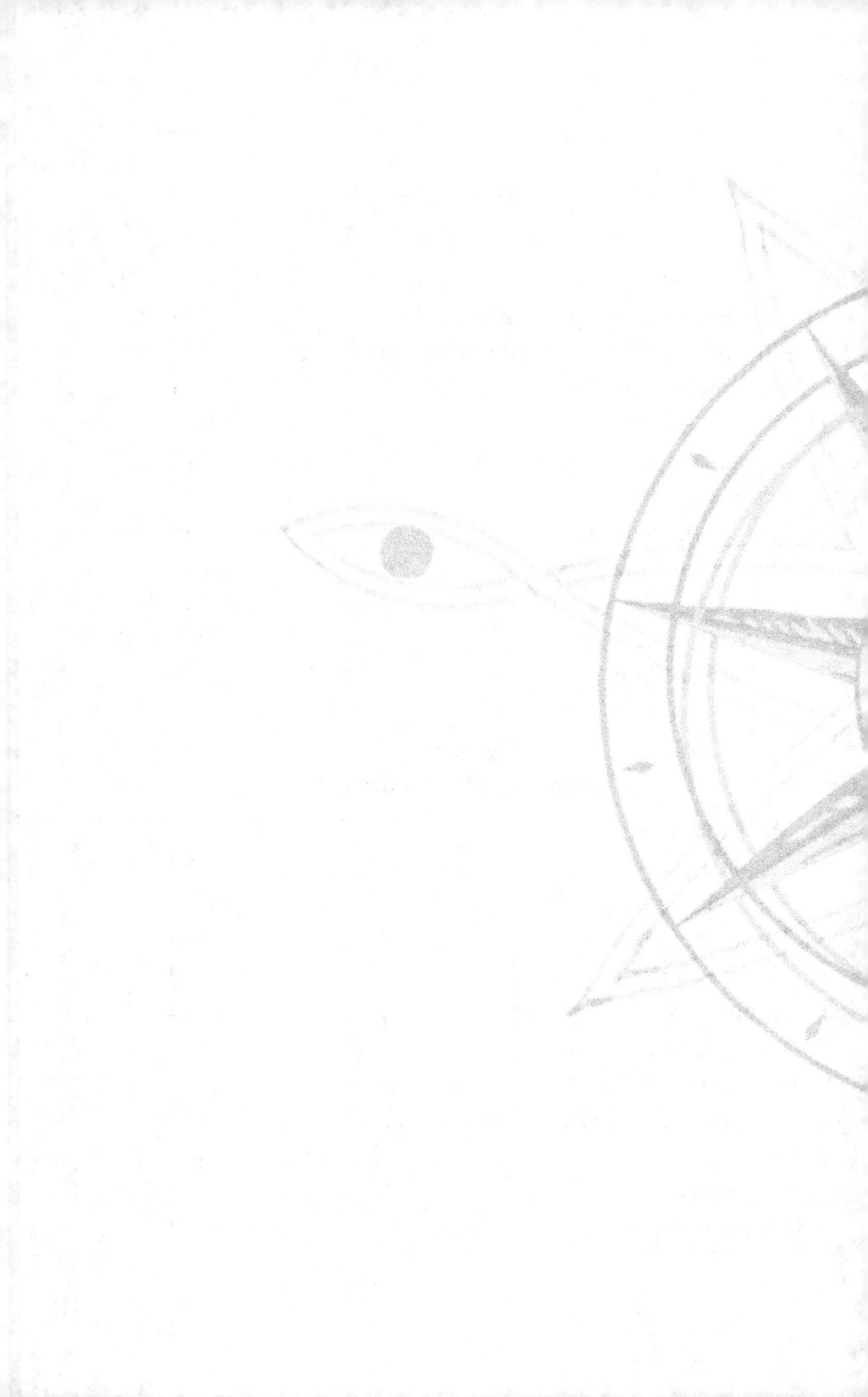

You know.®

How to Invite & Nourish a Relationship with Your Intuition

Foreword
(From a Skeptic)

When Jennifer Halls asked me to read her new book, I hesitated.

I had no knowledge of the world of intuition or the career of an intuition consultant. She said she thought I'd used intuition my whole life. Still, I had little interest. The topic seemed too foreign for my taste, and I was skeptical I could contribute anything.

But as I came to see, Jennifer chose me precisely for that skepticism, which is grounded in my long career as a newspaper journalist, including stints as a foreign correspondent, investigative reporter, feature writer and editor.

Out of respect for Jennifer, I eventually changed my mind. I'm glad I did.

As I worked my way through the book, I surprisingly found myself relating to a number of the concepts which Jennifer details in a concise and interesting manner. (She's an exceptional storyteller.) Significantly, I began to recount all the times in my life I subconsciously used instinct and intuition in critical, life-or-death situations.

For instance, on several occasions I was detained by armed militias in Lebanon during the country's 15-year civil war. Each time I managed to talk my way out of seemingly impossible—and potentially deadly—situations. This pattern continued during long overland trips reporting across obscure borders in Africa, Central America and Asia. Time and again, I had to make quick decisions that, if wrong, could have had disastrous results: Offer a bribe or not? Take this road or that one?

It's clear that I was using both instinct and intuition every time. As Jennifer writes, "Intuition can't be taught. It can be navigated, developed, understood and invited."

It was only by reading this book that I understood exactly what she meant. I had been following this path my entire life, but I had no idea I was doing so.

Inexplicable to me was the burst of creative energy I experienced as I read each chapter. Over a short period, I knocked out several satirical pieces, the concepts popping into my head from I'm not sure where, and completed a number of articles and photo stories for my overseas travel website, TheRoadBoomer.com.

Another reason I loved this book is because it's an honest and in-depth account of Jennifer's life journey. She invited me into her world and said: Here it is. All of it. The good and the bad.

Jennifer's vivid and descriptive prose elevates the content as do the stories of her many friends and clients I met throughout the pages.

In my mind, the combination of all those elements makes for a powerful narrative. Whether you're an outlier like me or an intuition insider, you're in for a treat.

George J. Tanber
January 2025

Foreword

(From an Intuitive)

As a Meyers Briggs INFP, I've always thought of myself as "intuitive," in a general, largely unconscious way (meaning, I haven't usually thought much about it). But Jennifer Halls' book reminds me that intuition is so much more than a personality subtype; it's a birthright. The remarkable stories and expert guidance Jennifer shares in these pages have renewed my relationship to intuition and stirred memories of its foundation in my life, including a particularly memorable happening during my early adolescence.

The bus for Jefferson Junior High stopped for me on school days around 7:35 am at the corner just across the street from the little house where I lived with my mother and younger sisters. I was the only junior high student on our street, so unless the grade-schoolers came to the stop early to play hopscotch and clap out their Miss Mary Mac-Mac-Macs, I waited alone.

One morning, a strange car pulled up to the stop sign where I stood by myself holding my books and brown-paper, lunch sack. The driver, a man I didn't know, got out, took off his jacket, and walked around the back of the car towards the curb.

Forty-eight years later, I have only the vaguest visual image of him. I remember that he didn't speak, and I know that somehow I knew I was in danger. My body knew. And it flew— at least, that's how it felt—over the car, across the street, and back through our front door.

My mother, who was already late for work, dismissed my fear. He probably just wanted to ask directions. You're being silly, she told me. By then, the car had disappeared. Like the good girl I was, I hustled back across the street to meet the arriving bus. I was safe. I made it to school on time. Nothing bad had happened, and I never saw the car or the man again.

Maybe my mother had been right. Maybe the guy had just needed driving directions. Maybe he was going to check a passenger-side tire. I was just a kid. Maybe I misread the situation.

So why does this non-event stick in my memory like a wad of gum on the bottom of a shoe?

Maybe it stays—not as a reminder that the world can be unsafe, not as an example of childish, overactive imagination—but because it's the clearest, earliest evidence I have that some part of me has access to awareness and insight that other parts of me overlook, dismiss, or deny. Maybe it stays because, on that day, I trusted my knowing. Maybe it also stays because on that day, my mother taught me to question my knowing. To doubt it. To tell myself, as I have done far too often in the nearly half-century since, You're being silly.

At 12, I didn't know to call this sixth sense "intuition." I didn't even know it was a thing. It was simply a part of me, as sure as my left big toe, my tongue, my love for turning cartwheels on the beach. Sometimes, like at the bus stop, it came as a warning. But, more often, it pulled me towards the people and things I loved—a book on the library shelf, my grandmother's lap, the arms of our giant Magnolia.

Intuition was (and still is) an embodied force. Indeed, the sudden desire to cartwheel across the yard was intuitive— an answer to my body's call for reconnection, grounding, or a fresh perspective. As a child, I answered these calls with little if any thought. As I "matured," however, I learned to delay my responses, to question their importance, to prioritize rational thought. I transferred my inner authority to those who "knew better."

You might say I had abandoned my most faithful companion. Not always. Not completely. Mostly, I honored her role in my life the same way I honored my best childhood friend: I thought of her fondly, but rarely called her to catch up.

Nevertheless, intuition never abandoned me.

Intuition has never been more than a whisper away, and connecting with it is as simple as leaning a little closer to listen. Of course, simple doesn't mean easy. As in any relationship, developing a real connection with intuition requires attention and practice, a willingness to listen actively and read between lines.

I credit this remarkable book not only for reminding me of this most important relationship, one I have too often taken for granted, but also for showing me how to practice being in that relationship. Or, as Jennifer Halls would say, showing me how to "invite" it.

Reading You know. is a spring afternoon front-porch visit with your wisest friend. In these pages, Halls invites you to sit and, before you know it, you're breathing deeper. She pours you a glass of lemonade, and you realize you're thirsty. She tells stories, and they resound in you, stirring long-buried memories and inklings to the surface.

Over and over, she invites you to simply be curious, to listen with your body, to let go of expectation. There's no "woo-woo" here. Halls' advice is nothing but practical. But gradually, as you accept her invitations, magic happens. Your senses grow sharper. The daily battle becomes less daily, less battle.

You find that maybe you do know, after all.

Kathie Collins
Co-Founder & Creative Director of the Charlotte Center for Literary Arts.
January 2025

Opening

I ntuition can't be taught. It is already a part of you. It can be navigated, developed, understood and invited.

Intuitive living is circular, enlivening, messy, and fun. Intuitive living pokes our curiosity and prods exploration. Intuitive living is easiest with a playful attitude. Intuitive living is wide, Soul-infused and we can all live it.

As you read, you will understand how you've already been following your intuition—consciously and unconsciously—your entire life. You will identify many ways your intuitive voices speak. You will release blocks to your intuitive wisdom.

I don't include lists of exercises because they often engage a habitual intellectual mindset. You will be able to extract some practices from the stories I've shared, but you don't have to. It may be hard to believe, but reading these stories is enough to connect to your intuition.

Stories enter our consciousness in ways that inspire our intuition to surface. These stories of clients, friends, and from my own life are curated from more than 25,000 Intuition Consulting sessions over the past 30 years. They show that everyone's intuitive connection engages a bit differently.

These stories also show real-life intuition. Intuition is not absolute—it helps in many situations but doesn't give us omnipotence.

There is no right way to connect to your intuition. Try what resonates. Have fun. While reading these pages, try different approaches and compare how you feel inside. Every story is an example of different avenues and perspectives. You may recognize your own story inside some of them.

Intuition cannot control everything in life. It is not an all-powerful, magic wand that delivers instant happiness. Sometimes the Soul wants to learn what our personality doesn't have any interest in. Maybe it seems impractical and/or will take too long to accomplish. As a matter of fact, writing this book was a 20-year intuitive journey that for 17 years I did not want to be on.

Soon after I turned 40, my friend and mentor Sobonfu Somé said, in a tone that conveyed impatience, "When are you writing your book?"

I was stunned. "What book? What are you talking about? I hate to write."

"You know what book I'm talking about and you need to write it."

That was all she would say. I asked her to elaborate many times. She'd just looked at me with disgust like I was pretending not to understand.

She was right in a way. I was pretending I didn't feel the book as a truth in my body. When Sobonfu said "you need to write it," her words smacked my core and resonated "yes." Her statement was the key that unlocked another door to my intuition, one that wouldn't close.

However, I was honestly confused. What was I going to write about? I lacked skill and interest. The very idea of writing a book was ludicrous. My annoyance tried to shut down that intuitive hit. I told myself she was wrong. I didn't have to listen. Yet something stirred in me that I couldn't ignore.

A few years later I was fooled into writing, *The Runes Workshop: A You know.*® *Intuition Workbook.* How was I tricked?

I was scheduled to teach a four-day workshop on how to make and use Runes for divination. I realized there wasn't a book that I could recommend that gave the range of definitions I'd discovered from using Runes since I was 19.

I spent eight hours every day for two weeks and put together a comprehensive reference book. I printed one for each participant. I left room on each page so they could track the experiences they had with the Runes. I also included information that I wouldn't have time to teach in the four-day retreat. Everyone in the class shared how grateful they were to have information to take home and continue to explore.

My friend Joanne, who was at the workshop, said, "You know this is a book, right?"

I tried to blow her off. "Nooo, it's not a real book. It's just a workbook."

"No," she said. "It's a real book and with a few tweaks you can publish it. I'll help."

Joanne did help. I published it and proudly gave my Runes book to Sobonfu, saying, "Here's my book!"

She smiled. "I like this book." Then in a singsong voice that was too sweet she added, "You know this is not the book I'm talking about."

I was pissed.

I knew I was angry because deep down I could feel she was right. I still had no idea how to write a real book or even what it would be about. I stewed for a year or three as my intuition continued to poke me relentlessly to write the book. Unable to ditch Sobonfu's intuitive bossiness, I finally asked Joanne to help.

She did. We spent a couple of years writing a book on intuition together. It was a good first draft, but it didn't feel right. We stopped, reassessed and decided to abandon our effort. I told her that I was going to try to write the book on my own. I didn't mean it, not really. I just wanted to drop the book idea. Or thought I did.

Sobonfu passed away in 2017. Even though I was devastated, the semi-constant intuitive nagging would not let me be. I wouldn't put it past Sobonfu to join with my Soul to badger me.

A few years before, I'd shared something about myself—I

don't remember exactly what—that made Sobonfu unhappy. She stopped, looked at me, and in a tone that came directly from her heart gently said, "Don't you understand? You are a midwife for the Soul."

I'd never thought of myself that way. It felt lofty and arrogant. Trying to hide my discomfort I jokingly said, "Can I quote you and put that on the book cover?"

"Put it on your book, your website, wherever you want. It's true." She was serious. As I started to understand and accept the title she named for me, I did put it on the website and now on the book to honor her.

In late 2017, I started to take writing classes. None gave me the training I needed until I found Charlotte Lit (Charlotte Center for Literary Arts in North Carolina) in 2018. I took one class there and then applied to be in a yearlong writing program. I was accepted to the 2019 Authors Lab, which changed everything.

Although I still did not enjoy writing, I was finally working on the book. When the year ended, I was a long way from being finished. I had an intuitive impulse to ask to join a writing group other students had started. Not only would my intuition not let me stop writing, these women wouldn't either. All of these talented, serious writers encouraged me, held me to deadlines, and gave feedback that helped me learn to write. It took three years before I started to enjoy writing—six to finally publish.

My intuition prodded me for the entire two decades. Because I actively invited my intuition to join me every day for work, I could not ignore the intuitive push about writing. Let me be clear. My intuition didn't make me do anything. It just wouldn't shut up. I wanted that intuitive voice to stop, so I gave in and wrote the book. I don't regret a moment of it.

Acting on intuition helped me discover that I was creating the book I wished I'd found when I started to explore intuition three decades ago. There were plenty of books with exercises, theories and seemingly easy ways to cultivate intuition. Those books, perhaps helpful to some, were not useful to me. I wanted to understand someone's real process. Maybe others are looking for the same thing today.

In my early 20s, I thought the purpose of intuition was to get the answer so I could fix the problem. I wanted to know beforehand what was going to happen. I wanted to control my destiny. Reasonable, right? Why bother cultivating intuition otherwise?

Intuition, thank heavens, gives me more than an answer. It gives me epiphanies, well-rounded perspectives and a felt direction to advance one step at a time. Intuition reveals options. Intuition is my Soul guiding me in so many surprising ways.

My mind thinks, I know the answer or I want the answer. Intuition, however, brings truth that resonates throughout my physical body and consistently refocuses my life in new ways, perspectives and possibilities. Writing is an example. It was something I never wanted to do, but it gave me a different understanding of myself and my work that I would have never had without intuition pushing.

I'm grateful I continued to listen.

I've said many times, "Intuition isn't our 6th sense, it's our Essence." I've heard intuition described as "a still small voice," so I understand why it's been diminished to a 6th sense—that's how people experience it.

However, intuition is infinite and eternal.

I am fully aware that people and systems like to separate, define and give hierarchical order to all of the things I'm about to name. I use all of these words to mean intuition: Divine, Soul, Spirit, Source, Higher Power, Love, Guidance, Collective Unconscious, God, and more. Intuition is the greater part of us that comes through to guide us. Intuition is a succinct way to describe where our intuitive self comes from and is compatible with most spiritual beliefs.

While reading this book I invite you to identify and substitute your source of wisdom—a benign power bigger than you—with wording that aligns with your beliefs. For example, if you believe that God is the source of your intuition, substitute God for whatever word I use to convey that larger power. Intuition is integrated communication with ourself and the outside world. It is not simply following our heart or gut. Intuition is the connection of our many parts that communicates a wider perspective in a variety of ways.

There are many different intuitive approaches that the stories in this book reveal. Everyone's intuition is unique in the way it communicates. You may relate to some and not others in each section. That's why I've divided the book into four parts.

Part 1, How I Learned to Embrace My Intuition, includes my personal stories. I share them in the hope that they might ignite intuitive echoes in your own life. These experiences— some from innocence, some from stupidity, some from pain, some from impatience, and a few of them embarrassing—all show I am just a normal person who has learned to invite and enjoy a relationship with intuition.

Some of the stories might seem magical. I promise it is only in the telling that I saw the magic. In the moment I felt nothing special happening. My guess is we all have stories where magic is revealed.

True stories about intuition, heard or read, automatically open our intuitive abilities. These stories are told as honestly as possible. They reflect the missteps and obstacles we unintentionally create to block our intuitive path.

Part 2, Intuition Building Blocks, includes stories that build upon each other when read in order. Each offers concrete ways to open a space of internal alignment where intuition thrives.

We are always opening space for our Soul-self to communicate. The variety of stories shared offers many different time-saving perspectives, not exercises, that my clients used to incorporate intuition into their lives in their own ways. Many of the stories show how to integrate and nurture an intuitive environment without sacrificing time.

These chapters show there is no one way intuition operates. Have fun. Explore different approaches while reading and compare how you feel inside. Every story is an example of different avenues and perspectives. You may recognize some. Others take less than a minute to try on.

Again, everything I've written in this book is true and told as honestly as possible. The stories come from transcripts of recorded sessions with clients, meticulous notetaking, and conversations with clients about their experiences. Others come from my own memories and perspective.

For reasons of privacy, I've changed most of the clients' names, as well as many identifying details, characteristics, times, and places. To facilitate an efficient telling of the stories, some examples have been compressed, compiled and/or altered slightly.

The teachers and friends whose real names are used have given me permission to do so.

The experiences, both my own and those of my clients, are meant to help highlight similar intuitive experiences in your own life. Some stories might illuminate situations or states of awareness that were unrecognized as intuition at the time. Pinpointing intuition in your own memories is a solid place to begin to understand your intuitive relationship.

Part 3, How to Navigate Intuitive Blocks, will help you discover your unique way of creating space for your deep knowing to surface. The whole book is about this topic, but these stories specifically show how those involved overcame blocks. You will find yourself learning to compare and contrast the way your body feels when intuition communicates.

Understand: Intuition can be blocked, but it never goes

away.

Pretend to trust what you're doing. You don't have to believe in what you try to compare the results of sensation. Opening the senses takes time. The more you let yourself notice and trust the subtle awarenesses inside, the more intuitive reception is built and wired into us.

There are accounts in some chapters that include challenging emotional states—especially the chapters Stand In the And, Change the Station and Paradox of Help. If the examples in these chapters or others elicit a traumatic response, consider seeking therapeutic assistance, especially for clinical depression, constant overwhelm, abuse, or chronic anxiety.

Part 4, Connecting With Guidance, gives you felt ways to connect directly to your spiritual guides. These chapters include beautiful stories my clients have shared about connecting with their guidance. I want to make clear that guides are not completely outside of us. The part of us that is Spirit is a part of all Spirit. Guidance is both inside and outside of us all at once.

At the close of every chapter, you will find an invitation that relates to the examples within the stories you just read. Invitations are one of the most effective and easiest ways to develop a relationship with intuition. I invite you to bring your awareness to them. They are to receive, not just to do.

With that in mind, each invitation is for you to accept, decline or read later. Consider reading these at a slower pace. It is easier to notice subtle sensory shifts by slowing down a bit. You may want to read them out loud. This will help you go slower and involve your hearing sense. Maybe read them more than once. Perhaps take a breath and close your eyes between each line.

Check your feelings as you go. Your mind might think that nothing is happening. That's perfect. You aren't involving your intellect. You are inviting discovery for your own intuitive workings through subtle, physical sensations.

Some find it easier to listen to invitations. If this is you, try recording them; almost every phone has a recorder application. Allowing your own voice to invite a connection with your intuition is powerful. Closing your eyes and listening to your own voice or that of a loved one can take you deeper into sensation. These invitations are designed to liberate the mind from expectation, judgment and conclusions. Your experience may be slightly or vastly different each time you read or listen.

Give yourself 10 seconds before you read the invitation to notice how you feel. Take 20 seconds afterward to sit and notice any subtle changes in your body. Resist judgment or analysis. Experience your experience—this is the fertile ground for intuition to grow.

At some point, describe what you sensed—either out loud to yourself or written in a journal. Be neutral. It might seem inconsequential to say, my tailbone relaxed, my brow softened or I feel heavier or more solid in my belly. Yet, naming an experience out loud over the long term has lasting results that are initially hidden.

The byproducts of noticing the subtle, sensory information each chapter invites you to experience are solid connections for your intuition to communicate. Your mind and body will automatically become more flexible to opening intuitively by reading stories and participating in the invitations. There is nothing to do other than read and breathe.

By sharing stories—mine and others—I hope to clear up misconceptions about intuition. My vocation evolved messily from a blend of studies and interests—visual arts, divination, energy healing, and a desire for a tangible connection to the Divine. Serious health issues were also a major catalyst. All of these combined in ways I never could have imagined. A relationship with my intuition has given me a life with meaning and purpose.

I am a very private, introverted person. I have chosen to be this open, especially with my personal stories, because the

Soul learns from unvarnished truth.

Sobonfu opened a door to my intuition that I could not open myself. My earnest wish is that something I share in these pages will permanently unlock many doors to the Soul communications waiting for you.

Have fun!

Jennifer and Sobonfu November 11, 2011

Photo by Jean Hollister

Part 1
How I Learned to Embrace My Intuition

1
Blind Calling

" **I** was *called* to it."

This is the most succinct response I have when my clients, who include—CEOs, lawyers, doctors, clergy, law enforcement officers—ask me how I became an intuition consultant.

But *called?* It's the truth. The trouble is the word *called* leads to misunderstandings and can sound a bit delusional. In fact, several people have interpreted my explanation as egotistical, implying I'm special, as if I'm saying God called me one day and said, "Get to work helping people with their intuition. Pronto."

But it's not like that at all.

Everything was going well. By age 24, I'd worked six months part-time as an assistant to the curator of art in a small museum known for its permanent display of the largest mounted collection of hooved African animals in the world. It also housed a planetarium and several art galleries with ever-changing exhibits. I was happy. I had just been promoted to a fulltime position, proving to my dad I could get a good job with an art degree. When I was a junior in high school, talking about going to college, my father told me to learn to type.

"You'll never be able to support yourself with art," he said. "You'll need to get a job as a secretary so you can find a man to pay the bills."

This, of course, made me furious, and it was the best thing he could have said. It gave me the drive I needed to obtain a career in the arts. I admit, proving him wrong felt good, too.

Fulltime employment included health insurance, which meant I could make appointments for long overdue medical checkups. I'd been feeling the need to go to the eye doctor for months. I wasn't having trouble with my vision, but I felt a recurring inner nudge that my eyes needed to be checked. The eye doctor I found had an immediate opening and although my routine exam was fine, he referred me to an ophthalmologist.

"There might be something going on here," the doctor told me. "I'm sending you to a specialist. He's The Best."

The optometrist's words were vague and noncommittal, but I wasn't concerned about anything being seriously wrong because it took two months to get an appointment. Once there, I relaxed in "The Best's" waiting room, eyes closed, as drops dilated my pupils.

To put my time to good use, I reviewed the placement of the paintings and prints I'd leaned against the gallery walls the day before. I've always had the ability to recreate the layout of rooms in my mind. I felt my eyes flow and land lightly around the gallery, imagining the blending of colors and themes on the walls of the exhibit. Following my eye exam, I planned to return to the museum to double-check my decisions before my boss's inspection.

Finally, my name was called, and I was led back to a darkened room with a single desk lamp turned on low. I sat in the dove gray leather chair and closed my eyes again. The nurse kindly reclined it for me as the doctor entered.

He appeared laid back and friendly. "I'm going to poke around a bit. Just relax and do what I ask, please."

With quick facile moves he strapped a small black tube the width of a fifty-cent piece perfectly centered on his brow. He then pulled what looked like a tiny telescope—actually called a fundus lens—out of a wooden box and held it to meet his left lashes. He leaned his face uncomfortably close to mine and flipped a tiny switch on the side of his forehead tube. An excruciatingly bright light burned into my right eye, blinding me to what his right hand was grabbing off the table.

I only got a brief glimpse of the flat metal instrument about the length and width of a wooden coffee stirrer, before he inserted the tip over my lid, deep into the top of my eye socket. The discomfort was so intense I felt like I was going to vomit.

"Look up. Good. Look up and to the right. Stay there. Good. Now look to the far right…"

Tears streamed freely all the way down my neck as he continued probing the circumference of each eye while giving seemingly endless instructions. Several times when he lifted the probing metal device to change positions, I squeezed my eyes shut, and turned my face away, forcing a ten-second break.

I knew this foreign exploration was a necessary intrusion. Still, my whole body felt vulnerable, exhausted, and the *back* of my eyeballs ached. It was all I could do to stay seated and follow directions until the exam was complete.

Finally, the doctor went over and sat at a black laminate wall desk. I heard the soft close of a box and the brisk scribble of his pen writing notes. I kept both eyes closed in relief. I heard the squeak of his rolling chair as he stood to step to my side again. My eyes half opened and looked at him with watery focus as he said, "I'm clearing my schedule this afternoon to do surgery on you. The retina in your right eye has torn to its limit and could completely detach at any moment."

He didn't offer surgery as an option. His warmth faded as he became detached and clinical. There would be no arguing. This was a command. He told me I was beyond lucky to see him when I did. I had a rare disease called *pars planitis*. Because it didn't show outward symptoms, I would have to see him regularly from now on.

"If left unchecked," he said, "you could go blind."

Blind?

As what he said sunk in, it instantly adrenalized me out of my physical discomfort to a frightening reality. My mind began to rapid-fire all the things I'd lose. Art. Work. Independence. Everything.

Then, just as quickly as the panic began, an inexplicable calm wrapped over my brain and flowed down my spine. My thoughts slowed and refocused on why I was there. For months, without any symptoms, I couldn't shake an inner nagging that I *had* to see an eye doctor. How did I know? I had no answer. All I knew was that if I had ignored that impulse, I'd have gone blind.

Seven years and two retinal surgeries later, I'm 31 years old I can still see. The exams were still very unpleasant, at times painful, even after more than twenty visits. My attempts at distracting myself when the eye-cavity poking took place were still unsuccessful, but I didn't jerk my head away as much. I was trying to relax my shoulders while my doctor checked to see if the current *activation* (the term he used for inflammation) in my eyes had diminished. Unfortunately, it had not. It was in both eyes full force. This hadn't happened before.

He frowned and cleared his throat. "The last four months we've tried medicated drops and a healthy dose of prednisone."

When he tried to project the severity of the situation, he used the clipped, no nonsense doctor's tone he was using now.

"What I can do is increase the prednisone to the maximum dosage. If the inflammation doesn't recede soon, you'll have to prepare for the worst. It's probable you will go completely blind. See you in a couple of weeks."

I was now an assistant curator of art. My whole career was visual. At any age, but especially at 31, I didn't expect to get this devastating news. I didn't know if my landscape would be dark in three months. The intuition that had led me to get my eyes checked so many years ago seemed to be silent about the future. My chest felt like punctured bagpipes. Heavy. No air.

No sound. What was I going to do?

Let me back up a bit.

Around the time I had my first eye surgery at 24, my friend Phyllis from the museum invited me to a guided meditation led by a woman named Elena. I was skeptical. How could you meditate if someone was talking at you? Wasn't meditation supposed to be quiet? Somehow Phyllis cajoled me into going.

I never would have gone if I'd realized it was forty-five minutes away. Agitated, I didn't think I'd be able to relax, let alone meditate. I took an open seat in the circle of 15 women and put on a good face while waiting for Elena.

It turned out Elena was already there. I was looking for a flowing skirted ex-hippie type, but she looked like a middle-aged Girl Scout leader, conservative from her short, light-brown hair and khaki pants to her sensible walking shoes.

She introduced herself, saying that her spirit guide would be leading our meditation. She would just be voicing what he said for us to do. We would have an experience and then share what happened to us with the group. While my face tried to remain pleasant, all I could think was, "I just wasted ten dollars on nonsense."

I couldn't leave so I followed directions. "Call on your spirit guides to join you and take a deep breath…"

"Now come back to the room still feeling what you experienced," Elena said.

What happened? The clock revealed that an hour had passed. I must have fallen asleep. Everyone shared some extraordinary things. All I shared was a question. "I came here tonight very stressed. How's it possible to be so worked up and instantly fall asleep?"

"It's the energy," Elena told me.

With no idea what she was talking about, I later told Phyllis that I was not going to spend money to go to sleep again.

Yet strangely, I was drawn to attend every month.

After a few months, I began staying awake and had experiences that validated some mystical things that happened to me in childhood, when I first felt there was something benign and bigger that helped us. It wasn't religious. Divine energy was the best description I could come up with. So, when I was invited to attend an energy-healing class that Elena and her partner Bud were teaching locally, I hesitantly said, "yes."

I didn't believe in hands-on healing. I associated energy healing with scam artists and slap-the-forehead evangelists. But there was a kind of energetic movement of power inside when I attended Elena's meditations. I wanted to understand more.

While in class, my body felt a new kind of density, presence and intuitive connection as I learned to run healing energy. I literally felt plugged into a source that felt like an electrical current that came through my feet, traveled up my body and out into another person. My hands turned into faucets of vibration I could feel but not see.

I also learned that my body had an intuitive knowing that my mind knew nothing about. My hands felt physically pulled, like a magnet, to hover over or touch the place that the person I was paired with needed support. Sometimes participants pointed to an injury or shared an illness, but usually we didn't talk about our minor aches and pains before treatment.

Not having knowledge of what our partners needed began to validate and hone my inner knowing to find and help someone heal. I didn't see the energy but the relief it brought was visible. Tight facial expressions would relax. Deep contented sighs were constant background sound. Comments such as "My back pain is gone," "My knee's stopped hurting" or "My sinuses are open," were common.

My skepticism faded as those inexplicable and unexpected experiences added up. When I learned to run energy to support a person's nervous system, my patient's whole body could feel ice cold even when the room was hot. They'd be shivering while covered with blankets, even as my hands were red with heat as I moved them around the body as we were taught.

As I experienced more evidence of an energetic world, my intuition ignited. I began to sense significant events from people's pasts. How someone had been in two car accidents as a child, or a loved one had recently died, or someone was calmed by playing the guitar. All were related to what was going on with them physically now.

It was strange to know things. Yet, it was gratifying to be of help. It was humbling and fortifying when the information I received was validated again and again. I was 26. My teachers, Elena and Bud, felt I needed more training and encouraged me to study with world-renowned healer Reverend Rosalyn Bruyere, author of, *Wheels of Light: Chakras, Auras, and the Healing Energy of the Body.*

Back in the doctor's office, I listened when he announced I could go completely blind. I took more meds, crossed my fingers and decided to ask for help. Fortunately, at that point I'd been studying with Rosalyn for five years and was already signed up for a healing energy workshop the following week.

At that workshop, I asked Rosalyn if she knew of anything I could do about my eye trouble. She generously offered to do an energy treatment on me as an example for the class to experience. This involved me laying still, fully clothed, face-up on a massage table with 80 people surrounding us.

I remember the cool pads of Rosalyn's fingertips barely touching my eyelids. Then slowly a light, warm sensation entered my entire eyeball, intense but not unpleasant. I saw flashes of fine, electric gold light traveling along the back curve of my eyeballs. A densely concentrated feeling filled the yoke of my eyes, relaxing a place I didn't know needed relaxing.

A slight amber scent filled the air, and I could hear the

quiet breathing of the class around me. I had no concept of time and was surprised that more than a half hour had passed. I learned more about what happened from author Chip Brown, who was in the room and later artfully chronicled the treatment Rosalyn gave my eyes in his book, *Afterwards, You're A Genius.*

My vision for days afterwards was altered. My depth perception changed, I felt like I was taller, and a glow encircled everything in my periphery. A week later, my doctor said I showed the first signs of progress. The reduction of inflammation was significant.

I mentioned I'd had an energy healing. His eyes rolled up as if searching for patience. I laughed inside as his reaction perfectly mimicked my initial disbelief in the energy-healing field. He paused. Then with a tone that suggested I'd lost my mind said, "Uh-huh, you've also been on 80 milligrams of prednisone. Continue it."

I did take the pills and more unexpected help arrived. Elena and Bud arranged for me to meet with a Native American healer who was flying in to teach locally. I was told to come to their home the day before his workshop. He'd agreed to meet me for about an hour and help me with my eyes.

We sat outdoors. His hair was white, jeans ironed, boots well-worn but polished. It took me awhile to realize his eyesight was impaired. His presence permeated everything around him. I felt uncomfortably and thoroughly seen.

"Tell me what you do," he asked.

"I'm a curator of art."

"Why do you do something you don't like?"

Startled, I protested. "I love my job. Okay, I don't *like* that I barely make enough money to support myself, but I love what I do."

He gazed at me with wolf-like intensity. "You will go blind if you don't start to see what your Soul wants you to do in this life."

The impact of his words hit my chest and gut.

Truth.

It reverberated through every bone. I vaguely remember asking, "How do I figure out what my Soul wants?"

I don't remember if he answered. I just remember shadows slowly reforming the ridges and valleys of the surrounding mountains. He spent hours talking with me and asking questions. He and the ever-changing light continuously altered my view. At one point he told me to look at the leaves on a distant bush up close for 15 minutes. I figured he needed a break. After I described the teardrop shape, thread-fine stems and mottled soft greens blending on the tiny surfaces, he changed the subject.

I wish I remembered the other specifics of our conversation. I do recall feeling different afterward—more whole but also uncomfortable that I'd taken so much of his time. He surprised me when he abruptly ended our chat and invited me to stay for dinner.

I watched as he went inside Bud and Elena's mountainside home and cooked for everyone. The foods he cooked were staples—steak, salad and potatoes. Yet it was like I'd never eaten them before. Every bite I took felt alive. Flavors felt like they were blooming on my tongue. I was rooted deep inside myself, aware of a vibrancy to everything around me.

I felt like a kid sitting at the adult table for the first time. I kept quiet and listened as the clinking of silverware, glass and stoneware became a concert. Time seemed to slow, and there was no reason to hurry. I was steeped in an enhanced experience where all of the hidden cracks inside of me were filled.

Going home, my awareness was completely altered for two sensation-filled weeks. There was a soft light around everyone. I saw and knew things about people I hadn't been told. Even my *hair* felt alive, which is an odd feeling.

Strange things began happening. A woman at work, who didn't like me, walked into the common room, stopped and stared at me. She then shared something deeply personal, burst into tears, looked horrified, abruptly turned and fled through the door, mumbling, "I don't know *why* I did that."

I stood there mystified as well. I felt only love for this woman who was typically abrasive and dismissive of me. My head reminded me that I didn't like her either. How could the rest of me feel only love? Something about me was altered. I didn't know *why*.

Near the end of the second week, a co-worker, Glenn, brought me deer antlers as a gift. He said he didn't know *why*. He just knew he had to give them to me. They were from a boyhood hunting trip with his father. They were precious to him, and I saw in his eyes that this gift was coming from his heart. I had a strong knowing I needed to accept them. But again, I didn't know *why*.

The next day, life faded back to the disappointingly normal, except I had a clear knowing I was being *called* to do something different with my life.

Looking back, I can only guess *why* all of that happened. I believe it was to show me what was possible. I remember wondering—and still wonder—if there are people who live with that kind of magical loving aliveness all the time. I've had many heightened experiences since but not for that duration. I also learned that *why* isn't always the best question to ask.

I didn't need to know why because my bones just knew my life needed to change. Questions of *What? How? When?* led me to knowing myself better. *What* was I doing at the museum? Did I simply want to prove my dad wrong? No. I didn't regret the curatorial path I chose, but I knew it was coming to an end. I just wished I knew what was calling me.

How did it feel to be a hands-on energy healer? Not right for me.

I'd enjoyed giving tarot readings for people since I was 21.

What did I like about doing readings? When information gave clients a different perspective.

When did I not enjoy tarot readings? When people relied on me to tell them what to do. I didn't want to disempower anyone.

How could I combine everything I'd learned into a career? No clue.

I was *called* to do something I couldn't name. I felt a constant, soft physical pull from my torso, as if my body was trying to turn right instead of moving straight. It was so frustrating not to understand, especially since I determined I needed work that I could do if I became blind.

I don't want to give anyone the idea that this introspection was orderly and succinct. It was long, tearful, doubt-filled and chaotic, though mingled with the love and support of many gracious people.

It took more than a year for the danger to my eyesight to abate. As my physical vision became clearer so did my life vision. I would travel and give readings that helped people connect to their intuition, their inner guidance.

At 33 I read a book about how to start a business. I called friends in five states who said "yes," they'd love for me to come and do intuitive readings in their homes for their friends.

I named my business InSight and gave notice to the museum so my last day would be on Valentine's Day (1997). I knew it was cliché but I wanted to say goodbye to the museum and jump into my heart's calling on a day known for love, devotion and an obvious symbol of what I was following. A fat red heart.

My carefully made plans started falling apart by April.

Friends didn't have as many friends who wanted a reading. I had arranged life so expenses were minimal, but I was barely covering those. If things kept going this way, I'd be filling out job applications by June. I was angry, embarrassed and didn't know what to do except to say to Spirit, "You want me to do this work? Show me how because I'm failing."

Not knowing what else to do, I continued to follow my April schedule and traveled to Virginia for a workshop. Some friends invited me stay with them. Before the workshop, we went to the home of their friend, Susan Hough, whom I'd briefly met before. I ended up giving her a reading, which I share in the *Spirit Babies* chapter, that had a profound effect on us both. By the end of the week, we agreed I'd come back in May, and Susan promised to have clients for me.

May arrived, and as I walked in the door, Susan excitedly thrust three sheets of paper into my hands. "Twenty-one scheduled and more people are interested. Those three days are full." She motioned to the papers in my hand and said, "I want to schedule you every month. I know more people, and I want you to teach classes, too."

Susan tallied what we'd make, and with her percentage she was able to quit her evening job. She could now be at home with her children. Scheduling me gave her the freedom she'd been seeking.

I still thank the Divine that my original plans failed. A much better plan existed. Susan welcomed me into her family and home as we worked together for a week to 10 days every month for 14 years. Neither of us would be where we are now without the other. We were *called* together, and we listened.

I couldn't miss my calling. Susan didn't miss her calling. You can't miss your calling. Your calling constantly redials. Your calling calls back until you pick up.

That's how I was *called* to my calling, by listening to my inner knowing over and over. We are always being *called*. That's what intuition does.

Intuition is your Soul's voice, *calling* to you. Always.

We all have intuition. Intuition can't be taught. It *can* be navigated, developed, understood, and invited.

I share stories, like mine and Susan's, to enter your consciousness as possibilities. If there's a likelihood for something similar in your life, stories help open you to receive the call. Or stories may jog memories from your past experiences and validate that you have listened to your intuition's call many times before.

I offer *Invitations* at the end of each chapter. Invitations will enter your consciousness differently each time you read them. These invites will lead to discovering *your* unique intuitive workings through physical sensation. This process begins to create the space inside for your intuition to easily surface. Read the *Opening* for more ways to use invitations.

Both stories and invitations will reenforce the line of understanding between you and your intuition, so you'll be more likely to take *the call*.

For now, see if you feel *called* to read the following invitation. If so, slow down. perhaps take a breath and close your eyes between each line and experience whatever happens. If you don't feel *called* to read this invitation, honor that and do what you feel *called* to do.

Invitation

Think of the last time an unwelcome call came,
By phone, social media or advertisement.
Check your body for sensation.
Is any part gripping, tense, cool or resistant to that call?
Notice how and where your body rejects that call.

Take a breath clearing that memory.
Now think of a time someone you cherish called,
In person, by letter, email, text...
Check your body for sensation.
Are any parts expansive, full, warm or softened?
Perhaps a place inside lights up?
Acknowledge how and where your body welcomes that call.
Where do you feel it?
Know this is the start of how to map
where your intuition speaks.

2
Stop Wanting & Start Inviting

E veryone wants their intuition to work. The question, which I get asked on a regular basis, is *how?* No one likes my answer, but it is a key to igniting and understanding our intuition.

"Stop *wanting* and start *inviting.*"

In my twenties, when my finances and health were bleak, I became interested in the philosophy of manifestation—the belief that anyone could attract money, possessions, perfect health and wonderful opportunities with the right attitude.

It was the 1990s. At workshops I heard other students regularly talking about the wonders of manifestation. Everyone seemed to have their own rules and practices. The bottom line was with the right belief and focus, anyone could attract *anything* they wanted. I remember being impressed when one woman claimed, "I had a day's worth of clients three months ago and now my calendar is full."

During workshop breaks, I soaked in convincing information from other students that I didn't need to live in such nominal circumstances. I needed to recognize I was a powerful spirit. I needed visualization—to not only see what I wanted in life but also feel it was already there. There was even a catchy directive: "See it. Believe it. And you will achieve it."

I didn't recognize until much later that the underlying message was *if you don't have everything you want, it's your fault.* Sick? Broke? Stuck? You aren't spiritual enough. You're doing life wrong.

The woman with the full calendar of clients told me to

make a very detailed list of what I wanted. "Think of it as if you're creating a work of art," she advised. "But the real trick to making your list come into being is reading your list out loud and feeling it's already happened. I see myself saying yes to new clients. I feel the sensation of holding cash in my hands and the joy it brings. I always remember, I already have everything I desire. Easy."

Wanting to do this right, I worked on a rough draft of my *wants*. I started small. I *want* a reliable car. I *want* healthy eyes. I *want* money to take more workshops. I *want* to eat healthier and maybe even eat out once a week. I filled an entire page. I was ready.

Out of the blue, I received three sample sheets of expensive deckle edge, off-white cotton paper in the mail. *Maybe manifestation was already working?* I hoped the luxurious creamy surface would amp up the mojo.

Feeling the paper's smooth weight in my hands, I read my carefully crafted list with all the feelings my *wants* entailed. I could see and feel the wants in my life. I just couldn't make myself believe I had everything already. I didn't. I *wanted* to believe, but I knew it was a lie. Faithfully, I tried every day for weeks. Lying felt heavy. So, I stopped, the list relegated to my to-do pile.

Many months later, a friend told me she'd read how to manifest something the *right* way. I needed to make a list and then put it away. "Let yourself forget about it, and the universe will answer."

Bingo! *Maybe I intuitively knew to do this already?* I dug out my list to see if the forget-about-it theory worked. Nothing had changed.

More months passed, my financial situation had worsened with more car repairs and medical bills. More manifestation advice arrived—switch the wording on my list from *I want* to *I have*. I rewrote my whole list. But writing "*I have*" felt delusional. Speaking it felt worse. "I have a reliable car." *My car was in the shop.* "I have healthy eyes." *The doctor had just prescribed more steroid drops.*

I sat there glaring at my original *want* list; at least it was true. The word *want*, appearing so often on the page, almost pulsed with ... *wanting*. Drawn in, all I could feel was a constricting sensation of *lack* in my chest. This had to be why I wasn't manifesting; my body wouldn't let me lie. But ... I did *want* a reliable car and healthy eyes. I did *want* more money. Yet, saying *want* kept me tight and *wanting*.

I was still wondering how to free myself from the crush of want when a friend's wedding invitation suddenly plopped into my head. It was so random that my desperate mind jumped to: *Maybe I'm about to meet someone and get married.*

Thankfully, my intuition intervened. The thought of my own nuptials began to fade as a calm expanded from my core. My mental need to analyze or draw a conclusion about the vision, be it right or wrong, dissipated as well. My body relaxed. Yet, the image of the ivory invitation filled my awareness.

A thought surfaced, not from my mind but from deep inside my core. *Maybe I could use the word invite instead of want?*

Intrigued, I rewrote the list on my last sheet of beautiful paper, changing every *I want* to *I invite*. I noticed I wasn't tense like before. Writing *I have* felt strenuous. Writing *I invite* was relaxing. The list felt hopeful. The feeling of lack vanished. I was just writing an invitation of what I'd like in my life. It was fun. It was true. I was curious.

This switch freed the pressure on my ego, my own will, to force an action. I ditched manifesting. I forgot about the list. My focus automatically shifted from *this must change* to *I wonder what will happen?* I'd found a useful way to think, perceive and open myself to possibilities with a simple invite.

I began to learn that invitation is an effective way to engage intuition.

All invitations are sent with the understanding that the

recipient—in this case the divine source of your Soul—has the freedom to say no like anyone else. Many people start the *I invite* practice only to feel ignored, that it doesn't work, that they must be doing it wrong, or worse, that a greater power doesn't exist. An impatient ego loves jumping to those defeating conclusions. Ego looks for *something to manifest* as proof until it's taught to recognize RSVPs.

Receiving no answer is a response. It could mean no. Or that a particular invitation is not what your Soul needs. Or perhaps the timing's not ideal. Or it often means something's already in the works that can't yet be perceived.

The purpose of *I invite* is to let go of exhaustive mental *wanting*.

I invite shifts your gaze from outside evidence, to your body's intuitive signals.

I invite is not a demand.

I invite is a request for Divine participation.

I invite welcomes the presence of someone or something desirable to come to your door.

I invite doesn't expect instant change or a phenomenal result.

I invite doesn't require you to pretend something is there when it isn't.

I invite welcomes unknown solutions.

I invite is patient and guarantees our intuition's participation.

I invite is an act of self-kindness because you're asking for more options to be revealed.

I wanted a reliable car, so *I invited* one. That freed me from the limited viewpoint of my expectations. I could relax. The when, how or if a car would come no longer was an action item to hammer away on. I wasn't passive either. While waiting, I was alert for RSVPs to check out.

Shortly after vocally inviting a car into my life, my little gray Volkswagen Rabbit died. I chose to recognize its death as an RSVP, which helped me to settle down inside. There, I felt an intuitive nudge to call my mechanic, Fred, instead of searching car dealerships. When I called Fred and asked about affordable used cars, he said, "Well, you are in luck, a guy just left his Jetta to be serviced to sell. Carz in great shape. Lot safer than yours. Even got a sunroof. Come check it out 'n I'll see what he wants for it."

The Jetta was under my budget and was still reliable when I sold it eight years later.

I viewed the death of my old Rabbit as life accepting *my invite* for a reliable replacement because action was required. The nudge to call Fred was easier to hear and saved me a lot of time and money. I did not manifest the Jetta. The invitation intertwined with my intuition from the start. Also, the knowing that I'd extended an *invite* helped me stay calm when my car died, a conducive state for intuition to operate.

Here's another way to think about invitations. What happens when you invite ten people to dinner and six say yes? You set the table for six. You don't set the table for the four that said *no*. Worrying why they said *no* is not a constructive action. You cook. You clean. You create a welcoming atmosphere. Whoever comes requires space, attention and conversation, which you'll miss if you focus on who didn't show.

Wanting focuses on who didn't show. *Invitation* sparks participation. It opens a space at your inner table for something new to arrive. You know at some point you'll get a yes, no, maybe or a different suggestion in response. That's the time to sink inward with breath, an awareness of physical sensation and the involvement of your knowing self to guide your next step. Just one step is needed.

Inviting a reliable car and healthy food into my life was a step. Yes, I still *wanted* those things; that's why I was *inviting* them. Not knowing the response kept my body open and receptive to intuitive replies instead of becoming tight with *wanting*.

Calling Fred was a step. That nudge felt right, first as a welcoming sensation in my body. Then my mind agreed. It couldn't hurt to call. I didn't need to know the result. I knew the first step.

Fred might have said it was cheaper to resuscitate my clunker. He might have recommended a dealership. He might have said he didn't know what to tell me. If that had happened, I would have asked if he knew of a reliable model to look for, or if he would make sure the car I found was safe.

Invitations voiced to something bigger—whether it's the air, the universe or the divine—automatically adjust perception to recognize and receive the RSVPs in our environment. The second step is to pay attention to your body's response to what you've received. An expansive feeling usually indicates alignment with your intuition. A tight feeling can suggest you pause and wait for other options. Noticing all sensation helps you discover and cultivate your inner knowing.

As I mentioned in the *Opening*, reading the invitations at the end of each chapter offers a different way to integrate the experiences of the stories shared. After you read an invitation, you might want to speak your experience out loud so your ears can hear. Hearing your voice say what happened, no matter how subtle, has lasting results that are initially hidden.

You may still be thinking, "I *want* my intuition to work… preferably now." Remember, *want* is stressful, tight and suggests there's not enough to go around. That's why *I invite* is important. Thinking or saying *I invite*, allows your mind to do something about your many *wants*. It anchors your connection to your intuition's RSVPs. You will live life wider, naturally manifesting the true you.

Invitation

Take ten seconds to scan the body.

Notice any sensation happening now.

Simply notice without trying to change anything.

Inhale deeply into the belly.

Hold the breath long enough to feel presence there.

Release the breath slowly.

Notice any physical change.

Think about something you want.

Breathe in that thought and say I want.

Where is the feeling of that want sensed inside?

Feel for anywhere tight, drawn in or pulled.

See if the sensation matches not having that want in life.

Now think about that same desire and say I invite.

Breathe that thought down inside.

Notice if there is any change in sensation.

Did the tightened place relax, open or feel a bit more spacious?

Exhale, releasing everything.

Now play—go back and forth between I want and I invite.

Take a few seconds for each.

Take several seconds to notice any subtle differences that occur.

3
Put the Hammer Down

M y mother sat cross-legged on the garage floor, eyebrows bent in determination. One hand gripped a hammer while three thin fingertips pinched together under the long pointy nail's head. She tapped through the metal lid then wiggled the nail upward and smiled a sigh once it was free. Radiant red hair fell forward as she aimed, and hammered again.

"We're going to have so much fun."

My job was to hold the glass baby food jar, which held a bit of grass in the bottom. After repeating the puncturing process until satisfied, my mother lightly returned the pierced lid to my jar.

"We're going to catch lightning bugs. Remember your jar is fragile and so are they."

The grass felt bouncy-thick as I barefooted my way across the lawn to the gathering that twinkled in our darkening yard. The woods were at the very back and, at age three and a half, off limits to me. Fortunately, the lightning bugs liked to hang out at the edge.

Careful not to startle the shining beauties, I tiptoed into their midst. There were so many. I stood still as they bobbled and hovered around me. I don't remember catching any. I do remember the expansive wonder of watching them. I felt special when they whisper-landed on my arms and shirt.

Later, my mom placed my baby-food-jar-bug-catcher on the nightstand and kissed me goodnight. She must have captured a few for me because we said, "Goodnight lightning bugs," as she turned out the light.

Awake with summer-sticky sweat, I stared through the dark surrounding my nightstand. I waited for my lightning bugs to glow. Nothing. Something else happened instead. I *felt the need* to let them go.

I didn't want to. I wanted to keep them forever so they would always glow me to sleep. Yet my belly squeezed tight, and I felt something bad would happen if I kept them. My sleepy mind settled the matter, *mommy said that lightning bugs would be fine with breathing holes and grass.* A part of me knew differently.

In the morning the heavy smell of green rot met me when I opened the jar to check on them. Dead. My first memory of knowing something intuitively and not listening.

I wish I could say those were the last lightning bugs to die in my bedroom. They weren't. A few from our next twilight excursion survived the night, safely released in the morning. Bigger bug catchers were made after more perished. I don't remember how long this went on. I do remember they never glowed inside their cage, regardless of size. I wanted them to light up next to my bed so badly.

My little girl logic said, *Maybe they'll glow and won't die this time if I treat them really nice.* Or, *Mommy said it was okay.* I kept trying—my well-meaning parents did too—our wants bypassed any hope of our intuitive voices showing up to stop us.

Like most people, I innocently ignored these and other small knowings that surfaced over time. They softly conflicted with my loud wants, again and again, until I rarely noticed them.

Our mind hammers holes in intuitive wisdom. When an inner knowing surfaces in our awareness, our mind instantly grabs it, and wants proof (*bang*), concise information (*thump*) and absolute clarity (*thwack*) from its catch. Intuitive information doesn't meet these rigid standards. The mind, now satisfied with its interrogation, labels the incident as fantasy.

Paradoxically, the mind knows intuition is valuable and desires to label it, tame it, *control* it. Our ego pounds away trying to nail down the rules or steps that will reveal how inner knowing works and where it comes from, unaware that trying to find the *how* and *where* of intuition suffocates the ability for knowing to emerge.

The mind wants to stuff the tiny lights that guide your way into a jar, hoping to get neon signs telling you exactly what to do. If you allow the mind to always take command, like trapped fireflies, your intuition won't light. You miss your body's intuitive signals when you allow your mind to hammer away while demanding answers. Thankfully, your intuition doesn't die.

Intuition has a lot in common with lightning bugs. It hangs out on the edge of your consciousness. If chased, it disappears into the woods. Your inner voice whisper-lands in your own backyard—your body—many knowing sparks wait to communicate. Intuition encourages you to slow down, get sensation-curious and wonder.

Intuition is subtle, not neon, though you really want it to be. It drifts into your awareness to glimmer for a moment then seemingly disappears. It reappears suddenly in a different place, sometimes hovering right in front of your nose. Inner knowing can't be caught and trained to light your way. It's your nature. It's always there. You just need to let its small glow tease you into the shadows to play and gently explore.

Let your hammering mind settle, and intuition will land.

Invitation

Let your mind drift like fireflies as you read.
Lighting on what seems interesting.
Invite a memory where your mind talked you out of a knowing.
Try not to judge it as good or bad, just notice.
Does a physical sensation accompany the memory?
Check the belly, chest or elsewhere.
Let yourself play, not grasp, as you see what surfaces
from the past.
Take a spacious breath.
Don't look for answers. They will either float up now,
later or never.
Allow questions to arise, this is a good thing.
Notice where there is sensation in your body now.
Ask that this feeling be informative.
Notice what sensations are experienced.
Remember very subtle physical impressions are information.
Don't try to know what they mean now.
Get used to lighting up snatches of information.
Learn how to play at the edges of awareness,
like lightning bugs.

4

Sensible To Be Sense-Able

I was three when I went to Grandma's house, alone, for the first time. Her two-story, sandstone-clad English Tudor home was a haven. In Ohio summers, Grandma and I ran around bare-footed on the massive front lawn with soft cut grass. We played with bubbles or rolled a big red ball to each other in the sun. The two of us wore oversized floppy brimmed hats to protect our pale tender skin.

In the backyard we wore shoes. The ground was covered with moss, roots, sticks and big bumpy lime green balls with a bitter-dirt smell that still calms me with one inhale. Just thinking about them, heavy in my hand, settles my limbs and brings me closer to myself.

Time with Grandma meant discovering birds, plants and trees. We'd look at how the bark pattern was different on every tree, feel its texture with the tender insides of our arms and try to sing the different birdsongs we heard. Her patient love of nature shaped me right along with her hugs and smiles.

My grandma told me that she used to have long red hair like my mother's, a shiny turmeric color. It was hard for me to picture. My mom had short straight hair, and I'd only seen my grandmother with short-spun, fleecy, white curls. Grandma looked different in other ways, too. I come from a tall, thin, jean-clad family. She was barely five feet tall, round and always wore a dress.

Grandma and I would go on long walks along the creek in the Poland, Ohio, woods. The trail was hard-packed dark earth that began right across the street from her driveway. She kept a lingering pace, squatting down frequently, even though she was quite round in the middle, to study the tiniest flowers, insects and fungi. We'd pet the soft mosses. I got to rub my cheeks against its cool spongy surface making my mouth taste rich with dirt moisture.

Each time we walked we would go a little farther, and Grandma would praise me for those extra steps, enticing me with arriving at the bridge someday. There were no trolls there. Yes, perhaps there might be fairies, though she hadn't seen them. One day she promised that in the spring the bluebells would peek out next to the bridge, "…but only for a few weeks in April. Do you think you'll be big enough to go that far to meet them?"

Meeting bells? Suddenly the bells eclipsed all thoughts of the bridge in my mind. All winter I imagined tiny blue metal-cupped bells growing up on sticks out of the ground. I hoped the wind would blow so that I could hear them ring. Was this how bells were made? Could I pick them and take some home? I didn't tell anyone about my imaginings. I was four.

Finally, April came. Grandma had gone the day before I arrived to make sure the bluebells were there. And they were. I was now much bigger and insisted upon carrying my own box of animal crackers for a snack picnic between bridge and bells. The shoelace handle on the cracker box felt thick in my hand as I tugged on her fingers to walk faster.

The bridge was so big it momentarily chased away all thoughts of bluebells. I reached the other side and was about to step down when I remembered. I scanned for bells. Nothing was there.

"Grandma, where are the bells?"

She looked at me, winked and pointed. We walked over to a tennis-court-sized area of deep violet-blue flowers that hung from delicate arched stems, suspended above leafy dark greenness.

Oh, I was disappointed. They were just flowers. No real bells and they didn't even look like bells. Grandma was so excited and happy to share this wonderful English bluebell sighting with me that I acted happy to see them. I opened my box of animal crackers and we sat at the lone picnic table. We rested for our walk back by nibbling on zoo animals, listening to the splashie bubbles of the creek, eavesdropping on birds and the chatter of squirrels. Then we bounced-walked over the suspended bridge for our walk home.

Expectation is a sure way to kill sensory exploration. There was no way those flowers were going to meet the expectations that blue bells conjured in my child's imagination. Bluebells don't ring. Instead of being curious, I immediately wrote them off as nothing special. They were *just* flowers. Their title kept me from experiencing the woods the way we usually did. My mind wasn't interested in something that wasn't as exciting as a bell factory in the woods. A disappointed mind, child or adult, isn't interested in exploring further with the senses.

Why is this a problem? Because, as I've said before, your intuition isn't your sixth sense, it's your Essence. Your Essence/Soul/Spirit communicates to you through all of your senses. If you are numb to your senses, you are numb to your intuitive receptors—well, you see the problem.

Expectation and naming things are the two main culprits of shutting down our senses. I'm not saying that we shouldn't give things a name. When I learned as an adult the lime green bumpy balls in my grandma's backyard were called black walnuts, it just added richer meaning to the magical sensation I'd experienced as a child.

When we give something a name *before* we've explored it ourselves, the mind oftentimes stops the inquiry and ditches the senses—even at age four. What the mind expects and names can keep you from connecting in the moment if you aren't careful to notice and redirect your interest.

Learning intuitive language starts with a vow from the mind to listen, to pay attention and let your senses speak. If your sensory awareness is dampened, so is your intuition's ability to help. You might not know the meaning of what your intuition is saying at first, but it's just like learning any language. You begin to understand if you're willing to not understand for a while.

People have expectations about how their intuition *should* look and feel. I understand. They've had an intuitive hit a few times and didn't notice that their senses participated in the information conveyed. And just like my expectation of bells, people become disappointed and disinterested when they discover the reality that our senses play a key role. I had one new client, after being introduced to this idea, say, "What do you mean listen to my senses? You're telling me I can pay attention to a smell and my intuition just starts working? I don't think so. How am I supposed to know what a smell means?"

This is valid skepticism. *Just start by experiencing your senses* doesn't make sense at first. Ambiguity is hard for most. Consistently accessing intuition requires a certain level of comfort/acceptance of spending time *not mentally knowing*. Yes, one of the secrets to active intuition is a paradox; to access your knowing you need to hang out not knowing. It's uncomfortable but true.

Here's why. When your mind lets go of knowing and directs its attention to full contact with the world, you receive input on a broader spectrum. This allows a many-layered knowing to permeate the moment you are in and focus on your involvement with the now. Try this: Feel the fabric on or beside skin, see where color touches your body, explore the sounds and smells around. This active involvement in *the now* is jumping jacks for your intuition. Full participation is how to feel more alive. It keeps your intuition healthy, pliant and receptive.

You're not supposed to know what a smell means for the future. You know what it means now—someone's making popcorn or the dog took a poo in the dining room. Your intuitive self astutely gathers all your experiences and retrieves them when needed. You want to taste the complexity of food and engage all of your senses in every delightful moment. It feels good. Embracing the nuances of being alive, without interpretation, is a simple way to jumpstart intuition.

How? Lingering in sensation without grabbing for meaning provides a foundational space for intuition to land. Releasing expectations and the need to name encourages your sensual curiosity to wake up and absorb a wealth of reliable integrated information. Your intuition processes the data when necessary.

Many are afraid and some know they'll find undesirable sensations when allowing numbness to lift. It's common to want to escape heartache, hardship and pain, but many of us tend to remember those moments in great clarity without effort. Later in the *Stand In the And* and other chapters, I share how intuition can help alleviate mental, emotional and physical pain.

In the woods I learned to absorb information by settling down by my grandmother's side and marveling at the tiniest curiosity. Feeling the faint ridges on shell-shaped fungus and wondering how and why it grew on old logs, without needing an answer.

The tiny teacup pink and sunshine yellow flowers, no bigger than the nail on my four-year-old pinkie, were invisible until my grandmother pointed them out. After sitting quietly with them, leaning in to see if there was a smell and gently stroking their miniature petals, I saw them everywhere.

My grandmother didn't name or try to explain most of what we admired. Perhaps she forgot or didn't know. Either way, it trained me to linger and learn though my senses at least some of the time. Names didn't clutter my experience of simply being with nature. When you name or explain something it can stop you from the wonder of experiencing it. Your mind is satisfied, so you stop paying attention with your senses. Adult brain says, "Got it. That's an oak tree. Let's keep moving."

Once you start pointing out to your intellect the subtle ways your senses are always communicating, you perceive more inner spaciousness and richer dimensions to your experiences. I remember all of these precious times with my grandmother in such detail because I was fully immersed in the sounds, smells and textures of life when I was with her.

I was with a friend of mine when she caught the scent of sweet grass. She stopped and immediately asked what it was. She was suddenly flooded with intricate memories of her time at "the bungalow" with her grandparents. The smell brought years of fond memories that she shared.

It started with her grandfather mowing the grass, and kept blooming into home remedies for sunburn, learning to make pies, feeling squooshie hugs and running with explosive laughter. She glowed with joy when she shared her memories, all filled with meaning derived from her senses. She didn't need a name; the scent alone opened chapters of her life all at once. Forty years later she discovered the name of the scent from her childhood, and her definition of sweet grass is much broader. It's blended with her experience.

It is sensible to be sense-able. The senses gather more multi-leveled information in one sniff than an entire dictionary. The ability to revel in your senses keeps you alert and receptive to intuitive knowings.

As much as your mind wants to follow a definitive line directly to knowing what it wants to know now, the process is actually more crooked, smudgy and interesting than straight. Being able to open your senses is like those once invisible tiny teacup pink and yellow flowers in the woods. Once noticed, your intuitive knowing will be everywhere.

Invitation

Feel the air come through your nose into your lungs.
Notice how all of your senses start to awaken.
Release your breath through your mouth
and notice the moisture.
Rest with an expansive focus through your torso.
Stretch your toes, allowing full body sensory awareness.
Slowly breathe in the scents around you.
Taste the inside of your mouth.
Let your tongue lazily explore the feel of your teeth.
Listen and invite every sound to come into your presence.
Marvel at the detailed texture of your clothes.
Linger in all of the sensation you've awakened.
Notice it is both normal and extraordinary.

5
Saving Lancelot

On winter mornings, the cold pressed through the windows at the head of my bed and hugged anything exposed. Never a fan of temperatures below 50, I cocooned deep under the covers. The side effect of three blankets and a bedspread was muffled quiet.

Normally, I slept through the creaks and clinks of morning. Normally, my mom peeled the layers back to slowly wake me up for school. Normally, it took a while to get out of bed. But that morning a scream, which started at a low pitch and quickly accelerated to high ear-piercing decibels, jolted me straight up to a stand.

I spun on the bed and looked down though the frosted panes to our driveway. Though blurred, I could see my dad opening the hood of our pumpkin-colored station wagon. The scream had lasted only a few seconds but had summoned the neighbors. I saw a few walking towards our house. Scrambling, I ran down the steps in my pajamas and stuffed my bare feet in snow boots, flung on my heavy coat, zipping it up as I pushed out the front door.

I slid in behind a couple of neighbors—all adults—now gathered at 7 a.m. around our car. The faint odor of burnt hair reached my nose. I blew the rankness out hard and fast, causing the frigid air to fog and swirl around me while I listened to my dad explain that Lancelot, our orange tabby, had crawled up into the engine of his car. He didn't know the cat was there until he cranked the ignition and cut it the instant he heard the howl.

The neighbors were astounded the scream wasn't human.

They chatted, guessing why the cat was in the engine and wondered where he was now.

"I don't know," my dad said. "Maybe he was trying to keep warm. He shot off that way." He impatiently waved his arm towards the left side of our house.

I looked and saw a few specks of blood on the concrete driveway heading towards the frosted grass. Seeing that small blood trail turned my insides very still. I was hyper aware of the situation around me.

Neighbors started going back to their mornings, promising to call if they saw our cat. They crouch-walked home, looking under bushes and calling, "Heeere kitty-kitty… Heeeerrre kitty-kitty."

I knew Dad had to be at work on time. A long search wasn't possible. My dad scanned the side yard, my mom the front. With only one car we had to find Lancelot now or he wouldn't have the option of going to the vet. He could die. I remained still and shut my eyes to concentrate on where he might be. But before I could think, an image of a stop sign hanging on a wooden board appeared in my head. A whole-body feeling of absolute certainty of Lancelot's where-abouts accompanied the image. I was a kid so I didn't think about consequences before I yelled, "I know where he is!"

My parents looked up, most likely noticing me for the first time.

"How do you know where he is? Did you see him run?"

"No, I just know."

"So, you know where he usually hides?"

"No," I replied, starting to feel uncertain and scared.

My dad cut to the chase. "I don't have time for this. If you know where he is go get him."

Hesitantly I told my dad I thought he was in our neighbor's woodshed inside their fenced backyard.

"Are you sure?" he asked in a brusque no-nonsense tone.

I was going to be in big trouble if I was wrong but I nodded. It was the only wooden place I knew that had a stop sign. With an exasperated, "Okay," he jogged next-door, opened the neighbors' gate and walked around their house to the shed.

I still remember the relief I felt when my father yelled, "Found him!"

My mother had grabbed an old bath towel from the stack in the hall closet—normally used to put our wet boots on—and tossed it over the fence to my dad to wrap around Lancelot. I watched my dad carry the big pink bundle with just a tiny face showing that he gently placed on the floor of the front passenger side of the car. He got to the vet and to work on time.

My relief was not only for our beloved pet—who survived eight more years until my high school graduation. I was relieved that I had been right.

Forty-eight years later I still remember the sickening fear—after I hollered where Lancelot was—of knowing I'd be in big trouble if I were wrong. Being wrong in this case meant my parents would have thought I was lying about Lancelot's whereabouts. Punishment followed lies. If I'd thought before I yelled, I'm not sure I'd have taken the risk to say I knew, when logically it seemed impossible.

I remember my mother's searching eyes on me when she later asked, "How did you know where the cat was hiding?"

"I don't know how I knew. I just did." I couldn't explain it. I didn't know the word intuition.

Recently, we talked about that morning. My mom remembered questioning me and laughed, "Now it all makes sense how *you knew*."

How can I have such vivid memories of the lightning bugs in the *Put the Hammer Down* chapter and the cat when so many of my early memories are gone or at best foggy? Intuition. My Soul registers them as important to retain.

It's why I've never forgotten the instant feeling of whole-body certainty that morning. Information that was desperately needed came to me. The flash of an image brought with it a knowing from out of nowhere. I didn't have to try. It was the first time I remember consciously using my intuition.

I also remember how quickly I began to doubt myself for fear of getting in trouble. I hadn't given myself even a second to think about it. It didn't feel like I was lying. But when my dad questioned me, I feared I might have been.

One of the biggest fears people have when intuitive information surfaces is that they're lying to themselves. If intuition does make an appearance, inner criticism shuts it down. We don't want to appear foolish. Or crazy.

Everyone has intuition. When people tell me they aren't intuitive they aren't lying. Their mind stops the flow of information before it even registers. My young self was so concerned about being right—and staying out of trouble—that this could have happened to me.

That stop sign not only saved Lancelot, it saved me. It gave me a real-life experience of intuition working. The image revealed the cat's location. For me, the stop sign shoved a foot in the door of my intuitive connection. It said, "Stop. Remember. This is valuable. This is *real*."

The future me needed to remember so I couldn't completely slam the door on intuitive data. Even though I had a lived experience of the power of intuition, it didn't stop me from feeling crazy or ignoring messages. I'm a product of a culture that dismisses intuitive knowledge.

That red octagon was planted as a message for me to *stop* and listen to another part of myself. A part that didn't have to try. A part with a different way of communicating. A part that wasn't afraid of making mistakes. A part that can—as religious texts teach us—*Be still and know.*

Invitation

Take several long softening breaths.
Let your consciousness ride the breath deep inside the body.
As you breathe down and in,
Invite a memory of having absolute certainty
for no logical reason.
See what surfaces.
A thought or memory that doesn't make sense could come.
There might just be an emotion or sensation inside.
That's okay.
Gently allow any subtle awareness to be noticed.
Give whatever comes space to breathe,
Even if you think nothing happened,
Note it anyway.
This way of focusing slowly changes us inside.
The start of tuning in has begun.

6
Sniff Some Dirt

T hanksgiving, many years ago, my mother's massive sixteen seat-er table shone with her love of making holidays special. Two large wicker cornucopias overflowed with colorful fall foliage, and bumpy orange-hued gourds sprawled down the center on a deep gold tablecloth. The whole display had a warm glow as thirty or more white candles, varying in size, were lit inside a menagerie of clear glass holders, artfully interspersed among classic bone china, silver, and crystal place settings.

Aromas permeated the whole house—roasted turkey interspersed with whiffs of red wine and cinnamon biscuits drawing us to eat. All the food was lined up on a long mahogany sideboard in a welcoming serve-yourself fashion.

My mother's three-story Victorian home, one she and her husband restored, was filled with people. My mom's smile and eyes revealed pure joy as she absorbed every person and dinner detail. She was fully present for the splendor she'd created.

We filled our plates and sat in our assigned seats. Acquaintances were sprinkled in with family. She wouldn't admit it to you, but my mother invited a few people with nowhere else to go on Thanksgiving because it helped my family, all of us adults, behave. This was the only time all of us got together. We disagreed about many things but spoke civilly in the presence of company.

Everything was going well until Bob, my aunt's second husband, started to talk about politics. This was a BIG no-no. Looking at my family was like watching kernels of corn about to pop. Faces began to turn red, eyes rolled, and everyone had a different kind of fidget. The conflicting views, first audibly expressed through table tapping and heavy sighs, quickly turned vocal, as snide comments and strong opinions crisscrossed the room. Sooooo much tension. Ugh. I tried to tune it all out.

For a good five minutes the anger roiled. Even though I had inwardly disengaged from the flying jabs, I was exhausted. My mother's strategically invited guests were now intently focused on their plates. Thankfully my brilliant and witty cousin turned the tide, pivoting with a smooth joke onto a different topic.

Phew. Remaining mute, I tried to imagine our family agreeably enjoying a peaceful Thanksgiving together. It was then that I was literally grabbed out of my fantasy back to the present. My sister yanked hard on my left wrist, under the table, and hissed in my ear, "If I have to be here, so do you."

I snickered. Though when I looked at her, she wasn't playing. Her eyes locked me to my chair. She was right of course. I had left. Not physically, but my presence was missing. At first it irritated me that she figured it out. Then I was puzzled.

She hadn't studied with healers, mystics and shamans about our energy being present. She had no interest in the subtle energy world at all, preferring logic, linear strategies and outcomes. My sister, the analytical businesswoman, called me on pretending to be present. How did she know I had effectively left the premises when I was still sitting there? After she exposed my disappearance, *I came to my senses.* Literally.

With a deep breath, I refocused on my weight in the chair, my sister's scolding gaze and the sounds of a now jovial family around me. That small shift in awareness was all I needed to leave the echoes of emotional turmoil and fantasizing behind. I was back.

I shouldn't have been surprised by my sister's admonishment. We might not admit it but we usually know when someone isn't really with us. Our culture is filled with sayings—*they drifted off, they're lost in thought, he's tuned-out, she's numbed-out, checked-out, closed-down, spaced-out or they're not all there.* We snap our fingers saying, "Come back to earth." Or whisper with eyebrows raised, "The lights are on, but no one's home."

We indicate we're not quite there by saying, "I'm wound up," or "I'm beside myself," about a situation. Only people you trust are in the position to call you on your absence of residence. It's too easy to deny. Saying to someone at the table, "Where are you?" can result in an indignant response. "I'm right here. What are you talking about?"

Turns out my sister knew me too well. I could not get away with disappearing while sitting next to her. I chose to disengage, she called me back.

Disassociation isn't always a choice. The inability to be present can also indicate a need for professional assistance. Constant disengagement is not healthy and can be a part of medical conditions brought on by traumatic events or physical pain.

A side effect of lacking presence, for some, is being unable to tell whether upsetting emotions are their own or someone else's. People have called me about this phenomenon thinking their intuition had gone awry. I tell them what they're experiencing is called being an empath—someone who can experience another's emotional state. A wealth of information can be found on this topic. Often when an empath has difficulty discerning what feelings are their own or someone else's *or* feel inundated with negativity and confusion, they aren't fully present. Developing a substantial presence alleviates that over-whelm.

Based on past Thanksgivings, I was *expecting* my family to misbehave, so I chose to remove myself. I was too busy *putting on a good face,* ready to block out negative comments that *might* be spoken, to notice what was actually happening. I spent the first half of the day anticipating what turned out to be five minutes of unpleasantness. I don't remember much beyond uncomfortable guests, my cousin's heroic redirect and my sister's yank. The specifics are lost. The table description is my after-yank memory, though not written in that order.

When we are *out,* imagining future or past scenarios, our senses are muted and there's nothing interesting to remember. Everyone does this temporarily; it's a problem when we perpetually analyze, are literally out of touch, and are unaware of our environment. The time we spend in our head can slip away. Unrecorded. Benjamin Franklin was right when he said, "Lost time is never found again."

Everyone knows it's exhausting to *put on a good face,* while our mind races through past and future events to avoid what's happening. In good-face state you tend to react instead of act. Your inability to take timely action indicates that you are disengaged or trapped in past dramas. When you aren't aligned with the present, your intuition has a hard time reaching you.

That is not to say you *should always* have a focused presence. You are more complex than that. There are many benefits to both mind-wandering and daydreaming. Some researchers say it's a natural resting state for the brain. Others credit that state with creative ideas, revelatory insights and aha moments.

It's common knowledge that great ideas and realizations come when the body relaxes while taking a shower, playing or during any kind of creative exploration. The mind meandering is not bad. Almost everyone has random intuitive realizations in that state. Your intuition thrives from a healthy balance of sensory engagement and rudderless focus.

When you reside in your senses, *your energy/spirit* is in touch with your current location. You are present. You are more likely to remember the details of your life. Your most vivid memories have dimension because more than one sense is involved. Senses have impact. You are more alive. When you are present to everything around you, including delicious food *and* disagreements, your intuitive self communicates more efficiently and effectively.

I know immersing yourself in your senses seems simplistic. It is simple. Your physical sensation is by far the easiest to access, acting like a magnet to the present. It gives you a broader perspective of your immediate surroundings that informs your logical and intuitive decision-making. The senses are the first step to a solid foundation for intuitive knowing, emotions and thinking are also important. I will be building upon them, story-by-story, in relation to intuition as well.

In my twenties I learned how powerful the senses could be. Before cell phones, I decided to go camping, alone in the Blue Ridge Mountains. No one knew where I was. I can't remember why this was important to me other than a test of my own courage. I know, stupid.

Choosing a time of year when the temperature was mild, I drove up into the mountains to intuitively find a place to camp. Late in the day I spotted a gravel parking lot and pulled over. A half-dozen trucks with horse trailers filled the lot, but there was enough space for my Chevette to squeeze in. It didn't occur to me that these trails were meant for horses, not people. I stuffed my tent, sleeping bag, water, and dry food in a backpack and started up a very steep muddy path. It was a rough, slippery hike for over an hour to find a flat spot for the night.

As the sun started down, I cleared away sticks and dried leaves, set up my sleeping quarters, and ate my almond butter sandwich and lunchbox sized Fritos, then zip-locked the trash away in my pack and found a comfortable place to meditate. Eyes closed, I felt alive sitting on the dirt, taking deep breaths under the trees. I didn't bring a watch but it was getting dark fast so I pulled out my mini-flashlight, took off my shoes and jacket, smiling as I snuggled into my sleeping bag.

The need to pee woke me. I started to shimmy out of my bag when I froze from a rustling sound. I envisioned bears stalking my tent and terror flooded my system. I lay perfectly silent. Still. Trapped in fear for what seemed like hours, I conjured all kinds of threatening scenarios, until my bladder reached a breaking point. This amount of fear seems stupid now, but I was terrified when I slowly unzipped the tent and peered into the night.

As cool damp air and rich soil replaced the new-tent-smell, relief washed over me. I felt suddenly solid. My terror subsided. My eyes adjusted in the shadowy light to quickly find a tree about ten feet away to relieve myself.

Back at the tent opening I paused, knelt close to the ground and breathed in predawn earth. Each sniff brought deeper awareness to my surroundings. My adrenalized hearing attuned to the night's true volume. Loud rustling became soft bits of chirp and chatter belonging to birds or squirrels, not bears. The more of that loamy surface I inhaled, the more I relaxed. I felt safe. The danger was conjured in my mind. Zipping myself back inside, sleep immediately took over. I've never been more thankful to *come back to my senses.*

The ground itself helped me ground. Since then, too many times to count, I've used this technique when *I'm feeling out of sorts.* Houseplants are the most convenient source of dirt at times. Watering or just digging in the pot with fingers releases a fragrance that brings me home when outside isn't available. Almost every friend and client I have has heard my advice to "sniff some dirt" at least once. It always works. When I told my friend Meredith, she said, "Of course it works. Everyone knows dirt is alive. It's the same stuff in our own guts."

Your senses dull for good reason when you are sick or in

physical pain. They dull when you are completely overwhelmed by a heartbreaking or devastating experience. You need to close down sometimes so you can process loss over time instead of all at once. The problem comes when disengaging becomes a habit that continually numbs your senses. You miss having a life filled with meaning and dimension. When you are dulled and not *all there,* your intuition has a hard time communicating with you.

There are many things we zone-out from habit. Congested places, interminable lines, anxiety, tension, fear, pain, anger, conflict or a myriad of other unpleasantries can trigger us to just go, tuning out the world around us. No one wants to endure any of that if we can escape by focusing on our grocery list, or daydreaming. The problem is that vacating your senses not only leaves you overwhelmed, drained and disconnected from your intuitive self, but unaware of what you need.

Yes, you might seem to get momentary relief from the screaming toddler in aisle four, but you lose more. Have you ever walked into a packed store feeling great and leave feeling tired or heavy, not sure what happened to your good mood?

The only sustainable relief you can find in an emotionally or physically crowded place comes by closely refocusing on your physical senses. The toddler's tantrum becomes manageable if you adjust your range of sound, touch and smell to the immediate space around you. Focusing on the sensation of where your feet land gives you stability, engages your intuition, and lets you know your on-the-spot needs. You realize you're hot and need shade, dehydrated needing water, discombobulated at Thanksgiving in need of a restroom for a quiet moment to gather yourself.

Also, intuitively you may feel the need to offer help to the overwhelmed mom in aisle four. Engaging the physical realigns you, helps you focus on your immediate sensations and not be overstimulated by the blurred cacophony of the masses.

Every time you leave the room while remaining in it, you pretend to be present. The person you fool and harm the most—losing memories, unaware of needs, dulled access to intuition, immobilized by fear and becoming exhausted—is yourself. The challenge is to know when you are pretending and *come back to your senses.*

Sniffing dirt brought me back.

My sister jerked me back. She returned me into the sumptuousness of Thanksgiving Day, the balanced weight of the silver in my hand, and the wonderful quirky attributes of people I love. I drank in stories, laughter and the rarity of being together.

I remembered. I came to my senses.

Invitation

Notice if your mind has wandered.
Now touch your heart with your hand.
Recognize, and say, I am here.
Slowly breathe in through your nose.
Feel the air touch the inside of your nostrils.
Feel your chest rise and your ribs expand as the breath fills.
Release your breath through your mouth,
sinking awareness deeper inside.
Ask all of your senses to open to this moment.
Let your eyes look at the words.
Now allow your gaze to soften and receive the words.
What textures does your wrist feel?
How many sounds are around?
Taste.

Notice different scents on the air.

Smile.

Curiosity in this moment has deepened.

Relax into the deepening by fluttering your eyes closed.

Rest.

7
Gaslighting

In the 1944 movie, *Gaslight,* a very young Ingrid Bergman (Paula) marries a dapper society man (Gregory). He tried to steal her fortune by deliberately doing things to make Paula believe she was going insane. Gregory repeatedly hides a painting and steals a locket he gave her, then tells Paula she hid the art and lost the necklace. He negates her experience of reality again and again, until she's convinced, she'd lost her mind.

Even though I had no monetary fortune to steal, I had a Gregory, (Greg) who hid things from me. He consistently sowed seeds of doubt in my mind. His deceptions made me question my perception. At the same time, it eroded my judgment and derailed my intuition.

When Greg and I began dating, I had just started taking classes on energy healing. Learning to sense and move energy had a side effect. I started to notice an increase in my ability to have accurate perceptions about things I had no way of knowing. My psychic intuitive abilities were expanding which was a lot of fun. I wanted to explore my newfound skill.

I'd play with the impressions I was getting with my friends. Their feedback was positive. The things I'd get impressions of were pretty benign and didn't seem invasive. Looking back, I should have asked their permission before I tuned into their life from the comfort of my home.

I'd tune in by feeling my love for them in my heart. As

I did, hazy images would flash up to my mind from my chest and I'd write down whatever surfaced. I'd randomly call and ask if my impressions were accurate. My friends were generous to humor my guesses. They'd confirm that, yes, they'd worn a striped shirt to work, had a new boyfriend, had a cold last week or no, they didn't have Mexican food for lunch. I was right about the trivial details of their lives most of the time, which was thrilling to have my far-away experiences confirmed.

When I was wrong, I'd start thinking maybe I was just lucky when I was right. Worse, I began to believe they were humoring me by telling me I was accurate when I wasn't. I was discouraging myself by lumping all of my intuitive perceptions as invalid because of a few misses. When I began defining intuitive hits as luck I stopped intuitively looking into my friends' lives.

Greg and I got serious quickly. I moved in with him, barely knowing him for two months. He seemed to like that I'd check out his day from afar; it felt like a special connection. He encouraged me and we had fun initially. Yes, he had to go to the mechanic unexpectedly. Yes, he spilled paint on his jeans. Yes, he was thinking about having spaghetti and meatballs for dinner and, "I can't believe you made it for me without asking."

I guesstimated that I was 90 percent accurate about the obscure details of his day. I stopped saying I just had a lucky guess and my confidence in my burgeoning ability was restored for about six weeks.

After about three months, my guesstimate with Greg dropped to five percent. He still asked me to try but, no, he didn't have pulled-pork for lunch, lose his favorite pen or forget something and have to go back for it. No, he wasn't late because he dropped by an old friend's house—he got caught at work, in traffic or at the grocery store. I had no evidence, but my heart and gut told me something wasn't right. Something definitely wasn't right with my impressions. I believed I'd lost my ability to tune into the people I love.

Greg was 10 years older. I was trying to be more mature and *act* how I thought a spiritually enlightened person *should* act. I wanted a relationship that was completely honest, even if it wasn't what I wanted to hear. Just in case he was afraid to hurt me, I would welcome truth. Thank him for correcting me. I'd preface conversations with, "Be honest. I won't be mad. I just want to understand you."

Occasionally I'd ask, "It feels like something about me is bothering you. Can we talk about it?"

After a particularly odd explanation about where he'd been, I asked, "Is something wrong? Do you want to see other people? Are you sure you're okay with our arrangement?"

All my questions were met with big smiles, hugs, kisses and assurances from Greg that everything was perfect. He *was* being honest. He was completely happy and would I, "Please stop being insecure and paranoid."

I stopped asking questions. I started to feel crazy. My chest and stomach would tighten when he walked in the door after *working late.* It didn't feel like he'd been at work. When I called to ask when he'd be home and got no answer, he'd say he was too busy to pick up the phone. Something wasn't right. But there was no concrete evidence of anything going on. How could I be completely off? Could I be paranoid?

Our romantic relationship ended after a year and a half when Greg admitted he had been cheating for most of our time together and didn't plan to stop.

During our conversation I was still acting like I thought a spiritual person should act—kind, understanding and forgiving. I pushed down the hurt and anger and pretended I didn't feel utterly devastated. He smiled at me lovingly and affirmed he knew I'd handle this well. Before he went out that Saturday night, he told me with a kind and gentle tone, "You can take all the time you need to move out."

Our future had ended but I was relieved that I hadn't been crazy. I knew! Why didn't I believe my chest tightening as evidence? I was mad at myself, having difficulty behaving the way I thought I should. I wanted to scream at him for every lie he told me. But I was rising above that kind of behavior. So, I was relieved when he announced he was going out that evening to, "…give me time alone to start thinking about where I was going to go."

How was I going to find a new affordable place that also took my Bassett hound Atticus? I crawled to the middle of our double bed, my mind churning. My body was numb. Desperation pushed me to find something positive to do. I sat still. I needed help. The "What am I going to do?" thought had taken over.

I couldn't stop that thought and it was gathering momentum. I flirted with doubt. Maybe Divine help didn't exist. Whether it did or didn't, *what am I going to do?* wasn't going to work. Maybe a prayer-ish request would. I asked, prayed, and then begged for help. "Spirit, please help me find an affordable place to live. Now. Right now. I have to get out of here."

Atticus snored softly, seventy pounds of solid muscle and 10 pounds of drool. He stretched out on an oversized khaki-colored canvas pillow at the foot of the bed.

I closed my eyes and sat still, hoping to see a new life that I couldn't imagine. To prod a vision, I squeezed my eyes tight and then relaxed them. Squeezed then relaxed, over and over. I had no idea how long or why I thought it would produce a result. It didn't. I tried to focus on nothingness. Something other than my determination helped me sit there, bored and sad and waiting. Other people got a heads-up about their future. I wanted those same magical visions.

Actually, I wanted the address of a house I could afford to appear in my mind. Now. What use was this woo-woo-weird stuff if it couldn't pony up with something useful when I needed it?

At some point I felt calm and still. My mind stopped the unhelpful swirling of, "What am I going to do?"

A garden gate emerged in my mind's eye. I knew something beyond *me* was happening. I wouldn't have imagined this scene in a thousand years. It was almost like seeing in a dream. The gate had an arch over it and a white wooden fence coming off either side leading into a hazy space. What did this mean? I couldn't afford to live somewhere with this kind of outdoor space. I stood in the gate's threshold but had no idea what to do next. So, I waited. Something bigger was present. Somehow, I had the ability to wait. At that point, patience alone was evidence of a miracle.

I saw spotty blurs of grays, greens and muted browns in the space beyond the gate. It sort of scared me. I momentarily felt the Divine had betrayed me by offering no clarity. I stubbornly sat and pleaded for clues as to what this vision meant. It was just beyond my grasp. Then I saw-felt a bit of space open to my right. Atticus, ears waving, was bounding through the gate in front of me. He paused, looking back at me with a thrumping enthusiastic wag that said, "Come on, it's time to go!"

My eyes popped open I was so surprised, and I checked to see where Atticus actually was. He had shifted to his back, in a dog yoga supine twist, head turned to look towards me. He opened one eye and went back to sleep. I was left with a peaceful feeling. For now, my worry was magically gone and I was okay. At least this was some kind of response to my request for help. Hopefully I would be able to get *actual* information soon.

The next day, out of the blue, a coworker told me a house was for rent across the street from her. "It's cheap and I bet they'd let you have your dog."

A week and a half later I was moving into a lovingly restored, sky blue 1908 shotgun home with a huge white-pillared front porch, oak floors, 12-foot ceilings, and a dog friendly fenced in backyard. The cherry on top was a dishwasher. I'd never had one before. The house didn't have an arched gate or white picket fence. I didn't expect it to. I knew the gate in my vision was symbolic, indicating I'd have everything I needed. As I walked through the threshold to my new home, I couldn't believe how fortunate I was that this turn-of-the-century slice of heaven was below my budget.

Greg actually helped with the move. He visited every day to pick up the boxes I'd unpack. He was being helpful and affectionate. I was still acting within my imagined rules of spiritual goodness. When I was almost completely settled, he said, "Being together is so much better when we aren't living together. Don't you think?"

I smiled but didn't agree so he continued, "Soooo, I've been feeling a bit guilty. You know that *women's intuition* guessing game you used to play? You were starting to freak me out, so I lied and said you were wrong. You were getting way too much right... Sorry."

The gaslighting about cheating was bad but I understood the desire to want to get away with it. Lying about harmless details was unthinkable. Sick. Especially when he encouraged me to keep trying. It was then I ended my mythical spiritual goodie-good act and shared how I really felt, ending my relationship with Greg.

Gaslighting is when one person tells another that what they saw, heard or experienced wasn't real, when it was. By definition, gaslighting makes someone question their own memory, perception and judgment to evoke personality changes such as low self-esteem using denial, misinformation and misdirection in an attempt to have someone question their beliefs. The person doing the gaslighting gains control with lies and misdirection, while appearing to be a caring person who's trying to help. The person being gaslighted loses the ability to have an opinion, objections, or make decisions without the other person pointing out they are unsound.

Looking back, I realize Greg was reflecting what I'd been doing to myself around intuition. I was afraid of being called a fraud, so I focused mainly on the evidence that suggested I could be a fraud. I had been gaslighting myself for years by negating my own accurate intuitive experiences with a few inaccuracies. I gave much more weight to my perceived intuitive failures than to my actual successes.

In my mind it took 10 correct impressions to negate one inaccurate one. I was more focused on fertilizing my doubts about my intuitive abilities, than nurturing and refining my accurate results. This kept me frustrated and blind to improvement. I made a huge mistake by dismissing all of my inner information as not real when most of it was.

Our culture raises self-gaslighters. We look critically in the mirror, and reality becomes distorted. Our minds magnify our flaws, failures and inadequacies, which squeeze out what's lovely, successful and brilliant in us. We doubt ourselves, making comparisons to an inner vision of imaginary perfection, so that no one can see themselves as they are.

The nature of critical comparison is a distorted lens if you place a fantasy or an outer ideal next to what is actually happening; you skew what's there. Part of self-gaslighting is believing the *shoulds* take precedent over reality. *Shoulds* erase clarity so you don't trust what's right in front of you. My skewed version of a truthful spiritual relationship was a *should*. I placed trusting his word over my own instincts. My mind ignored my intuition even though it was screaming, "Something is wrong!"

Subtle intuitive nudges don't have a chance when you live in *shoulds* and constant self-criticism. Self-doubt and misinformation are so loud everything else is drowned out. When you gaslight yourself, perceived imperfection keeps you in fear, locked into listening to your inner critic or inner what-am-I-going-to-do victim. It keeps you from reality.

You need to stop long enough and ask your inner compass for help. By breathing into the nothingness of your center, courage ignites and new questions and information begin to show up. I had no idea what was considered intuitive success.

After I left Greg, an old friend called because she thought I'd be interested in some studies she'd come across on intuition. It turns out that 65 percent intuitive accuracy is extraordinary. One hundred percent accuracy doesn't exist. I was under the impression that if I wasn't at 95 percent or more, I was a fraud. I gaslighted myself by believing what I thought *should* be a reasonable amount of precision. I never thought to look up actual facts or question my *shoulds*.

When Greg said my intuitive notions were constantly wrong, I lied to myself pretending [gaslighting] it didn't matter. I began questioning [gaslighting] the validity of every intuitive perception before anyone else could. It seemed like a good idea to not rely too heavily on outer validation. Unfortunately, I trained [gaslighted] myself to think my way out of my valid experiences. When my intuition failed, it became a reflex to challenge [gaslight] and often ignore valuable intuitive insight. I second-guessed [gaslighted] my memory, experience and positive feedback from my friends. I dismissed [gaslighted] truths that lay in front of me. I didn't want to be one of those crazy psychics who thought they were always right, though I was doing a good job making myself crazy by suspecting [gaslighting] every extraordinary experience I had was luck.

It's scary to think of the speed in which my inner gaslight became a reflex. I talked myself out of the evidence right in front of me, making it easy to disregard the many intuitive red flags around Greg.

If I could tell my 24 year old self one thing, it would be to write down every intuitive hit and put them in one place.

Concrete evidence is important. A few years later that's what I did. I used an empty wooden breadbox as a container to put scratched down notes about any intuited feeling I had. It filled with scrap pieces of paper, napkins and Post-its in a year. I added thank you letters people wrote me on how I helped them and printed emails of their intuitive successes.

My focus turned to remembering and cultivating success. I especially wrote down the intuitive advice I didn't listen to or follow. Many times, I had a *feeling* I needed to go a different way to work, not listening and finding myself stuck in stopped traffic, I'd check with co-workers who drove the other route. There were never backups on the way my intuition directed. My failure to take a different path to work reaped unwelcome delays but the result confirmed an intuitive win. I wrote it down and placed the story in the box.

Everyone has hits and misses. Sometimes what you think is a miss turns out to be a hit. You don't always have all of the information to prove your insights. It doesn't mean people are purposely lying to you. Hindsight always brings greater perspective. When I had a miss, I'd write that down as well, notice it, put it in a smaller box inside my breadbox. Then I'd read a few of the notes that were accurate to remind myself of the 65 percent study. My breadbox evidence visually showed a much higher percentage of accuracy and shifted my focus. I began to trust myself, which automatically stopped self-gaslighting and accelerated living intuitively.

In the movie Gaslight, Paula's fortune was saved when she finally saw and believed her own experience. Don't let anyone—including yourself—steal your fortune.

Invitation

Intuition is validated fastest by failure to listen.
"I knew it. Why didn't I do it?"
To fail to act on intuition is an important lesson.
Breathe in and feel this truth.
Let that thought that intuition isn't about perfection sink in.
Think of a time when this happened.
The feeling was right even if the action wasn't.
Intuition is working.
Breathe in and feel this truth.
Think back to a time when something didn't feel right.
There was no evidence other than a feeling of wrongness.
Remember the decision to act or not act on that feeling.
Go back to that moment,
That feeling of wrongness.
Notice where the body knew something was wrong.
Mark that place in your mind like a body map.
Realize this feeling will occur there again.
Breathe in and feel this truth.
Invite the mind to remember this sensation.
Invite the mind to remember that this feeling of
wrongness was right.
Breathe in allowing the mind to connect to this
valuable body information.
Invite the mind to take a different action next time.
Thank the mind for participating.
There is unimaginable power in simply being where you are.

Part 2
Intuition Building Blocks

8

Yes, but... What Is Intuition?

When I was reconnected with Sophie, an old friend of many years, she asked me what intuition was and how to use it. Overjoyed that she was interested in my work, I yammered on for quite a while about how to access and develop her intuition. Finally, I stopped long enough to ask if what I was saying was helpful.

"Probably," she paused, searching for what I assume was a way to be kind. "But I can't really concentrate on your suggestions... because... first I really want to understand... what is intuition?"

I had gone right to the how, so I tried again. "It's that sensation inside where *you know* something feels absolutely *go ahead true* or *grinding to a halt wrong* throughout your being, especially when it defies logic."

She sighed, "I know that. What is it though?"

Sophie wasn't being difficult. She really wanted to know the substance of intuition. She was convinced that if she knew exactly what intuition is, like muscle, she could find it in herself and make better decisions.

I tried metaphors. "Intuition is like the air that carries the music between the instrument being played and the melody arriving in our ears."

Silence. I tried again, "Intuition is like the old-fashioned switchboard operators connecting one person to another by plugging in wires on a board."

I heard a sigh and continued on. "Intuition is like the nerves delivering signals from the brain to the body."

"So is intuition the nervous system?" Sophie asked.

"No. It's not the nervous system but the nervous system can receive signals from intuition that informs the body."

"Why won't you tell me what it is? I can handle it," she huffed.

I wasn't hiding information from her or being vague on purpose. The nature of intuition isn't fixed. It's not a body part that can be found in a specific place. Trying to pinpoint intuition is like grabbing water with your fingertips, you can't hold onto it. This was the first time I realized that some people needed intuition defined. Webster's "quick and ready insight" wasn't cutting it.

Trying another angle I responded, "Some people like to say intuition is your sixth sense. I believe it's so much larger and more complex. Intuition is our essence."

She started to speak a few times, stopping as if trying to find the words she needed to get me to understand her question. "Okay if you can't answer what intuition is... then explain what 'our essence' is please."

"It depends on your belief system. I believe our essence is an extension of or a part of our Soul. The bigger part of who we are, that has access to something even bigger. Some call the 'even bigger' God, Source, Creator, universal intelligence, Divine, the collective unconscious, expanded awareness, angels, guidance, many different names throughout the world. It isn't the same for everyone, just use the term that works for you." Sophie made a *ummhum* sound for me to continue.

"Intuition is connected to that bigger wisdom that sometimes defies logic, reason and our inclinations. At its strongest, it is a deep knowing, an undeniable feeling that resonates in the body and mind so strongly it can stop us or propel us forward. At its weakest it is the faintest whisper, a fleeting question or a body sensation that's barely detectable. It is the place where you don't just think, you know."

I'll paraphrase the rest of the lengthy explanation I gave her. Intuition is an energy that receives valuable information then broadcasts it to the body on many different frequencies for us to pick up. Intuition is a receptor and connector. Intuition is an energy that receives insights from the "even bigger" and helps deliver those bits of data into our consciousness.

Intuitive information can arrive differently for the same person at different times. Clients often tell me that when they can stay curious as to what will happen, expectations dissolve and it becomes like a game to see how their body responds. One day the chest may tighten, the next the belly might feel heavy. Both were experienced as a warning to stop and pay attention. "That's why I was sharing ways to access and develop it," I said, wrapping up my explanation.

Sophie's response was honest. "Thank you. I always thought there was some secret place inside that people found through meditation or chanting or something. I figured if someone just told me what or where it was, I could bypass all of that woo-woo stuff and the knowledge would just... follow." She laughed. "Guess I have to figure out what I believe and work on it, eh?"

Sophie's assumptions about intuition aren't uncommon. Yes, meditations, yoga, and other practices help clear the mind and bring a focus to the body, which increases the chances of noticing an intuitive signal. The body, after all, is where we receive and understand deep knowing. Usually, the people who find me had an uninvited jolt of instant knowing that changed their life somehow. Or they had a grandmother who told them to always listen to their intuition and they couldn't figure out how.

Instant knowing does not need interpreting like other more subtle forms of intuition. Instant knowing is direct knowledge that resonates as truth in us so profoundly it often contradicts rational thought. It seems to come out of the blue and we listen to it or we don't. When we don't listen to it our sentences may later start with, *I knew it.*

A close family member had an instant knowing dream the night before her wedding. In her dream she walked into the church in her wedding dress and the only occupant was a large skunk in the aisle. She woke up knowing it was a mistake to marry. BUT everyone had flown in. She considered the caterer, the flowers, the expense and she couldn't disappoint everyone by calling it off. When she speaks of her first marriage her sentences start with, "*I knew it* wasn't right but..."

Another type of instant knowing is when we have laid the groundwork by studying and working hard in our career and a new job or idea magically appears. Author Cathy Pickens talks about how the idea for writing true crime stories "came in a blinding flash."

Pickens credits the instant success of switching her genre "to being ready." She had waded through the long process of finding an interested publisher when writing her fictional *Southern Fried Mystery* series, so she knew the process. A foundation can be important. The fact that Pickens acted immediately on the true crime idea and had a contract in a week shows she trusted that blinding flash of intuition. Knowing when to act can be the difference between slogging through or seamlessly making the change.

I hope, like Sophie, you understand the nature of intuition a bit more. Just a nuance of understanding is enough to explore the stories about the everyday practical habit of sensory listening. Perhaps you will recognize some of the different ways to act from an intuitive position. Perhaps you'll be inspired or intrigued to explore more.

I invite you to be open to the out-of-the-corner-of-your-eye messages that your body receives. Simply acknowledging your intuitive glimpses make the flashy aha moments more frequently available.

Value hindsight.

The *I knew its* are just as important as being able to follow through on an intuitive nudge. My relative admits her intuition was an undeniable knowing when she dreamed of the skunk. She made a choice that she thought was right for her at the time, a choice we all have to not act on intuitive knowledge.

Finally, like my friend Sophie, you can explore different beliefs until you find the *something bigger* that anchors you. Trusting the source of your intuition is an open invitation for wisdom to visit again and again.

Invitation

Feel the weight in your body and where it touches a surface.
Redirect the grabbing mind that wants to know now.
Inhale softly into several places where the body lands.
Let breath touch the hands, back,
and bottom places resting on surfaces.
Ask the body to remember a time of direct knowing.
Allow a memory to surface.
One you listened to or disregarded, it doesn't matter which.
If nothing comes, simply be with the nothingness.
From this place know that your intuition exists.
Take a moment and feel the truth of that knowing.
Allow a tiny experience to become something
bigger that contains wisdom.
One moment, no matter how fleeting,
know that connection is available.

Even if it is a belief that bigger place of wisdom exists,
That is the beginning of knowing and a
connection that is undeniable with body acknowledgement.

9

Where Does Intuition Come From?

Many people who work with me describe themselves as *spiritual, not religious.* Oftentimes their spiritual beliefs are a major factor in why they reach out. They want to connect to their intuition so that a bigger force can help them navigate life.

For the first 10 years of my practice, it was easy for me <u>not</u> to look any further than the Divine as the source of intuitive wisdom. It didn't matter what aspect or denomination. The idea that intuition is our Essence/Spirit/Soul, and has a direct connection to a divine Source seemed to work for everyone. Those who are non-religious to those ranging from Baptist to Buddhist, including clergy and nuns, agreed with that philosophy—intuition is the Divine communicating with us.

That was all well and good until I got pulled out of my comfort zone with a call from Victoria.

The first thing I do with a client is ask them to share their spiritual beliefs so I can adjust my language to fit their ideology. It doesn't matter what flavor of faith they have; to me all forms of spirituality stem from the same place. But, when I asked Victoria what her spiritual belief system was, she replied, "I'm not spiritual at all. I'm an atheist."

I was completely thrown.

What was I going to do with someone who had no spiritual beliefs? At all. Stunned, I blurted words I couldn't reel back, "You know who you're talking to, right?"

So. Horribly. Unprofessional.

Thankfully, Victoria has a great sense of humor. Her

laughter flowed through the phone. She told me she knew who I was from my website. Then she opened a door I'd never considered when she said, "You say on your site all we need to believe is that something bigger can guide us. I believe we all have access to the collective unconscious through our intuition. It permeates everything and makes more sense to me than a divine God or *something*. I'm pretty sure that's where my intuition comes from, so do you think you can help me?"

I wasn't sure, but her belief made sense. The Jungian idea that part of our mind can tap into the collective ancestral experiences from all humankind sounded possible. I'd just never given it much thought before. Research is starting to show that we get more information from our DNA than we can currently understand. Or perhaps there is an invisible web of all of our species' past experience. Why not? The idea that the past is somehow all recorded and accessible to us isn't out of the realm of possibilities.

I apologized to Victoria for my incredulous response and thanked her for being so open minded. I admitted that I didn't know if I could help and asked if she was up for an experiment. She was. Her yoga and meditation practice wasn't working to get her brain out of constant motion anymore. She recognized that she needed to find another route to the sensations of stillness and silence that jumpstarted her instincts. She was searching for practical steps to take in her career and personal life that would lead to more fulfillment.

Connecting to her intuition to access the ever-expanding collective unconscious worked for Victoria. Because thoughts and experiences were constantly being added to the collective, she felt there was always fresh data to access. Through monthly sessions, we experimented together for about a year. She began to trust her senses and gained a felt connection to the expanse of the collective unconscious. Just like my intuition's relationship to the Divine, her intuition's relationship to the collective unconscious came through physical responses and *aha* moments.

There was no difference in the process I used with other clients except vocabulary. I generally use different terms for the bigger-than-me sources anyway. We discovered many ways for Victoria to physically/sensorily experience full body centeredness before she made decisions. Her mind became calm as she tuned into choices that helped her feel settled and comfortable—her intuitive voice. It started to sing regularly. She learned to stay curious until the path "felt right on key." Every few years she still calls for a tune-up.

After working with Victoria, I had a new understanding that the only foundational belief needed to access intuition is knowing there is an accessible place of wisdom bigger-than-me. For an intuitive connection to be easily made you need to have a mental construct of an unseen place where insights reside. And, that place or space doesn't have to be spiritual. Your mind just needs to be curious about a place of knowledge that only your intuition can draw from outside your normal spectrum. The whole premise of intuition is that you are capable of receiving knowledge obtained from an invisible source. You don't even have to name this bigger-than-me place, though most times, it helps.

There are many bigger-than-me places intuition has the potential to access. Some can be daunting and difficult to believe that *little old me* has a direct line to God, Source, Universe, etc... People may have a strong belief system but find it uncomfortable to accept the idea that their intuition is gleaning wisdom from these huge places. Sometimes you need to find a vocabulary to help you fully settle into that connection.

The following stories can help to sort out the wording that feels natural and effective for you.

Charlene believes in God. It also makes her nervous to think her intuition has a direct link from God. "I think God has more to do than pay attention to me."

I would never say, *Charlene that's not true. God has limitless time for you. After all he/she/they is God.* That's not honest. Seriously, we both know God doesn't share an appointment book with me. It's not my business to change Charlene's belief. It is my job to help her find a more palatable idea or wording so she feels comfortable with accessing her bigger-than-me place.

Charlene and I went through different possibilities like benevolent spirits, divine guidance and heavenly helpers. None of them felt right. We both fell to silent searching. Suddenly Charlene exclaimed, "Angels!" She laughed. "How could I have forgotten about angels? They'll work. They are God's messengers, right? He's got to have a bunch of them and they're bigger than me. Let's ask my intuition to connect to them."

Angels continue to help Charlene.

Karen also believes in God. She doesn't believe in direct communication with God and has an aversion to angels. "Angels are the stuff of fairy tales. I can't connect to something I don't believe in."

She's right. None of us can connect when it feels like a lie. I asked her if she had any relatives that had passed on that hold her same beliefs. She didn't hesitate. "My grandmother. She was such a devout, good person. I know she's in a place where she can see clearer than I can. I'd love to connect to her."

Just thinking of her grandmother opened Karen's heart and gave her a receptive place inside for intuition to bloom.

Robin believes nature is her bigger-than-me source of wisdom. "I always get clarity after I go on a hike in the woods or walk on the beach. I want to get that same knowing in the city."

Robin now calls on the spirit of those natural landscapes to her intuitive link. "I close my eyes to gaze at my favorite tree, or sometimes I look at the ocean on my screen saver, breathe and ask for help to get clear on the decision I'm making. Most of the time it brings me peace. Sometimes it feels like a hug. I know I always get clarity shortly after I experience this space inside. Even if the clarification is, *it's not time to know.*"

So many traditions send us into nature to clarify our direction. Spend enough time in beauty and your intuitive receptors automatically get charged. Nature is an unlimited source of insight. Many indigenous people talk about how plants, rocks and land speak to them about healing. We know scientists still seek information from indigenous people about vegetation, bark and insects that heal specific disorders to test in our laboratories. We are all made from this planet. Maybe intuitive direction comes from the earth itself. The world is certainly a bigger-than-me place.

Rose has an inclusive belief system. Over a few months she tried asking for help from many places to experience which felt right. One day she called on the woods to help. Unexpectedly, a vision of a large grassy circle surrounded by old trees came into her mind's eye. Instantly all the tension drained from her body and she felt an overwhelming sense of love. She just sat there for a moment in disbelief as the feeling remained. Internally she asked, *What to call this place?* She felt a light happy dancing feeling and thought of fairies. To me she said, "A fairy circle? No way."

This challenged her practical business side, but she couldn't deny the experience. She tried and failed to create the feeling herself. But every time Rose calls on her fairy circle it comes to surround her when she needs direction. Sometimes she sees it. Sometimes she has a full sensory experience. "I know, to other people, a fairy circle may sound weird or just plain crazy. It did to me—but I don't care. I feel a large friendly green love surround me. It settles me down every time so I can *feel* my way forward."

Pam believes in a Universal Source of wisdom. "It just feels too big to connect to, I mean it's out there, with the stars and planets. I can't figure out how information transmits specifically to me from way out there."

Something made me ask Pam, "What's that song that says we are stardust, we are billion-year-old carbon?" She knew which one I meant, *Woodstock* by Crosby, Stills, Nash and Young, so I continued, "Science tells us that most of the elements that make up our body were formed in the stars—maybe the Universe communicates to you through those atoms?"

Pam shared that her whole body tingled then relaxed at the thought. "Now that you say it that way, I'm sure that's what my intuition connects to."

Missy believes her intuition sorts the data from what her subconscious gathers. "It's logical. I mean, studies show we pick up vast amounts of information every minute that never reaches our consciousness. I don't need any leap of faith to embrace science."

She's not alone in this belief. In 2016, researchers at the University of New South Wales* came up with quantifiable evidence that intuition—defined as unconscious information in our body and brain that helps guide us in making faster, better, more confident decisions—exists. They concluded that intuition not only exists, it can also be quantitatively measured.

Years ago Victoria knocked down a door I hadn't known I'd closed and helped me see that any bigger-than-me place is a valid link for our intuition to source from. You just need to feel that your connection to that intelligence is possible, comfortable and accessible.

I've learned that the mind can shut out just about anything. And we don't even realize it. When you allow your mind to explore comfortable names for the benign bigger-than-me consciousness your intuition connects too, it makes a difference.

You can't pay attention to information obtained from a place you don't quite believe in or trust. It may take some time to find what clicks for you. When you do, you are 95 percent open to living an intuitive life. The other 5 percent is learning to listen.

Invitation

Allow a few deep breaths.
Think of the oxygen entering the lungs.
Notice it is invisible yet sustaining.
Think of an invisible place or consciousness
that is huge and wise.
Ask, do I believe it's possible to access that wisdom directly?
Take another breath and allow the possibility
of that wisdom to ride in on air.
Do your muscles release or tighten?
Just notice.
Let go of judgment and embrace the felt information.
Invite yourself to revisit this invitation and discover more.

*Reference
https://www.psychologicalscience.org/news/minds-business/intuition-its-more-than-a-feeling.html
Lufityanto, G., Donkin, C., & Pearson, J. (2016). Measuring Intuition: Non-conscious Emotional Information Boosts Decision Accuracy and Confidence. Psychological Science. doi: 10.1177/0956797616629403

10
The Bottom Line

I n many of my retreats I give everyone a tennis ball.

Most stand, holding on to the back of a chair if needed to stay steady. Some sit, and we all place the ball under one socked foot. We breathe onto the sensation of the ball rolling back and forth, side to side and front to back. Stopping the ball under the heel of the foot, toes secure on the floor, we release our weight into the ball. We bounce and rotate around a bit, letting one heel press into the fuzzy surface for about 15 seconds. Then we roll the ball to the front of the foot and drop our heel to the floor. We keep bouncing the ball of our foot, back and forth, on the tennis ball for another 15 seconds. Keeping the heel planted, we roll the ball side to side under the ridge of the toes.

At this point people are laughing because someone's ball has shot across the room and others are bending to catch it without losing their own ball. The final flourish is to roll the ball anywhere on the foot that feels good, like a mini massage. The whole treatment for one foot takes less than a minute.

Before we treat our other foot, we get to *the bottom line* of the whole exercise. Standing still on the bottoms of both feet we compare, not just the difference in each foot, but our whole body.

The words people use to describe the foot that had been rolled are expansive, grounded, open, rooted, awake, planted, and alive. When I ask if any differences extend beyond the foot, yeses spring up throughout the room. Most express how shocked they are by how different they feel on each side.

One woman describes, "Half of me is full, comfortably

relaxed…solid. While the other half seems dull, up, not engaged with the floor."

Another says, "I feel weighted on the rolled side but it's not heavy. I'm connected with movement… aliveness is pouring into my leg, stabilizing my hip which isn't sore now. Can we please do the other side?"

Murmurs of agreement *let's do the other side* come from the rest of the class. Before we roll the other foot, I have them harvest more information. "The foot we haven't rolled is how we usually are all day."

Everyone's head nods in agreement as I share my experience. "The bottom of that foot feels like it has a barrier preventing it from connecting with the floor. The bottom of my rolled foot feels wider, like it's helping to open pathways of gravity that release tension to the parts of the body it can reach. Clearly our kinesthetic senses are feeling more. Are your other senses more active?"

A palpable silence swallows the room as sound, smell, and taste are investigated. Heads shake yes. Others give thumbs up. One woman flutters her hand back and forth, indicating just a little more sensory activity. She smiles and says, "My other side wants the ball treatment so I can be sure."

I take the hint and get everybody rolling.

This is the feeling of being grounded. Relaxing down into the bottom of your feet enough to receive the energy that's always there for you. We've lost touch with our exchange of energy with the earth because we haven't been taught to notice.

You see, touch, hear, taste and smell every day—yet your senses can atrophy when you are *doing* the head business of life too long. You are human. You get caught up in things and forget to be sensory curious—it happens all the time. You're not perfect and probably get bored with a continual focus on grounding. I know I do, but I like the feeling of being grounded much better once it's activated. The women in the retreat had a hard time waiting to do the other side. The rolled side felt so much better.

Here's the *bottom line:* multiple sensory *receptors* are open doors with huge welcome mats attracting your intuition. When your whole body gets involved, you receive from everything around you. You feel alive. Intuition is intrinsic to an enlivened life. Yes, intuition can enter your thoughts, but without the multisensory experience, you usually don't listen or trust intuitive information that comes only to your mind.

How do you get your whole body's participation? Start by feeling your weight drop down into your bottom like Weebles, the egg-shaped toys for children by Hasbro that *wobble, but don't fall down.* You need to connect to your weight and density, standing or seated, in the bottom of your body. Your contact with the world starts from the bottoms of your feet, the back of your thighs, forearms, wrists, any body part resting on a surface—including your bottom.

Sitting on your bottom all day is not the same thing as *feeling* the weight that lowers your sense of gravity. As Westerners, we primarily live in our heads. We were trained to live this way the moment we sat at a desk and had to keep-still-and-pay-attention all day in first grade. Now most of us sit in front of computers, cell phones, digital games, televisions for most or part of the day and we tend to interact from where our awareness resides the most, our heads. Getting in your bottom requires regular shifts in awareness—from solely thinking to embodied-soul being.

Right now your head may be probing which of your senses are engaged, as mentioned in previous chapters. Or you might be trying to analyze the current experience your body is having. Can you tell if you are observing from outside yourself, as if you're looking down at your body? That place is where your mind *thinks* it knows what you are feeling.

Or, do you drop down inside to notice which senses are

awake? Either way, soften your gaze. Now breathe in and back, feel the movement go all the way down your spine, inviting your mind to follow the breath. Do this a few times. Notice the way an inner awareness begins to relax down into your seat and other points of contact. Feel how shoulders come down a notch and how breath riding the spine down changes the openness in your chest. This is the beginning of being grounded.

Losing your body awareness isn't hard to do. Leaving full sensation can be a relief, especially during times of pain, illness or stress. You know the sayings *worked up, wound up, spun out, or out of touch?* That's the feeling of leaving your body. Also *space out, zone out* or *numb out* are obvious exits. The most difficult body exit to spot is when the mind takes over into get-the-job-done hyperfocus mode.

Trust me when I say grounding didn't come naturally to me. At 24, I was stuck in my head. In a workshop I was attending, the term *grounding* was thrown around a lot. I was clueless, oblivious to symptoms of being ungrounded—talking too much, the inability to calmly process an experience without jumping to conclusions and self-criticism.

David was grounded. To sit with him felt like sitting next to a gray-haired, neatly dressed tree. He was slender and not more than five foot ten. My mental whirlwind didn't ruffle his demeanor or perfect posture. He was always patient, kind, solid and direct with me. We met at a workshop. He noticed me struggling, introduced himself and asked, "Would you like some help?"

"Yes!"

Motioning me to walk outside with him, I started to excitedly explain what I needed help with.

"I just don't understand what being grounded means. I think I know but I don't feel it. The world dulls sometimes— like I'm out of or above myself. I mean sometimes I do get in..." I prattled on and on to David. My soon-to-be mentor listened to my rambling until I was talked out. God love him, it took more than a minute.

We sat down at a worn wooden picnic table out of the fray of students taking an outside break. He succinctly condensed my request, "So you want to understand what it feels like to be grounded and how to achieve that state consistently?"

"Yes."

"Okay. Take a few breaths and show me how you leave your body."

He was asking me to demonstrate how my energy moved up and floated above my head. I'd never *tried* to leave before. It just happened for as long as I could remember. Concentrating, I tried to move my energetic self up and out. I felt a brief gentle sensation lifting up and to the right side above my head. I don't know why I felt an inner movement up to the right, not left or just straight up. A soft stop followed about a foot above my right ear. I then felt a sinking back down into myself. "I'm so contrary, I can't even lea…"

David stopped me before I could go off on another tangent.

"Don't worry. Just tell me what you're feeling."

"It's like my belly and my legs were hollow when I moved up. Now I feel my weight on the bench and a kind of fullness coming in. I can smell jasmine."

I looked around and spotted its yellow blooms sprinkled along a fence quite a distance away. David had wisely walked me outside for our talk, where my senses would easily engage— sweet smells, gravel crunching, breeze on the skin, and natural beauty.

"Anything else different?" David asked. "Would you say you're grounded now? How do you know?"

Put on the spot, I started to feel the sensation of my weight lifting skyward, leaving my body.

"Now it's not working. I'm lighter. More in my head. I'll never get it…" My frustration fast turned to defeat.

David interrupted my critical verbal spiral. "That's good. You know where you are. Don't try to grab for the sensation to change it. Feel where your energy is going and let your awareness converge to be with the movement instead of directing or fighting it. See what happens."

I tried to be with my *moving energy*. "It's not working."

"Are you trying?"

"Yes. Of course I'm trying."

"You don't have to try to see me, do you?"

I shook my head slowly, "No."

I'd never thought of not trying. Or that there could be times I didn't need to try. "If I don't try, how do I do it?"

David easily kept me on track, "Okay, *try* to look at me…. Good. Now, just look at me. Is there a difference?"

"Well, when I *try* to look I feel pulled up… like I'm trying to go out to see you. The front of my eyes constrict, my eyebrows come together and my face feels tight… When I *just look* at you everything relaxes. I get a sensation of receiving your face through my eyes. My shoulders relax, my mind clears… I feel my weight, not heavy, supported… like I'm connected to the grass growing."

Over the years David taught me that there are many ways to access just about everything we need. Some of what he said about grounding seemed obvious. "The ground is always there. Gravity holds us. Let your whole body *feel* that supportive relationship you were born into."

I began to understand that when he said *feel* he meant it literally. Feel the contact points, the line of whatever I'm touching, resting or standing on. Touch and be touched. When

I let the weight of my awareness follow gravity to the bottom of anything that is supportive—my feet on the floor, my elbow on the arm of the chair or my bottom to the seat of a stool—not only do I join the line on which we meet, I get a sense of relaxed merging into my own calm center. In this place, if I have forgotten to eat or haven't moved in a while, I instantly know it.

You may not understand where your energy is but I guarantee you, you've experienced that surface self versus the deep down self. We all have had *a knowing from deep down inside.* This off-the-cuff remark is often used after saying that we believed one thing to be true but *deep down* we knew it to be different. This is an indicator of the direction our energy goes to find the truth. Inside. Down in our body. Not up in our head. It's that subtle awareness that just exists. It's one way we perceive energy. We don't have to try to feel it, if we come down in ourselves, it communicates loudly.

Even people with high body awareness have issues with finding their weighted seat.

A swim-team coach attended one of my presentations. I had the audience contract one butt cheek, then hold and release the same cheek several times. I had everyone compare how each side of their body felt. Uneven. The side that had a workout felt awake and alive while the other cheek didn't. When the audience gave the same squeezing treatment to the other side, they felt balanced. Not just in their buttocks. People spoke about feeling full and more centered in their whole body.

The swim coach spoke up, admitting that he initially thought the exercise was stupid and that he wasn't going to participate. But his curiosity eventually won out. He was shocked to discover he could actually contract one butt cheek at a time while sitting. He'd never thought to try before and was intrigued with the results.

"I know it sounds ridiculous, but as I was sitting there

feeling my body balanced by a few simple squeezes, a solution to help a team member improve his stroke came to me. I can't believe it! I've been struggling with how to help him for a while." He laughed then winked. "It's funny—I never thought my butt would *crack* the code to my intuition."

When he was experiencing his body, not *trying* to figure out how to fix a swim stroke, his intuition came through.

Those who spend extensive hours in front of a computer often don't realize how much stress is held in the neck and shoulders. When our head takes full control, we have very little awareness of the information our body is constantly providing. Sole awareness coming from our head blocks pain that signals we may need to stretch, eat or change position to keep us healthy and balanced. When we look at things purely from our head, we miss the wisdom the body offers.

Nan, a businessperson and academic, was completely unaware her neck was so stiff it was almost immobilized. During our first telephone session, her neck felt (to me) like a garden statue made of concrete. To confirm this feeling, I asked her to tell me how her neck felt. She immediately answered, "It's fine. Why?"

I asked, "Did you take the time to really feel your neck internally? Or do you *think* it's fine?"

"What's the difference?"

"Let's see if there is one for you, Nan. Take a deep breath and roll your shoulders. Now as your breath releases, allow a slow turn of your head. How does your neck feel?"

"I can barely move my neck—It's so stiff. How did I not know?"

Nan's energy was stuck in her head, bypassing the valuable information physical sensation that her neck was tight. This one-sided mental perspective turns into a habit when our energy moves up to dull or hide discomfort so we can get the job done. When we drop into ourselves with breath, we have multiple perspectives to gain insight from—physical, emotional, mental and spiritual—because everything is experienced in the body. Nan finally understood why she was so tired when she got home.

"Are you tired now?" I asked because our telephone session was at the beginning of her day.

"I don't think so. Maybe, I can't tell."

We worked on embodying her energy, grounding, so she could *tell*. She felt the weight of her body and was surprised to discover she had more aches than just in her neck.

"Yes. I'm exhausted." She sighed. "I have a ton of work to do. How can feeling how bad I feel help?"

I'd asked Nan earlier what she believed in that was bigger than her, that always helped her. "The Earth, being in nature always helps me feel better."

I had Nan close her eyes and see herself in nature. I then directed her to breathe into some of the aches in her body. "Ask the Earth's energy or Nature's spirit to come help to ground you and to help your aches. Just keep soft awareness of your body and tell me what happens. You don't need to do anything other than invite the Earth to help."

She took about a minute then reported that she felt peaceful, calmer and not so sore. As she told me, she noticed something else. "It sounds like my voice is a little deeper. Does it sound that way to you?"

"Yes, your voice has definitely lowered and you're speaking a tiny bit slower. A lower, more resonant voice is a sign of being grounded. I've heard some people's voices drop a full octave. Do you feel more grounded, centered, weighted in yourself?"

Nan took a minute to respond, "Sorry, I was really thirsty

and needed a drink of water. Yes. I do feel more unified in myself."

When you are conscious of your body, you take care of your needs as they arrive. You don't risk burnout because often being tired just means you're dehydrated. Simple everyday solutions like drinking water, having a snack or taking a five-minute walk can avoid long-term physical problems. As you know, the opportunity to hear your intuition exponentially increases with your senses awake.

Nan sent me an email two days later.

"I'm stunned. I have relied mainly on my head to make decisions and get me through my day. I guess I literally split myself in two and thought it was fine. After grounding myself for a day and a half, I feel completely different. I have more energy. My insight into situations is faster. I'm enjoying my day (Yes I'm drinking more water too!), not just getting through it. I'm more creative. Not integrating my head with my body underutilized my talents and was sabotaging my success."

Nan learned faster than most that sitting on her bottom is very different from sinking down into her bottom in a grounded way. Your physical body, however, must be activated in order for you to notice your intuition. Even if you are sitting in a chair with your feet on the floor doing work, you can still activate your body. Contract your right buttock muscles. Contract your left buttock muscles. Submerge your awareness into every place where your body has contact with a surface. Push your heels into the floor. Move any part of your body that you can move. Even if you are physically challenged, you can find muscles to activate and sink your weight into.

So many people in our culture feel shame about size and weight. Often, experiencing your dimension and pounds settle down inside is disconcerting. People don't like to feel heavier.

The thought alone can scare them into numbing almost immediately.

I shared one of my favorite ways to get grounded with my client Joanie who also didn't like to feel her weight. A partner in a law firm, Joanie was always working from her head and oftentimes running on fumes after 70-hour weeks. Of course she was out of her body. Who wants to feel all that stress? Unfortunately, this grueling, mentally-focused schedule led to her feeling anxious and overwhelmed all of the time. She wasn't thirsty or hungry. Physically numb on autopilot kept her blind to the symptoms indicating a total disconnect from her basic needs, let alone her intuition. She needed a fast way to ground, gain awareness and get some energy.

"Joanie, this sounds too simple but I promise it is gold."

As Joanie sat at her desk, I had her pick a side. She chose right. I told her to leave her left foot sitting flat on the floor. Then I had her focus on her right toes staying on the floor while she bounced her heel up and down at varying speeds for about 30 seconds. When she stopped, I asked her to compare one side of her body to the other.

"The left side feels dead. The right side feels like electricity is running up my leg all the way into my brain."

I had her switch sides and heel-tap her left foot. She remarked how quickly her whole body felt better. "I feel more awake—energized."

Her stomach growled and Joanie laughed. "I guess I'm hungry too."

When Nancy from my beloved writing group first read this chapter she sent me a note that she couldn't comment yet because, "I struggled with the concepts, not sure why, I just did." Later she wrote that she left the chapter for a week and when she read it again, "It made complete and wonderful sense.

Like you were speaking to me directly."

Grounding was exactly what she needed. "Any confusions I'd felt before were gone… I felt a clarity that I lacked and wondered to myself, 'Why didn't I see then what I see now?' You probably have the answer."

I don't have the answer, but I have a theory.

Nancy was willing to sit with her confusion and not push for understanding. I recently listened to *Think Again* by Adam Grant. In it, he says psychologists find that the hallmark of an open mind is being able to grapple with confusion. When you read something that is meant to rewire your thinking and the possibilities available to you, you need to digest it. Process it in your unconscious and then try again when the mood strikes.

I share this because if anything in my book causes you to say, "What the heck is she spewing here? This makes no sense," then wait awhile and read it again. Confusion is a valuable stew to put on your inner back burner. I hope you can be confused for a while. See if, like Nancy, it's just what you need.

You will not always feel the same groundedness every day.

It's a dynamic practice.

Some days you'll be surprised at how grounded you feel, other days, more curious about how your felt sense of density changes. Don't look for more—just know there are varying degrees of how heavy *in* your bottom you will feel. Like with David, my lower body felt weighted *and supported.* Nan felt less tired and more creative. Joanie felt electricity running up her legs. You never know what intuitive signals you'll experience when your inner compass resonates in a relaxed, grounded body free of expectations.

I have a blue racquetball, a bit smaller than a tennis ball, which stays on the floor by my sink in the master bath so it's the first thing I see in the morning. Sometimes I roll it while brushing my teeth. Sometimes I take more time to enjoy the massage. Sometimes my head takes over—*you don't have time.* This is when I need to get grounded the most. But I don't always listen.

My grounding practice varies throughout the day — comparing sides after cheek squeezing, heel bouncing, and ball rolling (a red Kong borrowed from my dog, Madison, works as a roller with a little different maneuver.) Long sensation filled walks, focused breath and calling on the Spirit of Gravity/Earth to pull my energy to the ground are other ways I connect.

So, what's the *bottom line* meaning of being grounded? I can't give you one. There are so many different traditions, beliefs and definitions of *grounded*. When I come across an unfamiliar way, I see it as possibility, another way to access my own grounding practice. I like different perspectives; an insight from someone else's experience can sometimes enhance my own. The welcome byproduct of being grounded is noticing more visits from intuition.

Maybe terms like grounding, foundation, the bottom line, and embodiment sound too much like rules and hard work. Remember there are no rules, just play. Experiment. Don't *try* too hard. Playing footsy with a ball for a few minutes brings you there.

Invitation

Start by taking a deep breath.
Notice how your body feels.
Follow your breath all the way down your body and up again.
Take another breath.
Allow yourself to feel the weight of your bottom.

Feel the weight of your feet on the floor.
Feel the weight of your thighs against the chair.
Keep your awareness on these areas as you continue to breathe.
Allow yourself to really feel your physical weight—
your bottom, your feet, your thighs.
You may have to adjust your posture.
Remember, if you are thinking about feeling your weight,
you aren't feeling your weight.
Bring your awareness to the lower part of your body.
Contract your left buttock muscle.
Contract your right buttock muscle.
Contract them both.
Relax them.
Continue to keep your awareness in your body.
Be aware of feeling your weight, your heaviness,
and your physical presence in your chair.
Lift your right heel, leaving your toes on the ground.
Lift your left heel, leaving your toes on the ground.
Gently drop your heels to the floor,
feeling the weight of your legs.
Breathe.
Feel your belly gently rise and fall with your breath.
Contract your buttock muscles again, feel your body's density.
Keep your awareness in the lower part of your body.
Notice any subtle difference in the way you feel now
Versus the way you felt when you started.

11

You Don't Say Hey

I sped north on I-95 pushing my little beige Chevette to its limit. It was early November 1983. I couldn't afford a speeding ticket, but my desire to escape overrode any whisper of common sense.

I was an overwhelmed college freshman with freshly divorced parents, running home from loneliness. The South Carolina state trooper who stopped me an hour and a half into my 12-hour drive ended up giving me more than I could have imagined.

When the officer arrived at my open window, he found me trying, unsuccessfully, not to cry. He asked for the typical glove-compartment documents and I blurted out, "I've got to go home. They hate me here in the South."

As I tearfully handed him my license and registration, he asked if I was in school and where. I told him the name of my small college, Coker. He nodded, and spoke in a fast drawl about Coker being a fine school.

When he turned to walk the interstate's gritty shoulder back to his cruiser, I sank into my seat and closed my eyes. My tiny car jiggled with every dieseled whoosh of eighteen-wheelers parading by. Exhaustion settled over me. All I could think about was if I had enough money for a crappy cup of gas station coffee. I needed to wake up.

When I heard the steady crunch of his hard leather shoes approaching, I straightened up. He handed me a ticket, then bent down to look me in the eye, "Now, sloooow down. Y'hear?"

I worried my way north and arrived home as a late evening surprise. After my mother's initial shock, she told me I could only stay a few days. Her advice was to finish the school year, and then transfer if that's what I still wanted. Miserable, I drove back three days later.

My dorm's resident assistant, Donna, a bouncy, pony-tailed-blond, leaned against my doorframe as I brought the last of my stuff back to my room. She looked me up and down and asked, "Why'd you run away?"

Sticking to the story I told when I left. I replied, "I didn't. I had an emergency at home."

"I *know* you ran away 'cause Gaye's daddy was the state trooper that pulled you over. She blessed him out for giving you a ticket. He said he had to give you one because you were goin' twenty-five miles over the speed limit. *Annnd* he only gave you one for ten miles over because you said the girls here didn't like you. He coulda taken your license, you know." Her perky tone held friendly concern.

I continued to unpack, avoiding her gaze.

Donna persisted, "You know where I live if you wanna talk."

I could feel Donna wanted to help but I couldn't imagine how. I thanked her but left it at that. She gave me a sad smile and nodded as she turned to go.

I shut the door, humiliated and angry with myself. *This. Is. Unbelievable. South Carolina is more than three times as large as New Jersey and I unknowingly blow my own cover story to my dorm mate's dad. I am an idiot.*

I felt stupid for coming to the South. I didn't know how to begin to understand the people here. Other students from Northern states didn't seem to have a problem. I simply didn't fit in.

The next day there was a rat-a-tat-tat on my door. A

bubbly girl with a huge smile vibrated in my doorway. The school was so small I'd seen her practically everywhere but hadn't been introduced.

"Hey there! I'm Kim and I figured out your problem: You don't say 'Haaaay.'"

What?

She floated past me and plopped on my bed, leaving a middle-of-the-day freshly showered scent in her wake.

"You don't say 'Hey.'" She shrugged. "That's why people don't like you."

I should have been offended. But somehow, I knew she was totally sincere and trying to help. I was clueless to what she meant. Evidently, she could tell and kept talking.

"Every time you pass someone you need to look at them and say 'Hey.'" Her thick Southern accent went up an octave and fluctuated, giving *hey* three syllables.

"I say 'Hi,'" I protested.

"You don't do it enough. You need to say it *every* time."

"You're kidding. I can pass the same person three times in five minutes."

Her buttercup hair bounced with quick affirmative nods. "Yep, *every* time. I've noticed that y'all up North don't do it and that's a problem here."

I don't remember the rest of our conversation. I hope I thanked her, because I followed her advice. I learned to say "Hey." and sometimes, "Hey you all," with a wave. It took a while to say a three-syllabled, "HaAaay y'all" and have it feel sincere, but I accomplished that too.

I started to notice that everyone in town said, "Hey" to each other as they passed. They said, "Hey" to me too, though I hadn't really noticed before. Because I didn't know them, I didn't think they were talking to me.

I had been taught to ignore strangers, to not make eye contact or engage because you could be taken advantage of, or be perceived as an easy mark. In high school if you said *hi* too often, you could be seen as needy or uncool. Besides, who had time to say hello to everyone? It might encourage them to stop and talk. I was too busy, always running late.

So it took some conscious effort, but learning to say *hey* turned the tides of my situation. Not only did I stay to graduate, I've called South Carolina home for more than *40* years.

Different places have different social norms. When visiting, you can accidentally offend someone. You don't mean to offend. My ignorance of Southern social norms led me to be accidentally rude to my classmates and made connection to new friends difficult.

So, what does this story have to do with intuition?

Think of the mind and the body as having different social norms. The mind tries to fix or criticize the body's appearance, uncomfortable emotions or physical sensations. The mind looks to connect with the body but goes about it the wrong way. Like my ignorance of how to connect with my classmates, the mind doesn't understand how to have a relationship *with* the body. Especially when the mind thinks the body isn't behaving as it should. The mind gets bossy and critical or, as in my case, simply ignores what's in front of it.

We all know *not* to speak to others in the harsh ways we speak to ourselves. It's more than impolite. It's offensive. Since intuition communicates through the body, you need to change old numbing habits and any abusive approaches. It requires shockingly minimal effort to transform inner criticism. You can begin by greeting whatever unwelcome sensation, emotion or thought that appears inside you—not fixing it, wallowing in it, criticizing it or ignoring it. A short greeting—"Hello"—is all you need.

This approach seems too simple to work.

Our judgey-self wants to correct, not connect. Just like acknowledging everyone I passed (every single time) launched the turnaround in my college social life, greeting my inner critic, my aches/pains and my emotional upsets continues to expand my intuitive life. I'm with what's happening now.

You know that addictive behavior (overdoing food, alcohol, television, social media…) is commonly used to numb our emotional and physical discomfort. When internal irritation won't numb, we often try to shoo it away with self-beratement.

A friend of mine regularly tells herself to, "Stop it. Just stop. Stop this—anger, hate, jealousy, sadness. You have work to do, and you're better than that."

The problem with her approach is that she's trying to fix the state she's in without greeting/welcoming/feeling it first. The emotion she's chasing away is a signal of pain.

Pain has a message.

When you scrape your knee, you don't say, "Stop it, you're better than that."

You stop. Assess the damage. Clean it up. So you can see what kind of help you need. Sometimes you need to experience emotional pain for a few minutes to gain the insight needed to take action or not. Even if it's to say, "I see you, Jealousy. Hi. I don't like you. I can sit with you for 30 seconds to feel if you have something to share. Then I'm going back to doing taxes. I won't ignore you. I'll check on you again."

When self-criticism pops up, you probably close down. Who likes to stop what they're doing to be with what's uncomfortable? You don't have *time* for self-pity or to fix what's going on. You have work to do. Unfortunately, over time desensitizing causes your mind and body to become strangers who don't speak to each other. You close down.

You can stay open by saying, "Hey!" to what's actually going on inside. Intuitive knowing appears when you have inner openness.

Like not greeting every person I saw every time, I also feared I didn't have time to greet everything going on inside. I certainly didn't have time to analyze every thought and feeling, and just like with school I didn't have to.

I played with waving a *hey* to whatever popped up inside. If an emotion is particularly bothersome, I try to revisit it later. I'm not going to lie; I find it impossible to do all the time. When I do remember, it continues to help create room for a reliable intuitive connection.

Intuition speaks through the body. That mind-body connection is crucial. You lose your intuitive connection when you become insensitive to your body's present state. When you deaden your senses, you impede your intuitive communication.

Jo was so disconnected from her body on the day we spoke that she didn't realize her shoulders were painfully tight. When I brought her attention to it, she wasn't pleased with the discovery.

"Oh, this hurts. How could I not know this was happening? It's depressing." Jo rubbed the back of her neck. "Now I feel stupid. No wonder I end up at the chiropractor so often."

I met her comment with stillness then said, "This idea might challenge you, but the first step is to say *hello.*"

Jo was incredulous. "Hello? Hello to what? My sore shoulders?"

"Yes. Say hello to the stiffness and to the feelings of stupidity and depression."

"But I don't want to say hello. I want them gone."

We talked about how the ability to disconnect from sensation—both physical and emotional—is meant to kick in for extreme survival conditions. This detachment becomes an issue if it's used every day, like Jo was doing. The cure is to feel what's actually happening in the moment.

"To reconnect with your intuition, you first need to connect to your senses. Our senses only operate in the present," I explained. "Your aching shoulders, feeling stupid and depressed IS what's happening now. That's why we say *hello* to acknowledge each. Recognizing what is happening inside aligns us with the present. You don't have to believe in it to try it."

We'd worked together long enough that Jo did try, a bit sarcastically, to see if anything happened.

"Hello stiff shoulders. Howdy to my feelings of stupidity, which I really feel now. Hi ya' depression for feeling stupid."

Jo paused for about ten seconds. "I can't believe it. I feel calmer, not depressed, and stupid is fading away. My shoulders are still tight but not as bad. I feel more 'here' in my chair."

This is just the first step. Saying, "Hey. Hi. Hello. Bonjour. Hola. Welcome..." is an easy way to be in sync with the present. Welcoming disengages resistance to experiencing unpleasant sensations and connects you with what's happening inside. I've had several teachers say, "What we resist persists."

You don't even have to believe *hey* will work to try it. Your resistance is what keeps you from *the now*. Knowing what's going on gives you choices. Feeling stupid and depressed faded for Jo when she greeted them and stopped wanting them gone. They were just signals to get her aligned with *the now*.

Jo knew she resisted feeling her physical pain. So, she started her workday by saying, "Hello," to it and continued throughout the day, every day for several weeks. She learned that her shoulders raised and constrained her neck when there was something she didn't want to do. Now she stretches, changes her posture, and then does what needs to get done with more physical awareness.

Sometimes she forgets to check on the state of her body for several weeks at a time. "I know when I've forgotten because it gets so sore, I can't help but feel it." Jo laughed, "Sometimes I even say 'thanks for the reminder' to the pain."

I've had people ask me if we need to say, "Hey!" to our good feelings and thoughts, too.

Sure.

Usually when good feelings show up, they're already welcome. But what the heck, find what feels good to you. Try this practice for a few weeks and see if you have more space inside. The more inner space you have the easier it is for you to feel your intuition kick in.

Part of learning to trust intuition is learning to say 'hey' over and over, to welcome all the body's emotions and sensations, even if momentarily. You constrict when you resist what wants your attention. It saps a lot of energy, too.

Embrace the good sensations and acknowledge the other ones. This clears the space for intuitive knowing. You might not always like the state you're in, but by greeting what's there you learn to get along. And just like the people in your life, you'll learn that some of your body's senses are more surface-oriented and others have something deeper to share. Welcome every state for at least a moment or two and see what happens.

You know that people in more than just the Northern and Southern states have different ways of operating. You need to remember your mental and intuitive states operate differently as well. No state is wrong. Yet if you want to live comfortably in different states, you need to welcome the local customs.

Assign your mind the job of *state* trooper. The mind

loves a job. Have your mind patrol the state of your body and emotions throughout the day by simply stopping to say, "Hey."

I'm so thankful Gaye's state trooper daddy stopped me. He probably saved my life that day. He also, unknowingly, gave me *the ticket* to living.

Stop yourself from speeding mentally through life, resisting a full sensory experience, so your intuition can take the wheel.

Invitation

Take a slow, welcoming breath.
Feel your body.
Let it get really comfortable.
Move around a bit and breathe to settle into your weight.
Say hey.
Invite your body to respond any way it chooses.
Value the feeling of how your body responds,
If your body feels good, quietly breathe.
Relax and enjoy your connection.
If aches and pains answer you, gently acknowledge them
by directing a gentle breath to each.
Enjoy the deepening connection to your physical self.
Say hey to all of the body's sensations.
Treat them like old friends.

12
Art Connects Us to Intuition

C reativity is a portal for the Soul's wisdom.

I can't remember a time when I wasn't making art. My parents and grandparents recognized something in me and always had crayons, watercolors and paper available for me to play with. By the time I was 21, I had spent thousands of hours drawing, painting and experimenting with other materials. Art gave me a strong connection to my intuition.

My mother was incredibly inventive, whipping up batches of homemade finger paints with corn starch and food dye. She found a recipe for homemade Play-Doh. She had us make cards and gifts for relatives and decorations for the holidays. When she made my school clothes, I sat on the floor beside her with my own needle and thread, sewing simple outfits from patterns she helped me design for my dolls.

For birthdays and Christmas, I received gifts of colored paper, markers, brushes and paint. I still love the smell of a new box of crayons.

In seventh grade, I won a scholarship to attend a still-life drawing class at the local museum. That class taught me that I needed to *see* in a different way to draw complex subject matter more successfully.

I enjoyed looking at the world differently and took every art class I could in middle and high school. I wanted to be a visual artist and received an art scholarship to attend college. Making art transported me into a space of timelessness and peace.

I also began to realize during my senior year in college that creating connected me to something mysterious. I had an artist friend, Ben, who mixed a particular shade of blue that was so vibrant he called me over to stare at it with him. "I can almost hear it buzz," he said.

Ben talked about how he wanted to taste certain colors. He really wanted to taste that blue—the color, not the paint. Planted in front of the canvas, he was so engaged it caused his mouth to water. In that instant, I saw how inspiration came over him. He picked up two brushes, lost in a vision. He was swept up. I quietly left. I don't think he noticed.

A few months later, I created several shaped canvases by layering old letters and cards together with plaster. I then sanded down the surface so different bits of color and words were peeking through the background. I didn't know what to do next, paint or draw? I stood and stared at one of the smooth, scarred surfaces. I recall picking up a piece of charcoal.

The next thing I remembered, I was looking at a painted drawing of a sleeping, nondescript adult with one arm hanging off of a bed, hand open and resting on the floor. Coming from under the bed was a spirit-like swirl of light entering the hand. I felt like I woke up to find this finished sleeping form in front of me.

I later told my art professor that I didn't remember drawing the image. He wiggled his fingers at me like a sorcerer in a Disney movie and said, "Spoooooky... I love it when that happens!"

At the time, I didn't understand what that drawing meant. But years later, when I started working in the spiritual realm, I realized that on that night my Soul took over my consciousness and gave me a clue to my future through the image of waking up to Spirit.

Working as a museum curator gave me the opportunity

to talk to many professionals in the arts. Over and over, they told me stories about how certain pieces gave them flashes of insight into their lives. I read interviews and attended talks where songwriters, poets and novelists spoke about how a melody or words would just come to them or seemed to be waiting for them discover.

I read about flamenco dancers and the phenomenon of *duende*, the idea that the larger Soul takes over their bodies and moves through them in the dance to affect all who see. Actors admitted to me that they felt their characters take over in a particularly good performance. Artists in peak moments becomes conduits for something much larger than themselves.

Even in everyday moments, making art of any kind, especially in commonplace creations like selecting a wardrobe, packing lunch, posting on social media and the art of a relationships, connects you to your Soul. The contact can be subtle. Yet, if you pay attention, you can feel energy moving through your body in silent support.

When I started intuition consulting full-time in 1997, I began facilitating art and intuition retreats. I've offered at least two a year ever since. Attendees receive multiple intuitive insights that transform their lives in positive ways, simply by engaging in an art project. Many gain clarity about what they need to focus on. Some of the insights are small, such as starting piano lessons. Some are major, like getting a new job and moving across the country. All come from listening with all of their senses while making art, sitting with what they've created and sometimes journaling about their artistic process. No one has ever told me they regret the life changes they made after one of these retreats.

Georgia, an accomplished visual artist, attended her first retreat with a desire to have Spirit make art through her. Her head was so fixated on this goal that she couldn't see that Spirit was already working through her. When I pointed this out to her, she said, "Yes, I know. I can feel my hands want to move in a particular direction. I just don't understand what it means."

When the Divine worked through her, she felt it in her whole body. But her mind kept negating her Spirit's influence because she didn't know what the resulting images meant.

Georgia was actually looking to understand what Spirit was saying through her art. After working together for a little while. I asked her, "Do you feel emotion in your artwork?"

Georgia's reply was immediate. "Yes, of course."

"When you let your hands and arms move to make marks and place color, do you feel a rightness or a flow anywhere else in your body?" I asked.

"I always feel a rightness in my gut. Sometimes my heart feels wide open and filled with something bigger. But I still don't understand what the images mean."

Georgia's mind was taxed with this need to understand she didn't recognize that 90 percent of her was already comprehending. Her whole body was engaged when she was creating. Her emotions were alive for the process. She spent many hours in trance-like states, which showed that Spirit was engaged as she constructed mixed media images in her studio.

Still, Georgia didn't know how to let go of her need to know. Her mind was gripping so hard for intellectual understanding of her imagery that the joy she always had felt making art was being siphoned away. It was as if Georgia was trying to get a drink by grabbing at a pool of water palm down. She would remain thirsty for meaning if she continued to grasp instead of receive through all of her senses.

"Try focusing on the 90 percent of you that does have contact with meaning. Hear that you are *here-ing*," I told her. "Say, 'I am here and hearing. My whole body is listening to understand.' This conscious recognition helps us open to the stillness of the imagination, which values wordless knowing. In that state, the mind automatically starts to let go, and more meaning becomes apparent."

When Georgia felt the truth that she was receiving meaning in every way other than her intellect, she felt inspired and left to make some art. Returning to the evening session of the retreat, she was smiling and very energetic. She shared her delight in spending all day playing with materials.

"Loving the feel and color of the pastels automatically brought me back to the moment. Here. When *here-ing,* I realized that more of me was *hearing.* I enjoyed just playing," Georgia said. "The few times my head wanted to understand something, I stopped and journaled about what I did know, the emotions I felt, or I described the colors, the materials and when my hands moved of their own accord. While writing, more meanings came. I got what I'd been wanting without trying. I had so much fun!"

In recent years, I've taught the basics of a detailed process called SoulCollage®. Created by Seena Frost, who authored, *SoulCollage®: An Intuitive Collage Process for Individuals and Groups,* this technique is an easy way to let our Soul speak to us through our creations. Everyone receives a 4-inch by 8-inch piece of cardstock, scissors, a glue stick, and a stack of magazines. Participants are given a limited time to pick magazine images that intuitively attract their eyes. They are *not* supposed to think about why they chose the photo or if the photo is beautiful or not.

Selected images are narrowed down to the two or three that they are drawn to the most. A collage is created on the cardstock and a series of questions are asked to uncover hidden personal meanings.

Profound insights and unexpected perspectives come from this deceptively simple process. This practice becomes another way to approach and gain Soul wisdom from visual cues, without the intellect interfering. SoulCollage® questions can be used with any visual medium to gather more intuitive knowledge.

The easiest, most fun way to develop your intuition is by participating in acts of creativity in any of the arts. Whether you make SoulCollage® cards, bake cookies, lay a rock garden, sing in the car, play golf, or dance in the living room, being creative generates awareness of the present and the well of wisdom deep inside.

Creativity has a detoxing effect. It releases energy from your emotions and expels what ails you.

One of my mentors, Sobonfu Somé, used to tell me to "go make art" to regain my balance. By pouring difficult, pent-up emotions into creative acts you clear yourself, making space to be healed and filled with more desirable energies.

For her, dancing and singing physically released *dis-ease*. On several occasions during Sobonfu's retreats, I witnessed people refuse to dance because they said they were fatigued or not well enough. Her response was swift and forceful: "Get up! You need to dance *because* you are sick. Dancing is medicine. Move slowly and gently if you must, but move. Keep sitting and it will be more difficult for you to heal."

Creativity and intuition come from the same place.

Creating connects you to the source of everything. When you create, you can choose what you want to grow in your life. The arts are directly connected to developing and understanding your intuition. What you focus on expands. When you engage in any of the arts, your Spirit takes that opportunity to download messages through your senses.

Focus on creating.

Art is an antidote that heals intuitive blocks and develops strong connections to inner wisdom.

Invitation

Think about the last time you created something.
Take a breath in.
If it was a while ago, breathe out limiting beliefs
of what creating means.
Breathe in ordinary creations.
As you breathe out allow more everyday creations to surface.
Breathe in those creations.
Breathe out judgments that accompany
your commonplace creations,
the art of a meal, the art of self-care or the art of friendship.
Breathe in memories of moments of fullness.
Know you participated in those creations.
Breathe out any doubts that daily ritual is not a creation.
Feel that we create our interpretation of everyday.
Breathe in and choose to see life as art.
Notice any differences inside from viewing life
with this perspective.

13
Imagination

Many times, when clients have an intuitive breakthrough, one of the first questions they ask is, "How can I tell if this is real or my imagination?"

What they mean is, "How can I tell if this is real or if I'm making it up?"

Depending on the situation, I respond to my clients' questions with my own. One is, "Are you generally able to imagine what you are experiencing now?"

When Jill asked, after intuitively seeing another way to handle a sticky situation with her boss, felt a sense of peace, confidence and safety envelop her body, "Is this real? Or am I imagining it all in order to be able to act from this different perspective?"

I countered. "Are you usually able to whip up this much peace and confidence when focusing on a difficult situation?"

When Jill said, "no," I wasn't surprised. I almost always get the same answer.

Jill's new perspective helped her navigate her office situation with a few adjustments and very little stress.

Sometimes I respond with a different question—one I ask when I'm sure no harm will come to my clients—since most messages are symbolic not literal. I will ask, "Do you want to test the intuitive message you received?"

I asked Natalie that question.

"I'm remembering a red label I saw on a probiotics

bottle in the vitamin store," Natalie answered, "but I already take a probiotic. Changing it isn't enough to help my situation... Why would I see that? Am I imagining this memory?"

"You're right in thinking a different probiotic might or might not work," I agreed.

"So why would I see the label then?"

"Well, sometimes our intuition starts us on a healing path that has clues to follow," I said. "It's possible, that while looking for the best probiotic for your system, you find some- one who can advise you on more support for your digestive challenges. Or, maybe you run into an old friend at the store who's been through something similar. Or, perhaps that brand of probiotic would actually help. It might be that company has other products for your condition. Or, or, or... Intuition works from a different vantage point than the mind. Look at that information as the first step in the direction of wisdom for your health and see what happens."

It's tempting to dismiss the literal interpretation of an intuitive realization and judge it as not useful. Using *or* is one way to open to many possibilities until something feels right.

Natalie researched probiotics on the web and became overwhelmed by all of the data. She had an "intuitive impulse" to look again a few days later. New information popped up about solutions to digestive issues that she hadn't seen before. It resonated and led to a healing plan that helped.

When Gwyneth wondered if her intuitive breakthrough was real or imagined, I responded by suggesting a test I often use on myself.

"I focus on day-to-day decisions like whether blueberries I might buy are sweet. If my mouth waters I've learned that means yes, and I'll buy them. Sometimes my belly tightens after musing about their sweetness and I still buy them, partly just to see if my body signals are still communicating the same way." I don't mind sour blueberries, especially when they validate my intuitive hit.

As I mentioned in the chapter *Gaslighting*, driving is a good way to validate/test your day-to-day intuition. When I head out of the driveway to a destination I've driven many times, if a different route appears in my head, I try it. Or sometimes, I purposely ignore the vision and travel the route I normally take to see if there's a delay. About nine times out of 10, when I take my regular route despite an intuitive warning, I'm detained with road construction or a backup. Now, I usually take the intuitive route. It seems to save me time and every once in a while, I'll get validation (from the news or a friend) that the other way was a mess. Getting validation on your perception of intuitive information continues to strengthen your ability to interpret invisible reality.

The most important response I can give to a client is short and sweet. "Imagination and intuition work together." When they look confused, I reassure them. "It took me a long time to understand how."

I had thought the images or sensations I was experiencing came exclusively from my intuition.

I didn't want to even think of imagination as being a part of that process. I associated imagination with fantasizing or making things up. I had too much experiential evidence that intuition was a very real part of my life to even consider its relationship with imagination.

I also knew that intuition wasn't taken seriously when imagination was thought to be involved. Including imagination as part of the intuitive process felt risky. I'd watched my clients struggle to tell the difference between the two. I remember having that same fear that I was making things up. Acknowledging imagination as a part of intuition would cast doubt, appear delusional or indicate that I was a fake. At the least, I'd be considered fanciful or at worst purposely deceptive.

It took time to see imagination as a space where different parts of ourselves come together. Imagination hosts every part of us in the past, present, and possible future, which provides infinite ways to focus.

For instance, when your creativity, emotions, thoughts, and physical sensations enter the imaginal space with a focus, for example redecorating, then imagination allows all of those parts a glimpse of the future. *How will this navy blue look in my bedroom? Too dark? Hmmm... this feels depressing. Let me picture sunny-day-sky-blue, aaahh, that makes me feel lighter. And happy. I can still use my white curtains so there's more room in the budget for that glass...*

Using imagination this conscious way is beneficial, essential even because it's so often used unconsciously. For example, it's wise to consciously reimagine a situation to learn how it might have gone better. However, be careful to release the situation you're reimagining. Otherwise, it can become a self-defeating loop of *I should have.* Or you can get caught in a patten of worry and fear, imagining possible nefarious motives or disastrous outcomes.

The way my imagination works with my intuition is similar to receiving a nighttime dream. I don't try or work for a dream. Images and sensations arrive. Sometimes it's difficult for my conscious mind to retrieve it before it disappears into the unconscious. Sometimes the dream waits for me to notice, get curious, and sit with it for a while, waiting for meaning to reveal itself or not.

Imagination is my front porch that receives and holds the package of Soul information until my mind spots it. My mind knows its job is to notice when a package (message) has been delivered to the porch (imagination) and bring them into the house (my body).

The body then opens the intuitive message and translates the information for the mind to explore (back on the porch) with curiosity, not analysis. The imagination is also a between space of communication where curiosity plays with and listens on all sensory levels to clarify intuitive messages. Frequently, the imagination delivers a message with an obscure clue to follow.

In response to a question from Melanie about her getting a new job, I saw the image of a minister. My mind wanted to tell Melanie, "I'm seeing a formally dressed male preacher holding scholarly books." But something about that wasn't quite right. I took a breath and listened with more of my senses and knew to tell her, "I'm seeing a pastor."

We talked a bit about how ministerial work wasn't something she felt called to do. Then I realized. Pastor was a pun. Melanie owned and loved horses. The message was directing her to start the new job process by looking in the direction of the *pasture*, something she loved. Where her horses socialize, play and feed. Where she'd be nourished in many ways.

She laughed, which released the seriousness and pressure Melanie held for an instant job change. I gave her more details about the *pastor*. He was holding large books, which indicated an education or research. Highly educated already, she hadn't considered studying something new.

Melanie's intuitive take-away was to not be afraid to change careers to something that might be a huge step down in pay, but would offer a richer, happier life.

Remember, the body is the translator for intuitive language.

We have sayings such as, "This situation doesn't smell right." Or, "This place leaves a bad taste in my mouth." Or, "That advice sounds *off* to me."

That's the body translating direct intuitive knowledge of the current situation. I'm not sure if imagination is involved in direct sensory translation. It's possible that your Soul amplifies the meaning of ambiguous information through your imagination. So that when, for no apparent reason, something "just looks wrong," it gets your attention.

You need to absorb the message into your senses. To do that, all you need is to notice a message has arrived without mentally jumping to interpret it. Be patient. The body automatically receives the message with a breath of awareness. Sometimes your belly clenches or your shoulders relax. And/or an image or old memory surfaces that's seemingly disconnected from the situation/inquiry. All are essential for interpreting the intuitive message. The mind is not in charge.

It has several important supporting roles to play.

As illustrated in Melanie's story, her mind served as the focuser (I need a new job). My mind used her focus as the noticer of intuitive information (I see a pastor). The mind's other role is to be aware of your body's response *after* your body has received the intuitive message. At that point, your mind reenters the imagination (back to the porch) and can brainstorm possible meanings while checking to see how the body responds (realizing the pastor pun). The mind loves coming up with great ideas in the imagination as long as it gives the body enough time to process. It can be instant realization (I love a pasture!) or take a lot longer (more education/research, money not as important). Imagination provides the space for the mind, Soul and body to align and communicate.

Once I made peace with imagination being an important part of intuition, I kept seeing the word, imagination breaking apart in my mind's eye. The main emphasis fell on *magi*. Like this, *I **magi** nation*.

Etymologists might cringe because the word *image* usually serves as the root meaning of imagination. *Magi* are usually seen as the three wise men bringing gifts to baby Jesus. The word *magi* is also plural for magus, as in seers, sorcerers, magicians, or anyone skilled in using supernatural forces.

Now, when I look at the word imagination, I define it as: *(I)* have several parts of me that meet to become skilled *(magi)* in interpreting the invisible language of Soul in this world *(nation)*.

Invitation

Let my mind focus on a situation where I could use some insight.
Just let my mind land there in soft awareness.
I invite intuitive wisdom here.
Breathe into my body the invisible message that comes.
Gently breathe.
Notice any information the senses are translating.
Internal body sensations.
Any change big or small
Any images or memories that arise.
Allow curiosity to surface and explore more internally.
Notice any emotion that arises and moves through.
Get curious about what's underneath the emotion
and the physical sensations that accompany the senses.
If images arise, allow curiosity to look at
what's to the far left and right of it.
Notice what's above and behind the image.
Notice small details and subtle sensations.
Release looking for an answer.
Notice any shifts in perspective over the next few days.

Allow the invisible to be indirect in the moment.
Allow wisdom to move you when it's time.

14
Know Your Neighborhood

When you know where you are, it's easier to relax into physical sensations, intuition's speaker system.

When I walk around my block, I look forward to our up-the-street neighbor's butterfly bush. They've trimmed it into an 8-foot-high rectangle, which keeps the bush perfectly aligned with the sidewalk. Perhaps because of the regular haircut, the bush's royal purple blossoms bloom and emit a comforting lilac-like smell into November. Other bushes of its kind are finished by September. If I'm off somewhere in my head, that bush finds me from three houses away, bringing me back from my musings to the sidewalk with full fragrant notes.

When you've lived somewhere for a while, knowledge comes from repetition. When everything stays the same, little changes in your neighborhood jolt your senses into action *because* they are out of sync with the norm. It wakes you up to the moment, to what's different.

If someone is grilling when I step out of my door, I notice, and without thinking I *find myself* scanning the street for the source. When I can taste and smell where I live, absorbing the world around me is a natural sensory response.

Your senses spread outward into your neighborhood to receive relevant information. The byproduct is a reciprocal inner expansion that opens your Soul wisdom/intuition. Often, you aren't conscious you've expanded, but a sense of flow, ease and alignment are signals that you've opened.

For 13 years I lived in a transitional downtown neighborhood, stereotypically, yet lovingly, referred to as *The Hood*. I'd been there for nine years when a guy who worked at the newspaper purchased the abandoned, dilapidated, turn-of-the-century shotgun home down the street. Our poet neighbor, Susan, insisted on introducing me to newspaper-guy, Michael, over a dinner she convinced him to cook for all of us. Her intuition was right on target about our need to meet.

I knew, liked and trusted Susan, and knowing she'd be there made it easy to accept the dinner invitation. The food smelled good, but to be honest, Michael's shrimp creole tasted like ketchup. It was his taste in comfortable antiques, artwork and color choices that kept my inner food critic from shutting down the rest of my senses, thank goodness.

I was open to feel his innate kindness and decent heart. His house, though still in need of a lot of work, focused my awareness and I knew there was more to him than his cooking. We fell in love, and I helped him renovate that rundown Victorian, graced with a huge white wraparound porch, into a stunning home. When restoration was behind us, we decided to invite 10 of our friends to a barbecue on our fine front porch.

Not being skilled barbecuers ourselves, we asked our longtime friend Dan, now a professional cook known as Dan the Pig Man, to slow cook something fabulous. He arrived early morning and soon a tantalizing smoke permeated the neighborhood throughout the day.

The weather was a perfect mid-September day in the South. A mild breeze whispered though the cherry red petals of our canna lilies, giving their six-foot stature a slight sway, as if moved by the succulent smoke. Most of the friends we invited came in short sleeve shirts bearing gifts. Wine, cold beer and the last of their garden's cucumbers, basil and heirloom tomatoes graced one long makeshift table.

Miraculously the last of the mosquitoes stayed away.

They were not the unwelcome guests this time. The hookers were.

"Well, hellooo there!"

As I opened the screen door with my hip, carrying more ice for drinks, my head swiveled, drawn by the friendly singsong greeting. Two brightly dressed women stood in the middle of the cement walkway that led to our porch.

My gaze traveled down the pumpkin orange dress that clung like shrink wrap, barely covering her chest and behind, to her worn spiked gold heels. My first thought was not, *What does she want?* It was, *How does she walk on these uneven, glass-littered sidewalks in those things?* Her friend was a mass of glorious hair, with enormous hoop earrings that poked an inch out in front of her face, in a shade that perfectly matched her violet tube dress. She wavered uncertainly on silver heels.

Michael joined me as Orange Dress asked, "This party for everybody?"

Huge coquettish smiles from both followed.

Most of the guests ignored them or pretended not to watch. Having lived in the neighborhood for a few years at this point, Michael played the game. "Noooo, this party is just for close friends, not for all of our friends."

The women bent over at the waist and laughed with their heads close together like they'd just heard a sidesplitting joke and couldn't hold it in. Amazingly, their dresses held tight preventing more exposure. Then they straightened, smoothing the Lycra over their bodies with quick hands and good-naturedly swatted a goodbye. Purple Dress voiced a parting, "We was just checkin.'"

Both of us called out, "We appreciate you checking. Have a great night."

We weren't expecting the working girls' visit, but it wasn't out of the realm of possibility for them to show up. We knew our neighborhood. We didn't get hooked into reacting. We just gently sent them on their way.

Michael referred to another character in our neighborhood as the Hose Burglar. This little old man who lived a half-mile away had a garden-variety obsession—with yard hoses. Almost every neighbor on our two-block street found themselves missing a hose at some point—including us. We made the mistake of leaving the hose out during a particularly hot day so we could easily water after work. After that hose went missing, our next hose was always tucked away safely in the backyard.

Scott, the novelist, lived next door with his wife, Susan. Once, while watering plants in the front yard, the house phone rang with a call from his publisher. He cut the water to take the 45-minute call and returned to find the hose gone. Scott was wise to the Hose Burglar's antics so he went to the sidewalk and looked up the street. Sure enough about two doors up, walking at the speed of a three-toed sloth, was the Hose Burglar with the missing hose. Scott sauntered after him and approached the man with a smile, "Hey there! I believe that's my hose you're carrying, sir."

" Oh… What… This?… It could be…" The Hose Burglar's response was slow and confused.

"Thanks so much," Scott said as he reached for the hose in such a way that the Hose Burglar could only hand it back.

Scott knew his neighborhood, which allowed him to correct the situation with little effort.

It's easy to respond to situations with kindness, patience and understanding when you know your neighborhood. My first thought wasn't fear or panic when the Orange and Purple ladies showed up. I was trying to understand how they navigated our battered sidewalks in heels. You can relax when you know what to expect. If hookers appeared in front of our current home, my reaction would not be as generous. The context is different.

Entering a new neighborhood or place can be stressful. Your senses are usually on alert, quick to judge what's going on and how to respond. You don't absorb much when you are figuring out context. You are more likely to close down and react instead of listening to your intuition.

One day, after a particularly rich walk in nature, I had a huge intuitive realization. I'd been responding to my inner neighborhood like it was unknown territory. I was reacting to internal circumstances from a place of stress. I had inner hookers and thieves that I battled constantly, as if I were in a new circumstance. I needed to change the way I perceived the mental and emotional disruptions that inhabited my inner world.

When unexpected, nuisance thoughts or disruptive emotions showed up, I began to remember the people in the neighborhoods where I'd lived. Some of my unwelcome inner neighborhood traits resembled characters I had funny interactions with in real life. I started to recognize my unappealing traits as my inner neighbors. This made me laugh and relieved some stress. The parts of me I longed to get rid of became less threatening. I began to treat the characters in myself with the kindness, patience and understanding I gave locals in my life.

To keep negative thoughts from *hooking* me as often, I think of the neighborhood working girls. When those colorful women asked for an invitation to the party, it wasn't to irritate us. They had smelled good food cooking all day and probably thought, *what the heck, let's give it a try*. When you are feeling good, all parts of you are going to try to score an invitation, especially the parts you disapprove of or don't like—such as negative thinking.

Now, when I wave off my unwelcome thoughts, I can imagine that colorful duo saying, "Hey, thought I'd give a mental takeover a try."

The trick is to be as good-natured as possible to your negative, judgmental thoughts, self-criticisms and little tantrums of unmet desires. *I want* thoughts, like *I want my intuition to work right now*, are best met with inner generosity. Deep down those parts of you know they are blocks to what's really wanted.

When your inner *wanton* ones try to hook you, respond gently and with kindness first. Unlike the hookers in my front yard who weren't going to cause trouble because they knew the police could come, your wanton parts have no rules to follow. They will try to take over, to be the most important thing you focus on or freak out about, because they haven't been policed.

You can *always* choose to police your inner unwanted's behavior with protective and kind boundaries. Dressed to attract attention these quick takeover thoughts and emotions aren't expecting kindness. They are used to being ignored or seen as a failure.

It's time to say, "Hello!"

Try to put a face on those intense thoughts and negative emotions. Maybe admit you're scared of losing control, so you'd like to know this shadowy side but not right away. You don't need to get rid of these inner parts you dislike, better to recognize them as inner neighbors. Start policing with kindness, "This good mood party is just for close friends, not for all of my friends. See you around the neighborhood."

Know that your critical selves are usually trying to protect you. The goal of self-criticism often starts as a message. *You can do better.* Sometimes you can. If your inner perfectionist/critic obstinately stays put in your inner sanctum, disturbing the peace, refusing to leave, then postpone the party. Think of it as a rain date and move on with your day.

Your useless inner dialogues, those slow-moving thieves, are a lot like the Hose Burglar. They steal time and energy you could use in fruitful ways. These inner mumblings disconnect you from your current experience and the power to direct your thoughts. Luckily, you can easily catch up with these thoughts which constantly operate in the back of your mind.

The ruminating mind hopes to gain connection to a solution, except our senses are robbed when we focus on changing the past, or what is out of our control. Often, we don't even realize what's mentally churning in our own brains. Understand, this disruptive part ourselves believes it's useful. It is. When focused creatively, we connect our hose to a source of energy.

Approach those long-standing, bothersome thoughts like Scott did with the Hose Burglar. "Hi there! I believe that's my time you're using. I have some quiet time, creative ideas and wonderful memories I'd like to use that thought space for. Thanks for giving me my thinking power back."

Kindness, coupled with intent, refocuses habitual useless thinking into new generative and creative pathways. You do need to have patience. It's hard to stop stealing hoses when you think you are gaining connections.

Instead, try connecting your hose to a fulfilling source— Soul/intuition. It takes time, curiosity and exploration to create that link. You also need courage because you don't exactly know what the new habit will look like; it can feel like you aren't making progress. Allow the exploration to be open to adjustments.

Only you know what drains or fills you. The first thing is to notice draining thoughts and redirect them to more positive memories. Focus on what you'd enjoy thinking about and have fun exploring. All thoughts are possible in the imagination.

You don't need to break old habits. You don't want to use your focus on the behavior you're trying to change. Susan

Harper, a world-renowned somatic movement teacher that I'm blessed to study with, says, "When you create a new habit, your focus is on what you are creating. The old habit remains, yet it will become less dominant because the new habit provides new skills that are more satisfying."

In the neighborhood where Michael and I live now, we have a couple of characters who have very loud spats. Mollie and Hank are brother and sister. I met them when I quickly turned a corner on my morning walk, surprising them. They looked at me, then instantly turned on each other, repeatedly bumping chests. Their combined yelling was a loud, fast, garbled, nonsensical language that ensued for exactly five seconds. They abruptly stopped and both met my astonished gaze, calmly facing me as if nothing had happened.

A tall thin man, with a kind face, stood behind them. He slowly shook his head, "I apologize. Hank and Mollie are siblings. They've done this whenever anyone approaches since we got them as puppies."

Hank and Mollie are Boston Terriers. They make me laugh. I look forward to seeing them as often as possible. Now their little black and white bodies wiggle when they see me, though seeing Madison, our old Labrador, still riles them up. Their smooshed, munchkin faces form huge smiles, before and after they argue. I know where my dog neighbors live, so I greet them by name and give them a pat no matter what mood they're in. Their behavior isn't about me.

Inner arguments, lasting five seconds or five days, keep you from your center. It is so much easier for me to stop inner (usually critical) scuffles with myself when I picture my arguers as Mollie and Hank, the bickering Boston Terriers. I start laughing immediately, which gives me time to breathe and come back to base, my center, where I am safe. Looking at myself humorously releases any harsh judgment, loosens me up to the space where intuition thrives. My Soul source is the part of me that observes everything.

Mental arguments cause internal constriction, which clogs both sensory and intuitive perception. My center allows me to see two or more sides without being taken over by one, or needing to push anything away. This stops the argument, opening space for intuition to thrive. The next chapter, *Stand In the And*, goes into more specifics about how to keep centered and have space for every thought and emotion without being overtaken by any of them.

All you are doing is falling in love with—okay maybe just falling in *like*—your inner neighbors by renovating your perspective and behavior to feel more at home.

Relax. Know where you are—it's your neighborhood. Remember experiencing your senses automatically expands your Soul neighborhood, reinforcing your connection to your intuition, the wisdom hidden inside.

Invitation

Allow a memory of being inwardly over-critical to surface.
Notice where the physical discomfort comes with it.
Furrowed brows? Tight neck? Clenched jaw?
Let the tension or stress be felt.
Observe the judgment over the emotion that comes.
Let it be uncomfortable.
Now wave hello to that judgey part.
Convey that its opinion, emotion and sensations are noted.
Let the judgmentally over-critical part know

it's free to move along.
Invite intuition to come where critical surfaced.
Notice if there is more comfort and ease.
Notice if there is resistance.
Pay attention to what's being paid attention to.
Either way, break the pattern by just observing sensation,
Neutral to either way.
This is the way to start to play.

15
Stand In the And

When you live in truth, you live in alignment with your intuition.

When you believe things about yourself that aren't true, you don't feel quite right and are intuitively misaligned.

Truth is complicated. What I *mean* by living in truth is to be aware of the spectrum of opinions and feelings going on inside and not letting one truth take over. When you anchor and align to your center, your perspective changes to include all of your thoughts and emotions, without being overwhelmed. That is living in truth.

Steve, a client I'd worked with quite a few times, was tired of the ups and downs of not knowing when he'd see loved ones during the Covid-19 pandemic. He worried if there was anywhere safe, how to make plans and the uncertainty of the future.

"I'm on a constant emotional roller coaster and I can't make decisions. How am I supposed to hear my intuition under conditions like this? I mean… now is when we need our intuition the most, right?"

"Yes," I confirmed. "When we are mentally and emotionally in a state of fear, pain, frustration, and distress, our body is in a constant state of restriction. We need our intuition. Unfortunately, turmoil suffocates our inner voice by actively putting us on high alert, spending our energy on every level, which leads to a state of exhaustion from constant bombardment."

Steve let out an annoyed breath. "So… *how* do I find space for my intuition when I'm in a constant state of overwhelm? Plus, I can't stop worrying about my mom." Steve hadn't been allowed to see his mother, a doctor working with high-risk patients, in two months.

"I agree with the policy that says my mom can't see people outside of the hospital. We don't know who's been exposed, but I hate it." He sighed. "I know I'm fortunate, so many people have it worse than me, but here I am complaining and feeling guilty about it."

Gently I said, "One problem is your *buts*. I'm sure you know the word *but* negates everything said before it. Your buts are negating the reasonable thoughts as well. Most of us only pay attention to what is said *after* the word *but*, including our own thoughts.

"For example, the thoughts having the most impact on you are, 'I'm worrying. I hate it. I'm complaining and feeling guilty.' While, 'I need space, I agree, and I'm fortunate,' have lost power to help."

But has its place, for instance, as a restriction. *You can have a snack now, but don't ruin your dinner.* Or, *but* can soften a difficult message. *You are so creative in your work, but you need to arrive on time.* There is nothing wrong with using the word *but*. You just don't want to use *but* to create an argument in your own head. *But* keeps you ping-ponging, your thoughts constantly competing to overtake the other, restricting the space for your intuition to operate.

This back-and-forth dynamic was responsible for the indecisive emotional rollercoaster Steve was on.

"I have a simple strategy to get the inner space you need." I said. "I call it *Stand in the And.*"

I asked Steve to close his eyes. "Imagine drawing a large circle on the ground with enough space for you to have a wide, comfortable stance. Imagine the word *And* filling the circle.

Step in. Feel your core get heavy and solid as you stand in that circle of *And*. <u>Only you</u> can occupy this *And* circle. Now, notice what shows up outside the circle."

Steve hesitated, "I'm sorry. I don't understand. What can show up around me?"

"Everything." I replied. "The nature of the word *And* brings us to a spacious place. *And* is used to include every word, person or situation, giving space for every complexity to be included."

"Okay. That makes sense, but what do I do?" Steve asked.

"Try saying, 'I agree with the hospital policy *And* I hate not seeing my mom.' Does using *And* feel different than using *but*?"

Steve thought a moment. "Yes. *And* feels better than *but*. But… And… I don't feel connected to my intuition. I know we've only tried it once, it's just hard to believe that using *And* is really enough for my intuition to work."

My initial explanation of *And* took Steve (like many others) to his head, trying to figure out if *And* will work. Mental probing left him unable to feel the intuitive space *And* creates. Knowing that the best way to help Steve feel *And's* potential was to give an example, I told him how I learned to *Stand in the And*.

Twenty years ago, I was working with a client, Linda, who was doing all she could to get out of a bad marriage. Her therapist was helping her see more clearly. Her friends were encouraging, yet this was a tricky situation. She was torn and in so much pain. I didn't know how or if I could help. We sat quietly. I tuned inside and heard a thought that wasn't mine, "Teach her to stand in the *And*."

I had no idea what it meant to *stand in the And*. I waited to see if there was more information. I felt a warm soothing movement inside my head that my brain seemed to absorb, a download of information in a matter of seconds. I was given a teaching that has never stopped revealing itself.

I didn't have words for what I'd received, just an understanding, so I asked Linda to start to tell me everything she felt frustrated about. Her lovely, smooth skin flushed into a mask of anguish as she rocked back and forth, head slowly moving right to left, "It's too much. It's too much. It's just too much."

"Can you share one or two things you're conflicted about?"

Linda let out a breath, eyes closed, gently nodded agreement, while her features morphed smooth. Her eyes opened out of focus, viewing the past.

"He hits me." She moved her hands from one side of her body to the other as she continued, "but he's always sorry."

She moved her hands back to the left as she spoke. "But it's not *that* bad. Some women are black and blue." Her hands shifted again, fingers splayed in emphasis to her right side. "But he's mean. He says horrible things to me."

Linda's fingers closed, as together her hands gave a short punch to her left side. "But I love him. How can I love him when he's so awful to me?"

Her head and hands pivoted, right to left, left to right, as she started to sob, "But I do. I feel so messed up and crazy."

Her body's back and forth reflected a tennis court of division. Linda feared she'd never be able to reconcile her feelings. I suggested that, for now, she not make decisions, that instead she allow every feeling and thought to have a place. "I think you'll see that you have space to hold all of your thoughts, feelings and emotions. Then maybe once you see it all out there, you can start making choices."

She worried about being overwhelmed. I described the image that came into my mind. "Pretend you're on base. Not a baseball game base, where you have to keep moving. Just a base that is always safe. It's big, round and on solid ground."

She closed her eyes, stilled, then indicated with a nod that she on base.

I continued, "The base is called *And*. It's the word *And*, and you're not going to move from it. Ready?"

I then repeated what she said before, substituting the word *And* where she had said *but*. "He hits me. See that truth come into the space outside the perimeter of your *And* base. Nothing touches base except you." I waited for her nod, "*And* he's always sorry. Give that truth a spot outside of your *And* base. *And* he's mean. Watch where 'mean' lands. Can you see those three truths around you?" I watched her eyes move behind her lids, as if seeing the thoughts she'd been fighting with finally stand still around her in different locations.

"*And* he says horrible things." I continued at a relaxed pace. Her shoulders began to release. "*And* I love him... *And* I feel messed up." Her constant fidget stilled. "*And* I feel crazy."

Her eyelids moved, revealing a map of this inner scene around her base. Lids remaining shut, she looked around, a stop held for each truth.

"Linda, are you still on base?"

This time her eyes opened and she was here, focused on the present. Calm and certain, she met my gaze. "I get it … It's all true."

Linda shared that she finally felt all of her thoughts and feelings stand still. She could see them and more. "*And* I'm a good person. *And* I deserve to be treated well, like everybody's been saying, but...no *And*... I can see it. That truth is standing big right in front of... well actually... all around me."

Linda described how some of the truths took on a shape and color in her mind's eye. "*He hits me* showed up about an inch away from my base. Very close, but not touching me, like there was an invisible barrier that surrounded my whole body, not just where my feet stood. Anyway, *he hits me* looked like a hot, red chair-shaped flame that scared me. I told it to leave me alone and it moved about ten feet away to my right."

Some truths came as memories. "I saw snapshots of scenarios in my relationship appear in my head. I'd think, *Get out of my head!* The images flew out to sit where I could see them. Almost like they took a seat in a theater but not as orderly."

Some emotions became smaller when placed, and some appeared bigger. Some of the thoughts she didn't need to move landed a safe distance away or simply appeared then dissolved.

Closing her eyes again, she described many of the colored shapes and sizes, some she understood and some she didn't. "All of my thoughts and feelings are there with space for more. I keep trying to find what's true. It all is. My thoughts aren't fighting." She slowly moved her head, her focus on an internal landscape. "I can make choices, I think. At least it …" A calm gaze met mine as she opened her eyes, "… feels possible."

Standing in the *And* was one of many tools she used to find her way when she finally made the decision to leave her marriage.

I can't begin to name all the ways that the perspective of *Standing in the And* has proven useful over the years. It's a book on its own.

The basic premise is that there is space for everything if you stand, your focus centered in *And*. You land on *And*, protected by the word's nature to separate itself from everything around it. The nature of *And* is also to connect. You can sense everything, yet nothing invades your And base to take over your thoughts or emotions. There is space for everything outside your center. *And* automatically grants perspective. Where there is space there is choice; intuition operates effectively in these conditions.

When you find yourself using the words *but, yet,* and *or,* replace them with *And*, see how it transforms your perspective. Notice if you feel more centered, still, grounded, able to make a choice instead of a thought or an emotion grabbing hold of you.

Annika was a client I'd worked with regularly. She started our conversation off with, "I know I should be feeling everything will work out, but I'm really tired and discouraged."

Annika had property for sale in a foreign country. The people wanting to buy it were a group of men that tried to bully her into a bad deal, beating her down with extension after extension, piling on new demands and lowering their offering price weekly with ridiculous excuses. She'd been working for several years to sell this property and these men knew it. They were doing their best to manipulate a deal far below the property's value by wearing her out.

She was scared to stop the deal because her land had been on the market for so long.

I asked Annika what her body felt when she made herself think *everything will work out.* "Ugh! Like a lie. Heaveeey. Tight. Tired. I'm so frustrated. It can't be good to continue to feel this way, right?"

"I never want you to deny how you feel," I said. "There is a way to play with these feelings that also helps to open space for your intuition's input."

Always up to learn a new practice for her tool box, Annika listened patiently when I explained the premise of stand or land in the *And.* At the end of my explanation she said, "So including everything actually gives me more space?"

"Yes. Try it. Unload everything you feel about these guys using the word *And* in between each description. Get it all out. Have fun with it."

"I feel frustrated *And* heavy. *And* mad. *And* bullied. *And* like I wasted time. *And* I want the sale to be over. *And* I know these guys aren't supposed to have this property."

I asked how she felt. Annika admitted she felt lighter

from unloading all of the negative feelings. I asked if she really unloaded them or did she just recognize them? "Maybe I recognized them. Is there a difference?"

"Nope. Unloading and recognizing are the same when using *And*. Sometimes negativity simply dissolves after being recognized. Maybe that's why you feel lighter?"

"Probably," she replied. "I'm not as worked up, though I'm still not sure about this *And* thing."

Annika loves jewelry. I asked how many bracelets she had on. She counted seven on one wrist and five on the other. "They're all yours right? As well as your rings and necklaces? Now imagine your jewelry as emotions, thoughts and opinions. They aren't you. You can choose which to wear and know the rest are in your jewelry box.

When we own a piece of jewelry, we don't become it, our own skin becomes base. When we *stand in the And*, we experience the emotion, we don't become it. This prevents the back-and-forth of battling emotions and thoughts. We might choose to wear a smile and let the rest be in our metaphorical jewelry box. There's space for every part of us if we don't fall into being only one part."

She got it immediately. "Unlike jewelry, my inner space can expand to have as many opinions or emotions as I have, as long as I recognize them from my center." She stopped and said, "I feel soooo much lighter."

I brought Annika's attention back to the last thing she said when she first played with *And*. "You said, '*And* I know these guys aren't supposed to have this property.' Where did that come from?"

"I think it's what my intuition has been telling me. It was just too scary to allow that possibility before. I still am going to take some time to sit with the idea ending the deal."

In our next appointment two weeks later, Annika told

me that *Standing in And* gave her the space to feel her intuition resonate throughout her body. This confidence coming from inside was new. The men were surprised when she ignored their demands and stopped the deal. "*Aaannndd…* a day later," she beamed, "another offer came in that's a win-win for all involved."

And also gives space for every one of your character traits.

Tonya and I had worked a few years earlier to sort through choices she was battling with by standing in the *And*. This time she was in a crisis of confidence that caused her to implode into shame and depression. She couldn't stop her inner critic. I asked what it was saying. "I am one big flawed character. I'm petty, jealous, mean and nasty—in my head. But I am always nice to other people."

"Okay," I told her. "Feel yourself stand on *And*. Let all of those traits, including nice, land around you outside of base. Imagine them. Then add embarrassed." She groaned. I continued, "Don't forget kind, healthy, happy to help others, caring, snotty…"

Tonya laughed recognizing snotty as how she described herself earlier in our conversation. Then she exclaimed, "Oh! *And* laughter! I'm good at laughing at myself. Oh… *And* when I do I feel okay. I don't have to be perfect." She blew out a breath. "Sooooo everybody has good *And* bad *And* everything, right?!"

I had Tonya close her eyes and imagine her character traits standing around, just beyond her *And* base. "Are any traits bigger than the others? How and where do they appear?"

Similar to the last time we worked, her traits showed up around her as words, some in all caps, others lowercase and tiny. Some had fonts that visually expressed the level of importance or type of impact the characteristic had acquired.

"Snarkyness is low to the ground in small caps off to my left. I even hear it hiss. Passive aggressive is in a thin, mousey gray, pointy typeface that's farther away, back on my right side. Kindness had large willowy letters creating a building-like structure, sort of all over, like a city."

"Where's laughter?" I asked.

"Laughter's right in front of me. It's big, blue and bouncy." Tonya sighed in relief. "Just getting a bit of distance from all of the ways I can be, I feel better. More like myself again."

Tonya found her confidence. By embracing her own paradoxes through seeing them outside of herself with *And*, she discovered authenticity. Landing solidly in her center kept her critical thoughts from constantly highlighting her inadequacies.

And is a lifetime practice. We don't always hear our thoughts clearly or register our emotions. Checking to see if your perspective changes by centering on *And* can be challenging to remember. One of the fastest ways is to notice when you hear yourself say or think the words *but, yet* or *or*. Inwardly arguing back and forth is another indication to check if you are tight or feel spaciousness with your position.

Another way to remember to invoke *And* is when you are taken over by an emotion. The other day I was so angry, I couldn't stop the feeling and knew I was being unreasonable. I took an evaluating breath and felt where the anger was in my body. I was feeling anger hot and tight gripping down my spine, around my left ribs and lower back. I found myself thinking, "Weird. I thought the anger was in my head."

I called on my *And* center and imagined peeling the anger from my body and tossing it off base. It was more of a sensation than a vision. I felt such relief. It turns out the perspective I needed was stopping long enough to locate where my body was being affected by anger. Once tossed, I filled the space the anger had been occupying by focusing on the beauty outside my window and choosing to breathe it down my ribs and back.

One of my powerhouse clients found *And* so useful, she made sure she couldn't forget to check where she stood. A tiny, ornate ampersand tattoo now adorns her inner wrist.

You can't escape what's inside. Pesky thoughts, traits and emotions will always find you. This happens to everybody. When you allow them all, the positive and negative thoughts, traits and emotions, one or two don't fight for the driver's seat. When all parts are included, your inner critic can't drive either. You don't need the cartoon visual that Tonya did to acknowledge everything inside. Don't pretend that you are above such nonsense, your own nonsense. Then your critic loses power.

Back to Steve's roller coaster. After I shared how I came to *Stand in the And*, he understood. "I feel better knowing that *And* gives me something to *do* to make space for intuitive input. I feel a lot calmer."

And includes all of your complexity. *And* is your core, your center, the nature of being human. *And* respects every thought, trait, emotion, and sensation, automatically giving space for your whole truth. *And* recognizes everything is allowed to occupy space. *And* recognizes and shrinks thoughts/emotions/problems to their actual proportion of importance. *And* provides the focus needed to alleviate inner arguments by welcoming all possibilities. *And* is magical. And holds the power for you to infinitely expand. *And* gives your mind something to *do* to access your Soul's knowledge.

At the end of the day, *And* is about integrity. When you

are aware of your inner spectrum, the different parts of you that have different beliefs, you are integrated with your truth. *And* creates the space for your intuition to have impact on your response.

Life aligns. *And* flows.

Invitation

Take a moment and look at your thoughts.
No need to judge, just observe.
Feel your breath ride down the inside of your spine.
Let it ride all the way down into both feet.
Feel yourself land on base.
Feel your standing in safety.
Invite the word And.
Ask to include all parts of you.
Even the ones you don't like.
Usually the demons are the most in need of help.
Invite help from the Divine for all of the parts
of yourself you don't like.
Invite help to all of the places you are judging.
You don't have to like those parts yet.
Maybe you can recognize they are wounded.
Invite the Divine to give attention to these rejected parts.
You don't need to know how to accept them.
Ask for help.
Ask for healing.
Feel the And, your center.
Then include everything.
Sink deep. There is space for stillness and peace.

16
Ancient Wisdom

T he word intuition came into use in 1450, according to the *Barnhart Concise Dictionary of Etymology*. Intuition was defined as an indication that spiritual perception and insight were being used to look at and *consider* a situation.

It wasn't until 1594 that intuition evolved into its current meaning of "knowledge that is perceived immediately." The actual Western word may have been formed in the 15th and 16th centuries, but the concept of intuition—as an invisible connection to understanding what's needed—is ancient. I like to think it's always been a part of human understanding.

The simplest and most powerful way I know to gain intuitive resonance came from my friend and mentor, Sobonfu Somé. She grew up living the ancient ways of the indigenous Dagara people in Burkina Faso, West Africa. The people in her village still live without modern conveniences such as running water or electricity. Hard to imagine.

Sobonfu's tribal elders sent her to the West to share their ways and wisdom because they knew their culture was dying. Her name, Sobonfu, means keeper of the rituals, an ever-present reminder of her purpose in the world to share the old ways.

Sobonfu always wore brightly colored traditional African clothing with a matching scarf wrapped around her head. Her smile was large and infectious. The gap between her front teeth only enhanced the charge of authority and unapologetic sense of knowing who she was in the world. When she walked into a room, her presence was felt before seeing or hearing her. Solid, yet quick to laugh, she engaged everyone she met. Even my Dad, who doesn't trust anyone new, liked and respected her instantly.

A practice to access intuition is included in Sobonfu's audio teaching, *Women's Wisdom from the Heart of Africa*. I suspect it is part of what gave her such powerful presence. In the audio, she shares that many people ask why she sleeps with her hand over her womb. Her response is that she finds comfort and clarity there, but it's more than that.

In her tribe, a woman's womb is a place of power. It is a part of Creation itself. It's a compass in a female body that processes information and gathers intuitive insight. Even if your womb has been removed physically, your womb continues to exist within you as an energetic field, giving you lifetime access to intuitive wisdom.

Sobonfu and I slept in the same room countless nights at our friend Susan's home in Virginia when our schedules overlapped and when I traveled with her as one of her assistants. I never asked why she rested her hand on her low belly in bed. It didn't seem odd so it didn't occur to me to ask. I'm sure her hand didn't remain there all night. I never realized placing a hand on the low belly was a daily practice for her. Truthfully, if I had asked, she most likely would have smiled a devilish grin and told me to find out for myself, which is what I did eventually.

A year after Sobonfu passed away, I was missing her, so I played her audio book for the umpteenth time. When I heard that to access intuition daily, women need to put their hand over their womb, I was stunned. How could her ridiculously simple technique not have registered before? When new information hits me, especially from a much-studied source, I pay attention. Usually, my intuition is pointing out something that's important for me to focus on. So, I started placing my hand on my womb to check inner alignment.

I learned that it's not a matter of slapping my hand over my lower abdomen and getting instant clarity. It's more about the presence of my hand guiding me to gently rest deep inside. My hand helps sense where I am. *Am I centered? Or a bit out of sorts?* I noticed that my senses registered more acutely. I heard the sounds of bird flutter and tasted the faint residual minty-ness of my toothpaste hours after brushing. After a few weeks, my palm's weight automatically directed my breath to accompany my hand, and I felt the beginning of a stable foundation.

I began to understand how just a few minutes of low belly attention from my hand and breath each day created a physical anchor for my awareness to rest. When I relax into that pelvic space, not judging how I am, but to access what I need, I find myself calmer, with a connection to a timeless space inside. My senses heighten and I have an innate knowing of how I am in relation to the outside world. At the same time, my inner world understanding and wisdom are more accessible.

When I read the above description of what I noticed, it sounds huge and profound. It wasn't. It's hard to describe how subtle those explorations were. I was intensely curious and alert about this process. But most days, even when my senses heightened a bit I thought, "Meh, this isn't doing much."

Every day for a month, I woke up and took a few moments to connect to my lower abdomen and appreciate my body being here. Hindsight kicked in and showed me my life had started to change. I noticed my interests had shifted. I began to eat healthier food and make visual art again. None of these things were a goal. The changes just emerged naturally. I observed them occurring instead of making them happen.

Since I'd started writing this book in earnest, I hadn't used my art supplies for four years, except for teaching retreats.

I found myself in my studio just touching the paint bottles, colored pencils and smooth, thick paper. My body walked into that room without prior decision.

An appealing online art class arrived in my email the day after my hands explored the supplies it required. I signed up. It finally occurred to me that I had been denying myself one type of art for another. All of the arts open the intuitive flow. This is the foundation of the retreats I lead and still I found myself blind. A few minutes a day with my womb-belly alerted me to what I'd done. I'd let my ego's goal *to hurry up and finish the book* slowly drain the pleasure out of writing.

Every day, I help free people from their constrictive patterns and blind spots that block their intuition. But I didn't see the same signs in myself even though they were obvious. I'd find any excuse not to write and my self-talk was abusive. "You've got to write faster. Stop being ridiculous, get disciplined and get this book finished."

I'd held myself to a standard I'd never apply to a client: *no project other than writing until the book was done.* Crazy. Every day I help clients find satisfying ways to include music, drawing, singing, reading, dancing, or golf in their day even if they only had five minutes. What we love feeds us *and* our other creative pursuits. Even my husband practices the art of his golf swing during television commercials. I did nothing else. I couldn't see that my ego hijacked my writing because the ego is stealthy. *Get the book done* was a story that was easy to believe and desire. Placing a hand on my womb revealed that I was stuck because of the way I'd been thinking.

When I realized what had happened, I felt ashamed of my blindness. *I should have known better.* Simultaneously, I recognized *should* as the ego casting a line to hook me into letting it stay in punishing control. Womb holding helped me see past the shame to my ego's attempt to take over and I found comfort. *It's okay, I'm human. I didn't know better.*

Holding my low belly helped me see that my ego's goal to *finish* the book held a destructive, limiting influence. Writing became difficult because my perspective was skewed from inward misalignment. My ego tried to discipline with bad parenting techniques like, "You will sit here until you write a chapter."

The more I scolded myself the more my intuition and creativity ceased to participate. For a few months, every single time I sat down to write, I fell asleep. The more frustration and disappointment I felt, the more out of balance I became and the more I avoided writing altogether.

It was around this time I was drawn to listen to Sobonfu's voice. I didn't know that placing my hand on my womb would help me get out of the debilitating situation I was in, but it did.

Having done the practice before going to bed and upon waking, I began to play with placing my hand over my womb throughout the day. Each time felt a bit different, but at no time did it *feel* remarkably powerful. I knew the practice was impactful because I was eating healthy, my writing was back on track, negative self-talk abated and I was alert to my ego's influence. Yet, the process itself still felt kind of normal—a combination of soft presence, comfort and centeredness, but without the *wow factor* that I'd expected to produce such incredible results.

The womb practice was the only thing new I was doing consistently, so I decided to try it with my clients. Everyone is unique. Processes that work for me don't always work for others. Sometimes though, I stumble across something useful that helps almost everyone. Typically, the easier it is to do, the more powerful the impact.

That said, easy things also awaken my too-good-to-be-true skepticism, which can be a good thing with spiritual/intuitive work. I believe one's inner skeptic is healthy as long as it is paired with a willingness to try new techniques.

I tend to attract healthy skeptics. My clients, like me, need to experience something to see if it works. So, I have learned to expect a few eye-rolls when I present an idea that seems too easy. Only a few rolled-eyes showed when I shared womb holding with sixteen women at a five-day retreat on how to open to more support. After I shared where the idea came from, we stood in a circle and all held our wombs at the same time.

"I know that simply placing a hand over the general location of the womb in order to center and connect intuitively seems too good to be true," I said. "It's not. Allow a settling awareness to accompany your hand and sink down with your breath." I demonstrated. "I've found it to be not only supportive, but transformative."

Every woman was surprised at how quickly she felt strongly present in her body. Many affirmative responses followed, some whispered, some loud.

"Wow."

"Amazing."

"Interesting."

Several women told me that they had felt a bit out of sync all day and this was a speedy remedy to bring them back to center. None had used this technique before and all were curious for more.

Womb connection in a group felt very different from practicing alone. More than comforting, it felt powerful. It had the feeling I was expecting when I started noticing my life changing.

It was so powerful, in fact that another woman and I experienced low back pain the next day. I had been numbing the sensation of low back discomfort, and my womb connection brought it to my attention so I could do something about it. I did some gentle stretching on a foam roller and received relief in record time. The other woman asked for help from the Divine to assist in healing the aches in her lower back, had fast improvement, and could move more easily.

I began, when appropriate, to introduce womb holding to individual clients. I was surprised when Ida said, "Yeah, I do that all the time, but I think of it as comforting my low belly. I've done it for years."

I asked her how she discovered it and what she used it for. Nonchalantly she said, "My chiropractor suggested I place my hand on my low stomach while taking several deep breaths to help me stop my mind from spinning and get back to an inner quiet so I can sleep. I tend to wake up in the middle of the night. Putting my hand on my belly works like a charm."

I asked if she had noticed any other results. "Well… there does seem to be a down side. The comfort of being held forces me to feel what's really happening."

"Why is that a downside?"

"Because sometimes, I know this sounds bad, but I don't want to deal with reality. When I am worked up from poor (work) habits or in a foul mood because of things I can't control… it feels good, initially anyway, to blame others for my snappish behavior. Easier, because it is so painful to see that I'm responsible."

We talked for a while. Ida admitted that sometimes she just wants to wallow in misery a little longer. Even though she knows putting a hand on her belly starts to calm her, helps her feel more optimistic and return to herself, she resists— thinking she's avoiding pain. "In those moments, I wish I could remember how much better I feel every time I do the stomach soothing."

I could empathize with Ida. I've wallowed or rolled around in denial when I don't want to acknowledge mental, emotional or physical pain. Many of us participate in this unconscious avoidance behavior because part of us always recognizes when we're headed toward discomfort. We want to avoid suffering.

Unfortunately, evading reality leads the ego to seize the reins. Our mind spins alternative *could*, *would*, and *should* stories or starts blaming others—instead of addressing the troubled place inside. When the ego is in control it's difficult to remember how much better we feel doing any centering practice such a walking, yoga, talking to a friend, or placing our palm on the low belly.

To prevent this memory lapse, consider doing this simple womb practice every day. It can thwart our fast-grasping ego from directing what we do, which results in overwhelm and stress. Think of placing a hand on the low belly as an experiment. The result might not always be natural balance and operating from wholeness, but we're more likely to get to a centered place that keeps us out of denial and helps us work from an intuitive perspective.

The unexpected benefits of this practice and the creative ways people have found to use it astound me. When I shared this chapter with my writing group, Meredith emailed me this note.

"I'm glad I waited to send this reply. This piece impacted me personally. Last night I couldn't sleep after being woken by thunder. My son Ben, along with two roommates, is on a 500-mile bike trek on the Blue Ridge Parkway. I realized he had not been 'trackable' (love the Find My iPhone App) for over 36 hours. He could be exposed to these extreme elements while camping along the parkway. I had no way to contact him to be sure. Instead, I tried your exercise. I could FEEL the energy running through both my hands and body. I was lying down with one hand on my lower abdomen and the other on my heart, thinking of Ben's safety. The energy felt like a light hum or buzz beneath my hands. I've never felt that before… it was connecting between my womb, where Ben once lived, and my heart, where he will always live. I'm tearing up just typing this! I felt more at peace about Ben and was able to go back to sleep."

Meredith sent this text the following day. "Found out this morning that Ben is fine and has shelter for the next few days. He'll be done with the trek in a week."

Sobonfu never shared with me an easy point of access to intuitive knowing for Dagara men. The space just below the navel is recognized as a center of power and an energetic foundation in many cultures. I encourage men to rest a palm there and notice if a settling, clarifying feeling comes to them as well.

Remember, we started with the original Western meaning of intuition as spiritual perception and insight being used to *consider* a situation. I had to look up the Latin roots of *consider*. Turns out it means, "together with the heavenly body."

Literally, it means to observe the stars by joining with them. It is a full-body-engaged way of studying or learning content. *Consider*, at its roots, is not simply to "think about something in order to arrive at a judgment or decision," as the current Merriam-Webster definition implies. It's recognizing the problem or situation is in you which makes it possible for more than your intellect to find a solution.

We all want instant results from techniques and imme-diate intuitive knowing. I hope you're beginning to see that this is an unreasonable expectation that keeps your self-important ego in charge. The ego-mind spins and tries to grasp at answers, which makes it even more difficult, but not impossible, for intuitive knowing to arise. It happens to everyone. We want what we want, and we want it now. That wanting knocks you out of sync, but it's still hard to resist.

Knowing this, the ancient technique that Sobonfu offers is *considerate*. It continually nurtures a balanced state that opens you to perceive with all of your senses. With just your hand you align with your essential self, so you don't need to spin and grasp at answers. The parts inside—those you've been ignoring or fighting—synchronize.

This innocent little practice quietly brings you to your core self, your womb, where you're literally connected to Creation. You feel your own stars, your own divinity where intuition resides, increasing the likelihood of instant knowing.

Invitation

Sit, lay down or stand in a comfortable position.

Bring the breath to the space below the navel.

Allow awareness to awaken the energy there.

Then bring attention to one hand.

Breathe into the palm, the fingers and let that hand

relax on the thighs.

Compare both hands.

Feel the aliveness in the hand that was breathed into.

Now let that hand lift and then connect gently to the low belly.

Let that aliveness penetrate to the pelvic space beneath.

Let the soft organs there feel the connection the hand is offering.

Let them join with the core self.

Let the anchor of the pelvis, the hand, and the core,

bring balance, comfort, and clarity.
Breathe deeply into the space around this anchor.
Relish the feeling of finding your essential self.

Part 3
How to Navigate Intuitive Blocks

17

I Only Smelled Roses

Once a month for 13 years I led an evening group called Tune-In Tuesdays in northern Virginia that focused on opening intuitive abilities. People would come to my friend Susan's spacious, light blue, brightly lit, living room and we'd sit in a circle on a mishmash of seating (couches, dining room chairs, floor pillows). Ten to 20 would show up to experience something beyond their everyday awareness. Participants closed their eyes and *tuned-in* to their insides as I intuitively guided them in three 20-minute experiential meditations. In between each round individuals shared what they noticed. Everyone's experience was different.

Some of the folks who came were visual by nature and they almost always raised their hands to share first. Their colorful experiences could sound quite dramatic. Initially, this caused others with quieter observances to shut down, believing they'd *tuned-in* wrong. Believing they should have experienced more. I curtailed this line of thinking by explaining our more dominant intuitive gifts are the first to respond yet oftentimes distract us from the nuanced cues that help give overall context to an intuitive message.

Since *Tune-In Tuesdays* were to broaden intuitive perspective, I invited everyone to direct their curiosity to discovering the smallest changes in sound, taste, smell, sensation, and inner vision. Exploring these subtleties makes your whole body alert to something new. This approach gives your inner wisdom more of a physical vocabulary to communicate through. Quieter nudges, when allowed a place of importance, help you develop a broad range of intuitive perception.

My standard line became, "The more subtlety you notice the better."

One night a pretty sandy-haired blonde named Cheryl came (I think her friend brought her.) The first time the group shared what happened for them personally, she kept silent. This wasn't unusual for a first-timer except that her body was rigid. Normally in these groups people relaxed; she was visibly tense. I wasn't too worried because I knew each round offered everyone more time to relax and dive deeper inside, which helped them identify subtle physical changes. This made it easier to find words for their experience.

I encouraged sharing because it's important to put words to what is wordless. Speaking out loud ensures everyone starts to create an intuitive vocabulary and increases the chances of noticing the softer nudges and subtle experiences again later, outside of class. Talking in a group helps other participants find words for their experiences as well. After the third inner dive there was a lot of what I call "Firework sharing," or big visuals with lots of colors and epiphanies. Each time someone shared, Cheryl seemed to shut down even more. I asked the people that hadn't spoken yet to voice something to the group.

"It doesn't matter if it's a negative experience or you feel like nothing happened. We'll still learn from it," I implored. "Whatever you did or didn't feel is information that is welcome."

Hesitantly Cheryl said, "Nothing happened. I didn't see or feel anything. I'm so frustrated." I asked if she had heard, tasted or smelled anything. She released a fast exasperated breath coupled with an eyeroll and said, "I only smelled roses."

Envy started to show up on faces in the group. I asked if anyone was wearing perfume. No. Rose oil? No. We all looked around the room, no sign of roses anywhere. I asked if anyone else smelled roses during the meditation or currently. "No."

Cheryl's eyes popped wide with disbelief. "No one else smelled roses? Really?"

She scanned the group, and then looked at me. "You mean that rose smell was something? What good is that kind of intuition? What does it mean?"

A big cuddly bear of a man responded that he'd smelled roses when his grandmother died before he knew she was gone. "Now I'll sometimes get a brief whiff of roses if I'm somewhere I think she'd like or if I know she'd want to help me. If I try to search for the source, the fragrance disappears. That's how I know she's really still with me."

Another woman said she'd heard that if you smell roses, the Virgin Mary is with you. I didn't say a word. Many in the group had never heard of anyone who could smell something not physically present. Cheryl shrugged her shoulders. "I guess it's good then, but I still don't get it."

Actually, she did *get it*. She got the experience. Her mind just wouldn't let her have *it*. She noticed the aroma. Everyone validated that it was something beyond what they could smell. What she wanted to *get* was an understanding as to what the rose scent meant. Even though she was given examples of possible meanings felt by others, her mind wasn't satisfied. Her mind took over and dismissed her experience as invalid because she didn't know why the rose fragrance came.

Cheryl got so focused on the why that she missed what was important. She had engaged and expanded her intuitive aperture to perceiving beyond the physical plane of existence. Her mind couldn't *get* the importance of this opening. Initially, many adult minds cannot.

The most common block to intuitive guidance is the mind getting grabby and dismissing intuition once it registers on your radar. You were taught to focus on *getting* the answer in school. To *get* the answer implies you understand. Our minds love to say, "I got it!" and check it off as done. Your intuition is never done. It speaks to you every day, all day, through subtle sensations that help your life.

Most times, we don't notice intuitive taps, especially when things are running smoothly. You typically wake up to noticing an intuitive signal after you don't listen. Like the other day, I purchased some nonslip dog socks to prevent our aging Labrador, Madison, from falling. Her back feet had been slipping on the hardwood floors. I felt my hand actually pause when I was about to cut the tags off. I noticed. I briefly acknowledged my hesitation, then my mind got grabby. "We're not going to return these. We measured and they look fine."

The tags fell onto wet coffee grounds in the kitchen trashcan. Half an hour later when the socks were uselessly spinning around Madison's feet, I thought back to my pause before cutting the tags. My intuition was trying to save me 12 dollars. I know, an outrageous price for dog socks. Also, outrageous that after 35 years of helping others with their intuition, my mind can still convince me to go against my own intuitive signals. That's called being human. I don't know anyone whose intuition doesn't get tripped up by overthinking. We've all ignored an inner intuitive directive if we've ever thought, "I knew it. Why didn't I do it?"

Your intuition is always working. Sometimes you don't know to or how to listen. Sometimes a soft message briefly registers but your thoughts overpower the signal (like me with the sock tags). Still, your intuition is always there.

Listening and then taking action, or not, from small sensory tickles has become a game I play with my mind all of the time. My mind's job is to pay close attention to any sensation while making decisions. It's even more important to notice when my mind takes over and tells me not to listen to those seemingly innocuous sensations. Like landing in stopped traffic, after ignoring an impulse to go a different route, proves my intuition was unequivocally right. My mind stopped me from acting on the impulse. My mind reinforces that it noted my intuitive impulse by saying, "Ugh, I knew it. Why didn't I go the other way?"

I've learned that lavishing my mind with praise, not criticism, when witnessing intuitive signals increases my ability to act upon them. The mind hates being wrong and loves to be right. My mind will stay curious and track the minute tweaks of my body, if tracking means my mind will be right, even if my mind made a convincing case to not proceed with the intuitive clue. I congratulate my mind for registering my intuition was active. I then ask my mind for help in pointing out signals next time and *remind* it that we'd be smart to listen.

One time I headed to the bank to get papers notarized. The document said it had to be signed in blue ink. Halfway to the car an image of a blue pen popped into my awareness. My mind noticed, then said, "They'll have blue pens at the bank. Let's just go."

I stopped, took a breath and felt a slight tug to go back in the house and grab a pen. I thanked my mind for acknowledging the tug. Then I told my mind it would only take an extra minute to go back inside and grab a blue pen. Thank goodness I did. This bank only had black pens. Employees weren't allowed to bring any other color to work. Crazy right? If I hadn't turned around for a blue pen, I would have wasted an hour waiting in line, had to rearrange my tight schedule and find the time to go back (and wait in line again).

My intuition was helping me be efficient. My mind got its way once, and cost me 12 dollars, but my intuition won twice because my mind noticed the intuitive input both times. The more your mind recognizes intuitive input, the more your chances increase that your minds will listen next time.

It's easy to dismiss an inner wave or second guess that you're having an intuitive experience, especially when you don't comprehend the message. It takes practice to speak to yourself with kindness when you realize you've dismissed an inner clue. Reminding your mind that the value of intuition isn't always to attain concrete information.

Intuitive sensations can help you experience something new, steep you in gratitude or be nourished by beauty. Your Soul gives little nudges to enrich feelings of fullness, widen your perception, receive the mysteries of your world and, dare I say, stop and smell the unseen roses.

I never saw Cheryl again. I'm so grateful she came that night. Her story has helped so many people get past the moments of I'm-not-getting-*it* frustration. *It* is intuition. *It* is subtle. Remember *you get it*. *It* is a part of you. Even when you miss or dismiss *it, you get it*.

Invitation

Take a slow breath in through your nose.
Smell the air.
Linger in the smells around you.
Invite the air to come alive with something especially for you.
Invite beauty and gentle joy to ride in on your breath.
Pause a moment to experience whatever came.
Remember nothing is something.
Take a slow soft breath through your nose.
Smell the air and rest.

18
How the Mind Helps Intuition

You need your intellect.

The mind is incredible at dissecting, analyzing and directing—separating ideas, brainstorming and filling heads with as many concepts that can be held all at once.

The intellect is even useful when working *with* your intuition—you just don't want your brain in *charge* of intuition.

When your mind appoints itself as the designated solver of a problem, its action-oriented role can stop the intuitive process. The mind likes to be on constant output, working all of the time to find a clear 2+2=4 answer for everything. Overactive thinking can override your senses and jam your intuitive knowing. This makes it next to impossible to receive the data your intuition provides.

The mind loves to look smart and be right. It often takes credit for intuitive insights. When an intuitive *knowing* permeates your entire being, your head unconsciously recognizes it as your Soul's wisdom. This phenomenon makes it easier to listen to intuition without inner argument. Submerged in *knowing*, your brain stops working so hard and relaxes. Full body *knowing* indicates to your ego/mind that it's about to look smart without effort.

Most of the time this type of overall *knowing* is elusive. To get your head to *want to* learn how to work *with* your body's physical sensations and find intuitive *knowing*, your mind needs a reason to change its workaholic habits.

I hadn't talked to my client Marianne for a year. She was

embarrassed to tell me that she believed her intuition wasn't working.

"I don't understand how to get my mind to work with my intuition," she said. "I can't stop questioning every sensation and intuitive hit I get. My mind is really bad, jutting out in so many directions, judging and then negating any intuitive information. I end up totally confused and constantly doubting myself. Even though I usually find out later my first impression was accurate."

"Our minds are a lot like untrained dogs," I said. "When the mind is put in charge of functions it can't fully understand, it becomes anxious. Our brain sniffs at everything and jumps around to different conclusions. Unable to settle, our minds can become unmanageable and even destructive, especially when we put our intellect in charge of our intuition."

Marianne told me she'd really never been around dogs. So, I elaborated with this story.

For two mornings one spring, we found our shoes, pillows, magazines, and garden tools carefully placed in a circle in our side yard. These items were stealthily taken from our front porch at night, as if the fairies had arranged them. We kept putting them back on the porch. On the third morning my husband solved the mystery by going outside very early. He discovered, inside the ring of our things a young black Labrador-ish dog sound asleep. After a fruitless search for her owner, we named her Louise and welcomed her home.

At the end of puppyhood, Louise had a bunch of energy. Perhaps from being abandoned she was also skittish. Inside the house, she behaved beautifully within the parameters we'd set. She learned very quickly to stay off the furniture, to only chew on her toys and to gently take a cookie from our hands.

Outside, however, Louise was difficult to train. She bolted all over the place when on a leash, often yanking me off balance. She was deceptively strong and no amount of scolding or physically holding her still could prevent her from enthusiastically leaping at a passerby.

I began to watch Cesar Millan, the famous TV dog trainer, for tips. The advice he gave that had the most impact was to give signals to your dog that you are the "pack leader." That's the strong guiding force that gives appropriate signs to help the dog relax and follow directions. We didn't know it, but we'd signaled to Louise that she was the leader every time we let her go out the door first.

We began to put Louise's leash on and then had her sit next to the front door while we walked outside first. Then we invited her to follow, signaling that we were in the lead. After a few weeks of this routine, Louise started to relax and sit next to the door when her leash was put on. She also began walking calmly beside us on our loop around the neighborhood. If she tensed to leap when another walker or dog approached, a small corrective tug accompanied by a brief sound from us returned her focus and calmed her down. When my husband or I gave the proper "pack leader" signals, she became a wonderful presence, and even helped me feel safe when I walked alone at night.

Louise was never being a bad dog, she wanted to please us. We didn't understand that we were sending her the wrong signals.

"Your mind isn't bad," I told Marianne. "It is yanking you all over the place and throwing you off balance. No amount of inner scolding or endless prove-yourself questions can prevent our minds from enthusiastically leaping at every intuitive passerby. Our Western culture puts the mind in charge of everything. Your intellect needs some different signals and some training to allow intuition to take the lead and release the stress of indecision."

When you leash the mind and invite your Soul through the door first, the mind becomes a useful companion. The mind relaxes when it can feel wisdom and act as a support for your intuition instead of an impediment.

When you consciously take in a breath and feel your weight settle with an exhale before focusing on your next step, it signals the mind that you want your body's sensory intuitive messages. When you then invite a source bigger than yourself to participate, your mind wants to serve because it feels something bigger and wiser is leading.

When beginning to work with intuition the mind has three jobs—to observe, to report and to ask for help.

Giving your intellect different tasks keeps it happy. Your mind enjoys variety, like the variety of objects Louise surrounded herself with in the yard. Your mind can find a center to rest in if the different jobs are defined. The parameters keep your brain focused, not distracted and overwhelmed.

There are a few steps you need to take to create a foundation for your mind to assist with translating the messages from your intuition.

First, observe and report on any intuitive wording you use. When you hear yourself say things such as, "Something tells me…" or "It just feels like…" or "I'm moved to…" these are signs for the mind to actively prepare your body to be receptive to intuitive information.

Second, pause and direct your mind to follow your breath inside to notice and name the physical sensations occurring throughout your body. This prepares you to investigate and clarify the intuitive communication your words have signaled. Observation must take place in the present moment and is reported by naming where and how the body reacts.

The mind usually tries to insert itself as leader by reporting on remembered sensations instead of current ones. For instance, when I asked a new client, Jenny, to let her mind follow her breath down into her body and tell me what she physically felt, she immediately responded with, "My lower back has been hurting."

I could tell from her quick response and wording that her mind had taken over. I asked her to take her time and describe what her whole body felt like *now*, not what *had been*. Her response changed dramatically: "My chest and arms are relaxed. My lower back is a tiny bit tight. I'm surprised, it's only a one on the pain scale."

I told her she was ready to do the next step--to prepare her body to process an intuitive message she received earlier. "We need to clear your body, to get it as close to neutral as we can, by asking a bigger source than yourself to help with your back. Then…"

She interrupted. "I've had this back trouble for a while, and I don't think it has anything to do with my intuition, and it doesn't feel that bad right now. Let's just get to the intuitive part."

Jenny's mind had taken charge again.

"Asking for help with any discomfort is useful," I told her. "We want our body to feel as clear as possible so we notice any physical change as an intuitive response. Asking for help with a long-term problem sometimes doesn't have much impact, but it's worth a try. Even though your back feels pretty good, let's see if asking for help makes it feel any better."

Jenny sighed and asked the Divine Feminine (her bigger source) for help. After about a minute she spoke. "I didn't move to try to change positions or stretch. A warm feeling came through my whole body. I feel unified and aware of myself. My back doesn't hurt at all. I'm shocked."

Jenny was now in a clear, receptive space—her body

primed to receive intuitive information. If we had ignored Jenny's back pain it could have been a distraction that took her attention away from the contrasts in the body that intuitive signals bring. By asking for help and receiving ease, Jenny received validation to trust that invisible help really was there. Asking for help is always an opportunity. If her back pain hadn't been eased, we could still navigate intuitive signals by observing responses in clearer physical areas.

Response from a mere request can be subtle or obvious. Either provides evidence and enhances confidence to engage with your intuition. When your intelligence is consistently directed to focus on what you say and how you physically feel, your observer and reporter mind get more effective over time, as do your requests for assistance.

The next step has many options and takes place only after your body has been helped to release (as much as possible) where it is tight or hurting.

Your brain can embrace the paradoxical like the examples given in the chapter, *Stand In the And*.

Your intellect can make comparative statements like the examples given in the next chapter, *The Power of the Penny*.

Your mind, like Marianne's, can review past intuitive experiences and discover through hindsight where your intuition was accurate. There are many other chapters that include ways your mind can support your connection to inner wisdom.

Marianne's mind thought its job was to interpret the intuitive signals her body received instead of simply naming the sensations. Jenny's mind thought it wasn't necessary to ask for help and to monitor her body's response. Perpetually redirecting your mind to perceive and name as much sensory input as you can *in the moment* is key to interpreting intuitive meaning. With practice, your head is reprogramed to easily report, not analyze, what your body is experiencing, which cultivates embodied knowing.

Embodied knowings are intellectual understandings that are revealed from wordless physical signals.

I've mentally walked the loop of my inner neighborhood countless times, leashed to my breath, continuously reporting observations and calling on help for large and small discomforts. My mind still gets distracted and wanders. When it does, I bring it back to the present. The only time intuition communicates clearly through embodied awareness is *now*. It's easy to remember because the word now is an integral part of *know*.

Often when someone tells me their intuition is wrong, their head has usually grabbed onto one fragment of information and created a whole story. The mistake your mind often makes is to jump to conclusions about the information given. Intuition helps you see the moment and the next step. Successful intuitive information is taken one step at a time.

But what about making plans? We have to take more than one step, don't we?

Not true; intuition signals in the moment when it's right to take action on something that takes place in the future.

A spiritual teacher I follow began promoting a retreat she was teaching out of the country. I had no interest at all. Yet, the morning she sent out the enrollment email, my whole body sparked. As I read the email my posture straightened, my chest expanded, I felt very present and alert. "Sign up immediately," my body conveyed to my mind. Out loud I said, "It is okay to revisit going to this retreat in two hours." I felt no constriction.

Later, when I checked my intuition from a neutral space, the workshop still felt right to attend.

My mind was not *in charge* of the decision to sign up. It recognized my body's 180-degree response compared to the disinterest I had when the retreat was first promoted. I couldn't miss the strong physical signals. My whole body resonated with "Go!" and I knew I needed to decide quickly for this particular opportunity.

Again, I breathed in the possibility of attending the retreat. I felt excited and an urgency to sign up now. My hands moved without thought towards the computer. I noticed a deposit wasn't required until the application was accepted, which allowed time to check logistics later. I found myself filling out the online form and pushing the button. It turns out I was one of the last people to get in. The workshop filled so quickly that if I'd have waited even 15 minutes, I would have been put on a long waiting list.

After I pushed the button, I felt even more aligned with my decision. It was then I engaged my brain to analyze if the retreat would be an unreasonable strain on my budget or conflict with my schedule. My calendar was open. The unexpected expense, coupled with an intuitive electric sensation running through me, felt significant enough to reconfigure my budget. My body felt ease as I paid the next day.

When the mind stops *trying* to think and shifts into a place of awareness, intuition becomes fully present at a cellular level, embodying knowing. You feel resonance in your whole body, your mind relaxes with wisdom present. Depending on how clear the signals are the next action can usually be taken.

With intuition you want to feel the good stuff. You may think to yourself, *Yaaay, I'm using my intuition, this is going to feel great*. Yet, it can be harder to navigate when your body starts to communicate through unpleasant or painful feelings, especially when your expectation is the opposite. Charlie's story in the next chapter, *How to Work With Intuitive Signals that Suck*, is an example of normally unwelcome sensations being integral to intuitive discoveries.

Intuition works best when it's given the space to

communicate in any way it needs, including through emotional and physical discomfort. When painful, irritating or troubling intuitive clues surface to help you with a problem, it takes practice to embrace whatever comes. If what you feel becomes too much, this might be an intuitive signal to seek support from a professional counselor.

The mind needs to learn that the best role it can play in seeking intuitive information is gathering data during the process. It just needs to be trained to recognize all of the senses as potential avenues of information. When your mind pays attention to the vast, subtle physical, emotional and sensory signals your body sends, there is a greater chance of intuitive direction guiding the situation. Even if you are only aware of a few signals, the process still works.

You know life is complicated. Your job is to remind your mind that it will feel smart if it lets intuition take the lead. Ask the mind to *remind* you to take time, give space to the present, and feel your breath move inside. Your mind has the ability to track the sensory information that might not have words but contains a fullness of knowing. Teach your mind to value mystery.

Your intuition gathers and integrates all of the known and unknown factors needed for transformation. The mind doesn't know, let alone understand, that many of the factors involved for your intuition to function even exist. It's a mystery how relief arrives. Just by asking the air for help, a feeling can change. There are many mysteries. Value them.

It's okay, even normal, to remind the mind of its jobs. Be kind to yourself, like you would gently remind a small child or a beloved pet. Your brain doesn't mean to forget. It's just hard to remember when you're learning and not in control.

Your intellect can't direct your intuition and deep down

doesn't want to. That would take away exhilarating epiphanies, *aha* moments of revelation, and the surprise when an undeniable knowing appears with a solution. Your mind loves being given a new direction, a next step or a solution to a complex situation that doesn't have one right answer.

Knowing that you don't know is an important knowing to embrace.

Your mind might never be completely comfortable with knowing that it's not time to know. That's the time to walk out the door first and take your headspace on a walk, around your inner neighborhood, to sniff out intuitive clues.

Invitation

Gently be aware of a situation intuition can help with.
Focus inward.
Feel your breath move your body.
Feel the pulse of your heart in your veins.
Notice whatever is happening physically now.
If some part of the body is uncomfortable, notice.
Ask for help for any discomfort.
Breathe.
Notice any change.
Invite a spacious stillness to encompass the body.
Notice any subtle physical changes.
Simply notice.
Let go of meaning.
Simply observe expectations.
If you are thinking, notice your thoughts.
Just watch them.

Bring focus back to the breath's physical movement.
Bring awareness to sensation, without judgment.
The mind stays current to all that happens within.
Notice spaciousness.
Notice anywhere constricted.
Simply notice what's occurring in the body.
By noticing the mind automatically reports the present.
Understand that nothing needs to be revealed now.
Just invite unified, neutral space.
The process has started for direct knowing, intuition.
Remind the mind that this is more than enough for now.
Embrace the mystery.

19
How to Work With Intuitive Signals that Suck

When Charlie called me the first time she said, "I want to learn to listen to my heart and my body as much as I listen to my brain."

Charlie said she'd never been able to feel her intuition. She wanted to so that she could balance her life with her clients' schedules. She constantly had "client stuff running through her head." She had forgotten how to focus on her own needs and thought maybe intuition could help.

We started by breathing down into her body. Charlie didn't know what I meant by "breathing down."

"As you breathe, feel how your breath affects your ribs, your belly, your hips, your legs." I explained. "Feel how the body moves by breathing. And just for the heck of it, ask your body to open to the earth's energy, even if you don't know what that means."

Charlie doubted anything would happen with earth energy, but she did it. "Oh wow. I can feel something buzzy going up my legs. That's trippy."

I asked if she was more aware of her body. She was. Then I asked if her body needed to tell her something. Charlie paused, took a breath and said, "I don't know. My stomach feels anxious now. Why?"

I suggested that her stomach might be trying to tell her something. She joked that maybe it was telling her "not to work on her intuition because she was fine before we started." I asked if that was her brain's interpretation, and she conceded it might be.

I then had Charlie ask the Divine to come and help her stomach's anxiety and to help her begin to understand what the anxiety was about. Charlie paused for a few seconds then said, "I'm anxious instead of excited about a lot of travel coming up, mainly business but some personal. I feel like a lot of people want a lot of things from me. I can't give everyone everything they want, but I also don't know how to say *no*. I don't like to think about it." She sighed. "Is this my intuition telling me I'm overcommitted? Ouch, now my stomach is nauseous."

I pointed out that when she asked for help with her stomach, she started thinking about the many commitments she couldn't say no to. Then, when she said she didn't like to think about it, her stomach went from anxious to nauseous. "So, you asked for help and the anxiety did change," I said. "Now, ask for help for the nausea."

Charlie was not happy with this process. "How can going from anxiety to nauseousness be a good change?"

I explained, "We're trying to understand what your stomach is telling you. The feeling isn't about good or bad, just notice the feeling changed and respect it. We aren't trying to get rid of the feeling. It's more valuable to ask for help after each change because it leads to more embodied information."

We asked for help for her stomach again, even if it didn't want help. Charlie told me there was no change. I asked her if she was still nauseous. "No. It feels very overwhelming. Like I want to cry or something."

Charlie sounded exhausted. I told her the change from nauseous to sadness was information. "I don't know what to do with this kind of information," she said.

I suggested she talk to her belly. "Say, 'It's okay that you're overwhelmed. It's okay that you want to cry. I'm asking for help for you.' This shows that you respect that your feelings are trying to tell you something. Then take a slow breath and tell me what happens."

"I'm nauseous again. This sucks."

I told Charlie that it's a habit for the brain to think, "This sucks." It's also this habitual reaction that makes our body unable to understand painful emotions. It is challenging starting this process when the brain doesn't know if it will glean anything from it.

When working with your intuition you want to discover any place that's uncomfortable. This way you can ask for help and sometimes uncover what's underneath the discomfort. Often, you just feel the nausea and don't take the time to ask for help. If you stop at noticing you're nauseous, you miss the opportunity to gain valuable information.

I told Charlie, "For now, say to your belly, 'It doesn't matter *why* I'm nauseous. I'm just asking for some relief and understanding.' Now you're going to breathe and feel if something happens... Anything change?"

"Nooooo change."

"You're still nauseous?" I prodded.

"No. It's more like a ball in my stomach. Boy these are really subtle changes."

Charlie huffed and said, "How do I know I'm really feeling these things? And my brain's not being like, just tell Jennifer what she wants to hear?"

I asked Charlie if she thought she'd be making up anxiety, pressure, overwhelm, sadness, and nauseas turning into a ball in her stomach. "Are these symptoms things that you tend to imagine and successfully create?"

She laughed and said, "No." This was not what her imagination liked to do.

I told her, "When you think you're making something up around intuition just ask yourself, *Are these things that I tend to imagine?* Then believe your answer."

Charlie reiterated that she felt fine before the appointment. I reminded her that she called because she wanted to listen to her heart and body, that she was so overcommitted that she was a bit numb, that she wanted to feel excited about her wonderful upcoming trips. I suggested that perhaps her overwhelming busyness suppressed or dulled all of her feelings.

"We want to feel the good stuff. We say to ourselves, *Oh, yaaay, intuition. It's going to feel good.* It's hard when our body starts to communicate through unpleasant or painful feelings. Especially when our expectation is the opposite," I told her.

Charlie agreed to continue and we asked for help for the ball that was still in her stomach. With this request, past client conversations came to her mind—ones where she had to tell her clients she couldn't help them because, being overwhelmed, "she didn't know her schedule." These memories, she noticed, "made the ball get harder and tighter."

Charlie talked about how more business was coming in and getting logistics in order was a priority. She went on to say she was slowly getting all of the detailed work for each client organized and on a schedule. As she spoke, she was surprised to find her stomach ball getting "loose and light."

I pointed out the timing of the tightening and loosening sensations. With practice, she would see how sensation connected to what she was saying was revealing important intuitive information. Training the mind to notice changes in physical sensation when you speak opens the door to valuable intuitive communication. Based on this information I asked, "Do you need to tell your clients that you don't know your schedule?"

Charlie hemmed and hawed but didn't answer. I asked, "When you talked about playing with your business logistics, the ball got lighter, right?" She made an affirmative sound. "Feel the ball and tell me if anything changes when I say to tell your clients, 'I'm working out some logistics in my schedule and I'll call you back.'"

Charlie took a deep breath and quickly blew it out. "Oooooh, I feel better!" I could hear her smiling. "The ball is gone! Wow. I *am* working on logistics. I never thought to tell my clients. I feel so good… open… better… I get it… and now I'm feeling excited about my overseas trip."

It's important to say that this is an abbreviated text of her session. Charlie didn't add up all of the information and think her way into this one conclusion. She morphed into an intuitive place of understanding. Everything from the session came together in that felt moment, and her head understood. Because of her unexpected joyful breakthrough, Charlie's mind was more willing to learn how to acknowledge and respect physical sensations/feelings, as opposed to ignoring or reacting to them.

Your intuition works when given spaciousness and many ways to communicate. In Charlie's case, painful feelings surfaced emotionally and physically to let her know there was a lifestyle problem that needed to be addressed. This is often the case; it takes practice to embrace whatever comes and to ask for big invisible help and notice the effect. Especially if your mind doesn't know if any useful information will surface.

Your intuition gathers and integrates all of the known and unknown factors needed for transformation. Charlie called me because she knew she was in her head too much. She wanted to operate with more work/life balance. She didn't know she was feeling anxious. Her brain had blocked out all sensation to avoid feeling the anxiety that her stomach revealed.

You never know how asking for help with uncomfortable feelings can illuminate the changes in perspective and behavior you need. The mind can't know, let alone understand, any of the invisible factors involved when you begin to communicate with your Soul. The mind can only be curious; to notice, to report what it observes, to have compassion with physical discomfort and to ask for help to aid aches and irritations.

Charlie learned the value of engaging body sensation to take the lead and let the mind support the process. Her body gave her positive clues when she spoke about logistics, intuitively indicating a solution might be found with that focus.

Her mind began to learn to value mystery. It is mysterious that nausea is trying to communicate something other than you had iffy food for lunch. I told Charlie to ask her mind to re*mind* her to take time, give space to present physical sensation, to feel the effects of her breath, and to allow her mind to track all sensory information without judging or disregarding what it doesn't like.

This process might not bring immediate understanding, but repeated over time, valuable intuitive communication occurs.

Invitation

Take a slow deep breath in.
When you release the breath begin to notice
the belly constricting.
Take in another slow deep breath and with it
Slowly shift your awareness down your body.
Feel your chest, ribs and belly rise.
Feel your hips expand.
Feel with your awareness your thighs, calves and feet open.
Release the breath tracking from the bottom of the feet
All the way up the body and out.

Breathe in and observe if there's any pain or discomfort.

Even if it's a minor constriction, notice.

Ask the Divine to help this place inside.

Notice the slightest change.

You and this place in your body might not believe this will help.

That's okay.

Invite the help anyway.

If your body tightens more in that area or in another

It might be signaling it doesn't want Divine help now.

That's okay.

Apologize to that place that you haven't tried to help before.

You know now and honor the decision

not to receive Divine help.

Sit there with the sensation.

Without judgment.

Without wanting to get rid of it.

See if any subtle change occurs.

When you're about to shift your focus,

Say you'll check on it again.

You'll offer Divine help again.

That you're always interested in the wisdom it is holding.

Then say thank you for its presence.

That you look forward to when it feels safe to reveal its message.

20
The Power of the Penny

My friend Glenn and I had a rare opportunity to go to lunch together. In those days, I usually packed my lunch to monitor every penny, so going out was a real treat. I had no idea it would lead to one of the fastest and most accurate ways to engage my intuition.

Two places were at the top of my list: Woody's and The Deli. Woody's was close, a dive that served the best homemade half-pound hamburgers with hand-cut, long, skinny fries.

The Deli was a 15-minute drive to a neglected-beige, one-story cinderblock, place-your-order-and-sit-in-uncomfortable-seats establishment. But in the summertime—it was July—their BLT was like no other. Garden-picked heirloom tomatoes and basil, generously stacked on fresh baked sourdough bread, with thick cuts of hickory-smoked bacon. Both places included whole kosher pickles with every order. I was torn.

I asked Glenn if he had a preference. Nope, either was good with him. So, I grabbed a penny and said, "Heads, The Deli. Tails, Woody's." I tossed the penny, caught it in my right hand, flipped it to my left forearm, slowly lifted my palm and announced, "We're going to Woody's."

Glenn stopped me. "Did you make the decision based on the coin?"

"Yes."

Glenn continued, "Because I use a coin toss to see what I really want. If I'm disappointed in the result, I know that in my heart, I really wanted to go to the other restaurant."

I was surprised to realize I *was* disappointed. How could I be blocked from knowing my real preference? Maybe part of me didn't want the longer drive to The Deli or maybe I was worried about disappointing Glenn. I didn't know. So, I stopped thinking about what clouded my preference and we went to The Deli. I remember being happy and satisfied.

For a time, the penny became a reliable shortcut to unblock my preferences and my intuition.

Choosing where or what to eat doesn't seem like a major life decision. Lunch, some might argue, has nothing to do with intuition. I thought the same thing until months later when I ignored the feeling of what *not* to eat.

That fall, I went out to lunch for a co-worker's birthday. The restaurant's special of the day looked good—artichoke, garlic butter, shrimp over angel hair pasta. I immediately thought, "I'm having the special," and my stomach gripped. I ignored my stomach and searched for another menu option for penny-tossing purposes. The toss fell on my second choice, Greek salad with grilled chicken. I glanced at the coin and ordered the shrimp special. My belly's reaction and the penny's outcome had no impact on a stubborn mental decision. I thoroughly enjoyed the pasta until the food poisoning hit.

Later, lying in bed, I had plenty of time to think about the penny's real power. Did it connect me to my intuition, my preferences or both? I remembered how my stomach had given me a gripping jab long before the coin toss, right after my head had said, "I'm having the special."

The statement was key. When I thought about the past, I remembered how making a decisive statement, out loud or not, produced a clear, intuitive sensation. Like thinking, "I'm having the special," followed by a stomach cramp *I wish I hadn't ignored.* I realized the penny's power actually came from the statement the flip elicited, not the flip itself. A choice stated in the form of a final decision held power, even if the decision was momentary.

Until the penny, my decision-making had always taken the form of a question. I had never purposefully vocalized a decision unless I'd made it. Saying *I am going to* was natural after a coin toss. Saying *I am going to* in order to gauge my disappointment without a coin toss was a revelation. I finally had a way to make complex intuitive decisions easier.

The penny depended on binary thinking, an either/or choice. A coin could still be useful in making a quick decision with mundane questions. "Where do I want to eat?" "Which grocery store line is the fastest?" or "What outfit do I wear?" I only had to limit the choices to two, flip the copper and see if I was relieved or disappointed with the outcome, remembering to pay attention to my body's reaction.

Now curious, I started playing with statements, shelving the penny. I'd say to myself, "The left checkout lane is faster." If my body responded with happy chill bumps, I'd get in that line. If my body's reply was neutral, heavy-shouldered or gave a constrictive twinge, I'd make a statement about a different line. It became a game to see if my intuition was accurate. It was, 80 percent of the time. When I found myself in the slowest line when I'd made a clear statement, I started to wonder why.

I remembered that intuition was my Soul guiding me. It's not about being right or having my wishes fulfilled. There are unseen benefits to being caught in long lines. The important thing is to pause, gather yourself, and allow your larger wisdom to weigh in.

Your body is able to accurately communicate in response to a statement because your intuition is commenting on one thing. The vocabulary of your senses speaks clearly when giving feedback, one situation at a time. The body can't give a clear answer to a complex question. It can only respond to what is. The fastest way for your intuition to send precise signals through your body is for you to make every statement as if it is the choice you are making.

Do I want to go to Woody's or The Deli? At least three statements can come from that question. I'm going to Woody's. I'm going to the Deli. I'm going somewhere else. Your body will give clear results because it is a single focus in the present moment.

My longtime client, Sheila, told me she uses statements all the time; she calls it her "little secret joy." Once she was in New York City during a snowstorm trying to fly home. The gate attendant announced that her flight was delayed but still scheduled to depart that night. She got a funny feeling in her stomach when she heard the announcement.

"I felt like my intuition was commenting on my flight information, but I wanted to be sure. I took a deep centering breath. Held my cell phone to my ear and made some statements."

I imagined her commanding presence in her tailored navy suit, surrounded by frustrated flyers as she spoke with purpose into the inactive receiver. She continued, "My options now clear in my mind, I said, 'I'm flying home tonight' and felt my stomach tighten. I took a moment. 'I am flying home tomorrow morning.' My stomach contracted again.

"I remembered to breathe down in my body to feel *very* centered before I said the option I really didn't want. 'I am flying home tomorrow afternoon.' My stomach *and* chest, that I hadn't realized were tight, immediately relaxed. My shoulders felt light and my head was clear. I secured a room at my hotel and switched to a 2:00 flight the next day."

What happened? Her original flight, and more, were canceled later that night. Many who expected their planes would leave had to spend the night at the airport because hotels were full. The following morning flights were over-booked.

Sheila, her seat secure, had a nice dinner, a good night's sleep, finished some additional work, and boarded her afternoon flight unhurried and rested.

Part of making statements is the ability to remain open-minded while saying things you really don't want to happen. Sheila wanted to be home. She hated the thought of waiting until the next day, but she didn't want to be stuck at the airport all night either. Instead of shutting down with anger at the delay, she took a breath and opened to the options available. She was willing to accept the consequences of listening to her intuition.

Had the snow storm continued, the flight she let go of might have been the last plane out, leaving her stuck for days. She knew there were many outcomes that could occur from an intuitive decision. She trusted her body's clear response would be favorable for her, no matter the result.

Choosing to believe your intuition will lead you in the best possible direction fosters the ability to find ambiguity interesting rather than frightening. That's not to say that embracing mystery is comfortable, but a willingness to make statements anyway strengthens your courage to act from your intuition.

Eve, another high-powered client, was trying to get home to the East Coast from a winter business trip in the Midwest. The snow was falling heavily and many flights had already canceled. Her flight was still scheduled to depart but no one knew when. One of her business associates whose flight Eve was on, was going to chance it.

Eve wrote to me, "I tried to breathe and feel my weight, which was a challenge in the midst of airport confusion. I felt a tiny bit centered and spoke softly to myself, *my flight will get home this evening.* I felt neutral. Then I tried, my flight will get home tomorrow. I still felt neutral. Since this seemed to make no difference, I tried a different approach. *I will stay the night.*

I felt light. *I will go home tonight.* I felt heavy. Even though I would have loved to have tucked my kids into bed, I decided to switch my flight to the morning.

"I was surprised to discover the outcome. My flight did leave late that evening, but the snowstorm had continued moving east. Although I would have arrived at the airport without a problem, I would have been very tired driving home on icy, treacherous roads. Even though I thought my statements were about my flight leaving, I realize now I averted a dangerous car trip. Thank you for teaching me statement-making! My intuitive decision eased my stress and my family's worry."

Eve was tenacious in making statements. By changing her words from *my flight* (the plane's action) to *I will* (her action) made the difference in her body's capacity to respond. This is really important because neutral so easily translates into "It doesn't matter. Or it must not make a difference." Rarely does a neutral sensation mean any choice will work. Most often it means, *Make a clearer statement.*

When making statements, keep it simple. State different possibilities starting with, "I am…" It worked for Eve to use "I will…" but I don't recommend it. "I will" indicates the future, not the present. Intuition's clearest reply is in the present.

Statements work for making plans because you are making decisions in the moment. For example, if your intent is to avoid traffic or a long line going to the pharmacy, say, "I am going to the pharmacy at one o'clock today." Take a moment to let your body respond. "I am going to the pharmacy at one thirty today." Always give yourself a quiet moment to listen to your body. See sensation as wisdom. Then take a deep breath to clear yourself for a new result from the next statement. Make as many statements as you need, at different times, different days or in a different location.

Sam also used statements in a stressful airport situation.

"I said, 'I am going home tonight.' Then I tried, 'I'm not going home tonight.' My body felt more open and relaxed to staying and waiting for my delayed flight. I felt light and kind of smug sitting in that crowd of people knowing the flight would take off."

He looked at me hard and said, "You cannot imagine how pissed I was when my flight cancelled. I thought 'Did I mix up my body signals? Is my intuition broken?' Then I thought, 'This woo-woo shit doesn't work.'"

Then he laughed and said, "Don't worry. I found out woo-woo shit does work."

After his flight got cancelled, Sam started towards the pickup area in search of a hotel. What he found was a surprise. While looking down at his phone, he literally bumped into an old friend. They lived in different cities and hadn't seen each other in more than five years. The friend's plane had been canceled as well, so together they found a hotel, had a wonderful dinner and spent the whole evening catching up. "We've stayed in touch since." He laughed, "I couldn't imagine a situation where I'd be happy my flight was called off. But I was."

I need to point out a potential problem with Sam's second statement. He said, "I'm *not going home* tonight," instead of, "I'm *staying here* tonight." You provide your body with the opportunity to respond with greater clarity when you state what you *are* doing as opposed to what you aren't.

I know crafting statements seems picky. I used to think that my intuition should just know what I mean. It does. Your body doesn't. Learning to present statements clearly, so you can understand your body's insights, is the key to opening the container of *knowing* you are walking around in.

Sam's experience is the magic of intuition's hidden wisdom. There was zero indication that reconnecting with an old friend was a possibility. Because he waited for his flight, the timing was perfect for a reunion. Magic.

Life has many ambiguous situations where there is no clear path. Facts are missing and there is nothing obvious to help you decide. A penny flip is a valuable place to start. Practicing statements with the mundane when the stakes are low builds the confidence needed to use statements for more important situations. When I remember to make statements, especially in seemingly unimportant matters like when to run errands, I make better decisions. Life flows more smoothly.

Statements are a way to connect to the unseen bigger picture. Intuition points towards things that your rational mind can't possibly detect or understand. It takes practice to make very simple statements that engage your Soul's advice, so be gentle with yourself if there are missteps as you explore this process.

My intellect would have never suspected that the coin with the least monetary value could lead to something priceless.

So next time you pick up a penny, change the old line, *penny for your thoughts*, to, *penny for your statements*. Then small change will always remind you of the power you hold inside.

Invitation

Take a clearing breath.
Breathe deeply into your head.
Release the head breath down through the body.
Breathe into the neutral space inside.
Feel this space of no decision.
Feel it as a place of wonder,
A place of potential,
A place of mystery.
Say, I am comfortable here.

Notice the body's response.

Respect whatever sensation you receive as information.

Take another clearing breath.

Land in the inside space of neutral mystery again.

Say, I am uncomfortable here.

Be open to experience the body's input.

Respect the valuable information given.

Take a soothing breath.

Ask for help to enjoy this process.

Take a moment to receive the help asked for and smile.

21
Wishing Well

While dictating a response to a client's question, my phone decided to mess with me.

I simmered in frustration as yet again the words I spoke to it were misconstrued. "Intuition… Intuition… Intuition." I said trying to get the desired response. All the phone would spell was, *into Wishon… into Wishon… into Wishon.*

This went on for weeks.

I was fed up until I slowly realized I wasn't walking my talk. If this were happening to a client, I'd have them check if this was a message from their intuitive self. Was I pronouncing intuition a bit differently? Or, is it possible the Soul can influence technology? I don't know.

The how wasn't important. I googled Wishon. Turns out it's a surname. I didn't know anyone with that name. I did, however, find the pun *wish on* curious. "What do I need to *Wish on*? What do I need to get *into* about wishing?"

I took a few breaths and settled myself into my hips and belly. An almost holographic projection of a long-forgotten memory drew me in.

My client Mary was beating herself up for "wishing her life away." I countered that she might instead be "wanting her life away."

Wishing is different from wanting.

Many have written that "wanting leads to more wanting" and keeps you in a state of want. *Want* doesn't create a space to receive your desire. *Want* is a squatter, taking up all the room inside, constantly on the lookout to grab what you are wanting.

Wishing occupies your inner space long enough for your desire to form. Then your wish leaves, trusting and welcoming what you really need to take up residence.

I suggested that when she found herself wanting, Mary could let it be a signal to take a bit of time wishing. "Notice what it is you *want* and replace that desire with the word *wish*. Feel the difference."

This is not magical thinking. The way we express something is powerful. Your body responds to the words you use. Those words can support or close you down to possibilities.

Mary didn't know how to release her wants. I said, "Learning to release can actually come from listening to the word wish. When you put a bit of breath behind the word wish, your desire lets go with the sound... *whish!*"

We played with the sound and Mary felt an inner space open just a bit. Still, she wasn't convinced about wishing or about the idea that carrying or holding a want removed space inside for it to happen. She said the conversation was sounding "a bit airy-fairy." We moved on to other topics.

A few months later, Mary told me about an uncharacteristic note her father had written her for her 40th birthday. I knew of the hardships she faced with an overly critical father who never applauded any of her decisions or offered support. But in the note, her father validated her in ways she never expected. His letter brought the start of a deep healing to their wounded relationship. I asked her if she'd ever wished her father would validate her like this before. "*Most of my life!*" she said.

I asked when she let go of wishing for his validation.

"Actually, not long.... Oh my God... So, are you saying that when I actually let that wish out into the world what I needed found me?"

"It's possible."

My phone was reminding me that wishing helped me walk around feeling lighter. After all, you usually place your wish *on* something. A star, an eyelash, dandelion seeds, a wishbone, coins, the tiny flame of birthday candles—the very act of wishing implies you can't hold on because you attached the wish to something outside of yourself, something that might actually know how to grant a wish.

It's a mistake to make wishes and hold onto them. This creates fear. Fear that you won't get what you want if you let go, and then you're right back to wanting. You get tired of *wants* infiltrating thoughts and complaining they're unfulfilled. If your brain keeps thinking about wants, reforming them *into* wishes helps.

This way of thinking isn't about never having wants. You can use *want* as a reminder and a focus for wish-making. A wish is not definite or absolute. It's risk-free and fanciful enough to say, "What the heck, let me try it."

I shift my focus from want to wish because I don't *want* to waste my time on the dissatisfaction that *want* carries. Dissatisfaction tightens my insides while gratitude expands. Expectation tightens. Wishing expands. Wishing opens a space for something to come in. Perhaps it's peace of mind or my intuition directing me toward the thing I wished for.

Looking *into* what I *wish on* taught me to wish well.

When unmet *wants* take hold for too long, exhaustion and hopelessness move in. They foster an unhealthy inner mindset where there is no room for your true needs to be met or to find the energy to take action.

Wishes, when used well, create a welcome healthy space for what's *really* needed, your wish or something better, to move in. Wishing requires playfulness, flexibility and whimsy. This is powerful, preventative medicine for your well of intuition to thrive.

By the way, my phone hasn't made the error *into Wishon* since.

<u>*Invitation*</u>

Think about something that you want or desire.
Let yourself focus and feel the weight of, "I want this."
Now change your focus to, "I wish this."
Notice any differences in your body's sensation.
Inhale and hold your wish in your chest.
Feel its pulse.
Now breathe out your wish and let it fly on the air.
Whish!
Pause and feel the internal space created.
Let your belly soften.
Let your breath bring possibilities to this space
you can't imagine.
Smile and feel well.

22
Skylight Expectations

When my husband Michael and I moved from our Victorian home, we missed the covered outdoor space of our wrap-around porch. The remedy was building a roof that connected our new house to the garage, 25 feet behind it. We added two skylights to the vaulted ceiling the roof created and hand-finished it with soft pine beadboard. The wood's red-golden hue lent coziness to the space. We relaxed and entertained beneath it for three seasons of the year.

We loved everything about that open-air porch except hummingbird season.

Michael, raised by a family active in the Audubon Society, is an avid bird watcher. We both love the magical antics of hummingbirds, bright little jewels flying forward, backwards, straight up, down, and sideways. Amazing. Except when they encounter skylights. Ours were positioned 18-plus feet from the ground.

My heart broke watching these tiny creatures, able to fly in any direction, only fly straight into the glass again and again. My husband and I witnessed moths, horse flies and on one occasion a wood bee fly up to a hummingbird on the brink of exhaustion, circle it, then fly down and out to freedom. It appeared these creatures were trying to guide the stuck hummers, yet we never saw one follow. Those bitty birds would rest on the miniscule tongue and groove ledge, then try to escape through the surface of the glass again.

When we would spot one, we dropped everything to help. Because of the height, Michael figured out a way to save some by gently spraying the hose so it would rain down on the hummingbirds. The water eventually became heavy enough to cause them to float down within reach. We'd cup them in our palms and take them to safety. Unfortunately, we buried about as many as we saved.

Skylight moments happen to everyone stuck in a narrow focus, seeing only one way something can be done. On those occasions, we become deaf to and perhaps afraid of those who offer assistance.

You have blind spots disguised as windows. You think you know. This state of mind is usually triggered by expectations. The brain flies around trying the same thing over and over because it *should* work. *Expectations* forfeit curiosity and cause you to forget to get out of your head and engage your intuition.

Hannah had skylight vision when it came to things she didn't want to do. "My mind knows I need to buy a new-to-me car, but I hate shopping for cars. I can't make myself do it. I feel paralyzed, even though my car is in the shop again. I have bad car karma."

We had been talking about how expectations, good or bad, can narrow our view of the possibilities around us. I asked Hannah if she needed a working car.

"Yes."

"Then if that's something you need, ask your intuition for help."

Out loud Hannah said, "I need a new-to-me car." Then she whispered to her intuition, "I opt for a new way. *Please show me a fulfilling way to navigate this situation.*"

I encouraged Hannah to notice what happened when she shifted her focus from getting rid of her stress and frustration to the possibility of a new way. She discovered that buying a car felt stressful because she believed it was stressful. With that realization, she suddenly knew she could make a choice to explore the new or expect the worst. Now curious, she got out of skylight vision and began to research cars online. Finding a model that met her mental checklist, she made a reservation to test drive it at a local car dealer.

When the salesperson pointed to the car she reserved, her eyes were drawn to the SUV next to it. "I instantly became aware that choosing a car wasn't just mental reasoning, it was also physical. My eyes and belly felt pulled to the car I didn't reserve, like a magnet."

She drove the car she'd reserved feeling uneasy and on edge, but this wasn't unusual when driving a vehicle that wasn't her own. She pulled back into the same space, next to the *other car*, an attractive Subaru. Her whole body felt drawn to drive it. She asked if she could test drive it, but it had already been sold.

"I didn't even think about it. I just pulled out my phone and Googled to find that year and model at another dealership. A new impulse! In the past I'd typically be disappointed that the car I tried didn't work and go home. But I think my focus on a *fulfilling way* made me more receptive, open and strangely relaxed. I was clear, not murky at all, that something inside had nudged me. I needed to know how that other car felt to drive."

It turned out Hannah had briefly researched the Subaru online weeks before. It was rated well and had features she liked, but she hadn't explored further. In person, seeing it next to the car she'd reserved, the contrast helped her physical-intuitive-wisdom engage. She drove straight to the other dealer.

"I'd never driven a Forester before, but it felt like I'd driven one forever. I wasn't on edge at all. I discovered features I'd really wanted but had overlooked online. I *love* this new car! It was interesting letting a new way unfold simply by following little impulses as they appeared. I couldn't be happier."

Hannah's skylight was, "Buying a car is going to be a nightmare."

By realizing there might be another way, she challenged that expectation. By paying attention, even though she didn't expect a different way to arise, she became curious about it. She held such delight in her voice when she told me how much fun it had been to unexpectedly find her perfect white pearl-colored car. The best thing about releasing expectations are the surprises that follow.

Rachel was caught in two stubborn expectations. She could only see one job she was qualified to do—teaching, and she didn't like it. The second, even though we'd worked together off and on for several years, she confided that she didn't think anyone could help her. Her skylight of *no one can help me* blocked possibilities, perspective and intuitive input.

Rachel had mothered four children, thoroughly enjoying the full-time privilege for 17 years. Her first-born was entering college soon, and she needed to go back to a paying job to help her husband with the costs.

"The only thing I'm qualified to get paid to do is be a teacher, but I don't want to go back to that."

With a defeated tone, she explained that teaching drained her.

"It's the three P's: Paperwork. Politics. Pass out after dinner every night. But there's no other way. I try to focus on the positive. I'll be on the same schedule as my kids. There's a teaching position open that's mine if I say yes. It's all pretty easy because I continued to recertify every five years. I wanted to be prepared just in case I went back but..." She slumped, covered her face with her hands, and started to cry.

I waited until she settled a bit. Then I said, "Take a few breaths. I'm going to make several affirmative statements about your decision that will contradict each other. You'll repeat each back to me. Pay close attention to how your body responds to each statement."

She rolled her eyes, then took a few determined breaths, and nodded she was ready.

"Close your eyes and breathe slowly down inside your body. Feel the weight in your bottom. Really feel yourself anchored to the couch. You're going to repeat whatever I say, no matter how much you disagree. Out loud, so all of your senses can respond. This will help your whole self listen, okay?"

Rachel nodded, took another deep breath and became visibly more centered. "Ready," she whispered.

"I am declining this teaching position." After she repeated this, I asked her to tell me how her body responded.

She frowned. "My stomach gets tight. My throat constricts and my head hurts. Weird. I thought I'd feel happy or at least relaxed by saying I wasn't taking the job."

After double-checking to see if her body had any other sensations to share, I said, "Perfect, now breathe down inside, allow your breath to clear out all of those inner responses. Focus on being heavy and centered. Signal when you're ready for the next statement."

Rotating her shoulders and blowing air out like a jogger getting ready to run, Rachel shook her head, reset herself and nodded.

"I am going to look for another job in a different profession," I prompted.

She shuddered when she voiced those words. "God no, that felt awful. Like I couldn't even stand the words on my tongue. There's a painful kind of numbing stiffness in my whole body." She stood up, rolled her neck, and said, "This is not fun. Can we stop now?"

"Let's do one more. If it doesn't work, we'll try something

else," I promised.

She closed her eyes, drew in a few more breaths and gave me a thumb's up.

"I am taking this teaching position." As she repeated the words, I watched her body relax and her face briefly soften before her eyes sprang open. "What the hell? That can't be right. I need to do that one again," she said.

I asked her what had happened and she ignored me while repeating, "I am taking this teaching position." Again, I saw her relax, then straighten quickly. "My body is a traitor! How is it that saying, 'I'm taking the job,' feels better? I can breathe freely, nothing is tight, and it almost feels … good."

She stopped, closed her eyes and turned her attention inside again for about a minute. "Yep, no resistance in my body, just in my brain."

Rachel still didn't like the thought of the teaching job, but she couldn't deny her body's positive response. Even after receiving such a clear physical message, her worrying mind took over and she fast-asked me a number of questions, ending with, "What would we have done if I had conflicting sensations?"

"A great question," I said. "It's usually an inaccurate or ambiguous statement that produces vague or conflicting physical answers. But in this situation the statements were easy to define. You were either declining, looking again or accepting the job. With conflicting sensation, we would've paused. I would have asked you questions designed to reveal more info to make different statements."

I sat with her question a bit longer, to feel how I would have proceeded if further questioning didn't glean new information. "The other reasons the body may not give a distinct reply is expectation or timing," I said. "We first took care of expectation with breath. You breathed down inside your body and landed in the sensation of your own weight. This got you out of your expectant head and into physical sensation. With timing, you or we would try again in the future and honor if it wasn't yet time to know. Usually, if the block is timing, more details about the situation arrive that clarify the statements needed for a definitive visceral reply. But Rachel, you're not in that situation."

To get her out of her worries and back in the moment, I asked, "Do you enjoy teaching the kids? Just the teaching part."

Her posture straightened. Her shoulders relaxed. Her face glowed into a smile as she said, "I love working with the kids and the actual lessons."

As Rachel walked to her car, she let me know she was irritated by our session. She still didn't know how to proceed. I called out, "It's normal for our heads to vacillate with decision-making. Keep checking into your body. You'll know."

She laughed and shot me the finger. I laughed and knew I deserved it. No one wants to hear, "You'll know," when they don't know.

The ancients believed in the power of language. Words vibrate in a way where the Soul can actually feel aligned or misaligned. When you pay attention, words vibrate the senses. Your ears can hear when you say something that is true or inaccurate, like a note off-key.

Words have resonant power when you expand your attention to include your body. Making a basic statement out loud (especially one where the mind disagrees) is an efficient way to engage an intuitive response, *if* you are anchored inside before you speak.

The first thing I had Rachel do was breathe *down* into her body and feel her weight, to land like an anchor. When words are spoken from a weighted place, your body's response is easily registered. You notice inner restriction or expansion as a reply to what you said.

Basically, expansion usually indicates a *yes or proceed* message from your intuition. Sometimes only parts of your body relax and the rest remains neutral. That's still a good *yes* indicator, especially if the other statements cause gripping in any way.

Restriction is an indication of *no, not now, or make a clearer statement.* An inner tightness is a little trickier to discern, but the main message is stop or approach from a different direction. For example, the statement I had Rachel say, *I'm looking for another job*, was a different direction than the obvious statements, *Don't take the job or take it.*

If you are aligned with your insides when you are statement-making, it's harder for your skylight expectations to get in the way of your corporeal/physical perceptions. Expectations keep you operating from old information and closing doors to clues your intuition sends. The mere act of acknowledging your expectations, then following your breath down inside, creates a crack for new information from your intuition to redirect you. The crack, in Rachel's case, was telling me that she thought she couldn't be helped.

I saw Rachel a month later.

"You won't believe it!" she announced, even before walking in the door. "I took the teaching job. At the last minute they switched me to a different classroom. The teacher who worked with learning-disabled teens quit. I had credentials so I was asked to cover the class. At end of my first day, the principal gave me the option to keep that position. I did and it's perfect. I can be creative, and I really feel like I'm making a difference in these kids' lives. I never understood why I took special-needs training. I hadn't used it before, but I'm so happy I did. I took the job!"

She was beaming as she took off her denim jacket and plopped on the soft lichen-colored couch. Rachel eyed me.

"You can say I told you so."

"What? I never said you had to go back to teaching."

She flashed a disbelieving face and said, "Yes but you made me do those statements. I figured you knew I'd love teaching again and were making me work for it."

"Nope, it's all you," I said. "You felt it. I just prompted you so you wouldn't doubt your decision."

She laughed. "But *I did doubt it* when I was driving to work that first day."

"I'm not surprised. It's easy to get stuck in our expectations. Our minds love to second-guess our knowing. How long did it take for your intuition to be proven accurate? Sometimes it takes quite a while to get the evidence. Did it take a few weeks?" I asked.

Rachel replied, "At lunch, on my first day, I realized I had more energy than when I'd arrived. I was *expecting* to be exhausted, and I was actually excited. There are challenges, but every day I look forward to being with those kids."

She leaned toward me, slowly shook her head and continued. "It's still just crazy that by saying a few words my body knew what was right for me, you know?"

I share these examples because intuition often isn't a direct fix (the way we *expect* it to be). I think that's why the mind grips so tightly to flying up against windows, to what we can see versus what's possible. Your mind wants *it, whatever it is,* to be fixed. Now.

Noticing expectations, sometimes disguised as beliefs, provides the possibility of other options, sometimes clear, sometimes unknown, sometimes both. These minor shifts in perspective awaken curiosity, and curiosity evokes possibilities, questions, solutions, new avenues of thought, actions, and room for surprises. Rachel took the simplest step by asking for help when she didn't believe anything could. That single act created a sliver of space for her intuition to slip in.

When you feel like you have no other way to go, imagine you are a focused little hummingbird in a three-by-four-foot skylight. Ask your intuition to help you see more than the impenetrable sky in front of you. The hummers under our roof had two exits, both more than 12 feet high and 25 feet wide. They, like Rachel, like all of us, needed to land closer to the ground to sense them.

Think of options as openings. Hannah gave her intuition a gap that freed her paralysis and guided her through the fear of a terrible car purchase. She consciously chose to opt for a different way; she chose curiosity, even though she didn't know where it would lead.

I like to remember that something as small as a moth, a horsefly or a bee can guide our path.

Inspiration shows up in unexpected moments. There are always more ways available than can be seen through a window.

Invitation

Think of the mind as being in the sky and ask it
to nestle down in the body.
Feel the weight of gravity.
Notice any limiting expectations.
Breathe them out.
Release.
Breathe again.
Allow the earth to absorb what's useless.
Ask if there's a limiting expectation inside not willing to let go.
Breathe to turn that expectation over.

Say,

"I am weighted in gravity. I am anchored in myself"

Taste the words to see if they resonate as truth.

Ask intuition,

"Help me sense other options.

Bring options that harmonize with my Soul,

And gently open fulfilling possibilities."

Make the statement,

"I am able to receive guidance."

Recognize curiosity entering all of the senses.

Let something intangibly new surround you.

Breathe it in.

Smile.

Know you'll know when it's time.

23
5-4-3-2-1 Be

I came across this simple technique on social media as a way to center.

Curious to find who developed it, I found similar instructions on many websites, never discovering the origin.

The American Bar Association says this process helps with focus.

Several hospitals offer this practice as an aid for anxiety.

A slew of other sites promote this exercise to assist with meditation and grounding.

I find the 5-4-3-2-1 a fast and easy way to embody and intuitively listen with all of my senses. This can be done with more than one person. It's especially fun to do with kids.

The idea is to fully engage with each sense during the countdown.

5: *Look at your environment.* Describe five things you see, out loud or silently.

4: *Listen to your environment.* Speak four things you hear, out loud or silently.

3: *Feel your environment.* Focus on three things you physically feel.

2: *Smell your environment.* Take a whiff and discern two different scents.

1: *Taste your environment.* Name one flavor in your mouth.

My examples come from a day I spent with a friend who lives on a large bay.

I *see* ripples of different shades of blue from the wind brushing across the water.

I *see* the thick, deep green, oval leaves of a bush.

I *see* sandy land around the water in a snaking pattern.

I *see* a small streak of brown, black and white stripe scurry by, a chipmunk.

I *see* the bone white, square patterned tile of the floor beneath me.

Next, I *hear* the rhythmic running of the refrigerator.

I *hear* a sea gull's demanding, repetitive call.

I *hear* the click of my short finger nails on the keys as I type.

I *hear* the wicker couch creak as my husband shifts positions in the next room.

Moving on, I *feel* the cool, metal edge of my laptop against my lower wrists.

I *feel* my elbows resting against the hard, painted wood of the rocking chair.

I feel my toes pushing from inside thick socks to move the rocker.

I take a slow, deep breath and *smell* the beeswax candle burning beside me.

I *smell* a slight mustiness from the rug, wet with sand, inside the porch door.

Finally, I *taste* the cheese dust flavor of the Goldfish crackers I snacked on earlier.

After completing 5-4-3-2-1, I like to rest in the sensations and allow myself to discover more. Here by the water,

I found myself taking several minutes to digest and settle into the beauty all around me. I heard more sounds, absorbed the changing colors and realized I needed to shift my position and get some tea. On the way to the kitchen, I noticed more smells and sounds, which accompanied my deep feeling of calm.

When I'm at home, I may spend only 30 seconds to settle in and inventory my surroundings. It's one of the many options I use to center before I begin my workday.

Colleen was exhausted. The day before, she'd driven 10 hours straight after a taxing week with her sister. "She has the television blasting all day long, it's never quiet… constant chaos. She complains about feeling stressed. I told her she might be able to relax if she shut off the stupid TV. Nope. I could hardly wait to get home."

"How are you feeling now," I asked

"Tired. Numb, and my brain won't stop," Colleen responded.

"I have a simple countdown that might help you feel better. Want to try?"

When I started Colleen through the numbers, she had very brief descriptions of what she saw: "Dog, tree, wood floor, fridge, plant." It can be tempting to rush through the process. I encouraged her to allow a bit more time for detail.

She began again, "The birds are making noise." By the time her three feelings came around, Colleen's descriptions reflected the good sensations she was beginning to feel. "A lovely heaviness from a soft, yummy blanket is covering my legs. I feel the thick, puffy hold of my socks keeping my feet toasty warm."

She continued more slowly, lingering in sensation until it was time for taste, "Yuck. I had coffee an hour ago."

We both laughed.

I suggested Colleen take a few breaths now that her senses were heightened. "Do you notice your environment any differently than you did before?" I asked.

Colleen's response was immediate. "Yes. There are a bunch of different bird songs in the branches outside my window," she said. "I hadn't noticed how many before. I can't believe that it took me so long to identify two fragrances. Now I can still smell a hint of the delicious curry I made last night."

She paused then said, "I'm thinking I need more variety of smell in my life. I have a selection of candles and essential oils that I forget about. I'm going to get them out today."

Even if you rush when describing what you see, this countdown will heighten your senses. Narrating what's around you with the tiniest bit of detail brings you all the way home.

Your pathways of intuitive communication stay clear.
Your wellbeing is increased.
Your ability to *be* present for life awakens.

Invitation

Breathe in.

Describe something you see while breathing out.

Breathe in.

Describe something you see while breathing out.

Breathe in.

Describe something you see while breathing out.

Breathe in.

Describe something you see while breathing out.

Breathe in.

Describe something you see while breathing out.

Breathe in.

Name what you hear, breathe out.

Breathe in.

Name what you hear, breathe out.

Breathe in.

Name what you hear, breathe out.

Breathe in.

Name what you hear, breathe out.

Breathe in.

Feel and name what your body is touching, breathe out.

Breathe in.

Feel and name what your body is touching, breathe out.

Breathe in.

Feel and name what your body is touching, breathe out.

Breathe in, find a smell on the air.

Breathe out.

Breathe in, find another smell.

Breathe out.

Breathe in.

Notice a flavor in your mouth.

Breathe out.

Take some slow sweet breaths in.

Allow a bit of time to steep in sensory awareness.

24
Change the Station

During the fall of 2020, in the midst of a polarized election made worse by our physical separation and isolation due to the Covid-19 global pandemic, I was getting a lot of anxious calls from normally non-anxious people.

While so many businesses were struggling, Maeve's high-end boutique was a profitable unicorn. "My life is good," she said. "Why am I consumed with anxiety? What's going on? I need to make some decisions. But my mind can't focus, and my intuition is hiding."

"Take a few breaths in. Expand your stomach and ribcage," I said. "Then breathe out, relaxing into your body's weight."

"I've tried breath and a bunch of other things that usually center me. Nothing works," Maeve said. "I can't stop wondering about where this anxious feeling is coming from."

Origins of emotions can be tricky. Sometimes emotions are our own. Sometimes emotions belong to someone else. Sometimes emotions slip in from our surrounding culture.

Maeve had experienced the disorienting feeling of someone else's emotions before. The first time it happened, she walked into her friend's home and suddenly felt depressed. She rarely felt this way, was confused and used a smile as a cover. While they caught up on each other's lives, her friend admitted she'd been feeling very blue and instantly Mauve's gloom lifted. Initially she couldn't believe the emotion wasn't hers, but it wasn't.

Now she was feeling anxiety. She didn't understand how that was possible. Maeve hadn't been in the same room with anyone for almost a week.

We didn't need to know where Maeve's anxiety came from in order to release it from blocking her intuition. But she was jailed mentally by an all-or-nothing pressure to find the source. I promised Maeve that the cause of her anxiety would be revealed if we asked her intuitive guidance to shift her *just a little bit* into body awareness. It worked.

"Okay, ask your body where the anxiety stems from," I said.

"My stomach is tight, but it feels like there's an amorphous buzz surrounding me," Maeve answered.

"Now ask your stomach what started this anxiety," I said.

"I have to vote today. I realized I didn't want to and that's when the anxiety started."

I asked Maeve to change her wording from *have to* vote to I *choose to* vote and see if it made a difference.

"Yes, my stomach feels more relaxed. But I do *have to* vote and I don't want to be in the lines when masks aren't required... Oh no, my stomach is tightening up again."

"It sounds like you want to vote. The conditions to vote seem unsafe and your anxiety might be magnified by others in your community who feel the same way. How does your body feel when I say that?" I asked.

"That rings true." Maeve exhaled with a sound of relief. "Knowing there is more anxiety than just mine releases most of the tension, like air from a balloon. But I still have a little trepidation."

"Let's ask your intuition for the best time to safely vote today," I said. "The best time could include very short lines, a fortuitous meeting or maybe you'll effortlessly get all of your errands done along the way. Numerous possibilities."

Maeve took a deep breath. "Maybe I'll say, 'Help me be more fluid and guide me where I need to be.'" She took a moment to see how that landed inside. "That's good ... calm and spacious in my belly. But what am I going to do when anxiety strikes again? I don't know how to get out of it in a different situation, especially if the anxiety's not mine."

Part of what's scary about strong debilitating emotions is they displace us. You can't feel where you are, let alone connect with your intuition, because you are occupied in a struggle to escape your unease about the future. Emotions aren't bad. Often, they have hidden messages and need to be navigated.

As uncomfortable as it is, if you let yourself observe and sit with the emotional discomfort, you start to steer your way out. It doesn't matter whether you know if the emotions are yours or someone else's.

The first thing to do is recognize where you are by saying, "I know where I am. I'm in anxiety (or some other uncomfortable emotional state)." Voicing that you know where you are starts to form a map with exits.

Maeve sank into the moment and identified that "I'm in an anxious place." That recognition helped her remember that when she makes restrictive statements like *have to*, she feels trapped. Anxiety then has the opportunity to get a foothold. This is pretty common.

I asked Maeve to go inside to observe where the fear she had about future anxiety traps was located. "Describe the physical sensation while noticing you are in your room, on the phone with me," I said.

"There's a discordant feeling, a buzzy vibration all over...

I don't like it. My stomach gets really clenched again," Maeve said.

I shared a vision that came to me of an old car radio tuning itself into a station. "The anxiety station," became a crackling voice in the vision. If you haven't seen an old 1950's car radio before, there's a round knob to the left of a line of numbers. It rotates to move a dial (usually a vertical red line) through the numbers, left and right. Buzzy static is heard until a clear frequency on a desired station is found. Maeve seemed to be caught in the static between stations.

"A vibration is just a frequency, so why don't you say out loud or inwardly observe, 'I know I'm in anxiety.' Then ask your intuition to help you tune into a better station. Extend your senses to both sides of your body. Notice if you find a different vibration. Or picture yourself rolling an inner dial to your right or left side."

Maeve was silent for about 30 seconds, then said, "I felt myself standing in the anxiety vibration, kind of bumpy and rough. To my right, I saw/felt a smooth vibration. I just asked to internally shift to the right. Everything changed. I felt peace slide into me. I feel more solid," she said.

We practiced a few times by thinking of things that made her anxious. We discovered that saying, "I know," was important. When she knew where she was by saying, "I know I'm in anxiety," even if it felt bad, it gave her a stable presence to shift into. Without that knowing, it was more difficult to change stations. Eventually, all she had to do was picture turning a radio dial to change her internal state.

Unsettling emotions can spin you up into the false belief that you don't know anything. Often, *I don't know* triggers fear and traps into the repetitive thinking of "I don't know how to get out of this state."

Instead, if you take a moment to identify your emotions

and where you are physically, the present returns. "I know I'm in anxiety. I know I'm in fear. I know I don't know. I know I'm in some emotion I can't name. I know I'm sitting on the couch. I know my mother knit the blue blanket covering me ..."

When you're in the moment, you always know where you are *now*. Remember, the word *know* has *now* in it. Any unpleasant emotion can become a signal that there's a need to anchor to the *now* so your intuitive knowing can operate.

That day, Maeve kept tuning into and out of the same smooth, comforting station. We spoke about how there are endless stations available, and the importance to remain curious about which station she needed in the moment. If she *expected* the smooth comforting channel all the time, it could lead her right back to the anxiety station if she couldn't tune in that day. The feeling of expectation often has the same restrictive effect as *have to* and *got to*.

Remember, Maeve began our appointment by saying, "I don't know why I'm feeling extremely anxious. It doesn't feel like mine, but how can it be someone else's if I haven't seen anybody?"

It is possible to take on other people's emotions. That's the trait of an "empath," someone who experiences emotions belonging to other people as their own. An empath may or may not know if the emotion is theirs, when or where the emotion was picked up, or if it's a specific feeling in the cultural air. This is different from being empathic, which is more universal. Most of us have the ability to understand what someone else is feeling without simultaneously feeling it ourselves.

Other's emotions can definitely amplify your own. You experience this at concerts, parades and celebrations where good feelings are magnified, uplifting and unifying everyone.

Unfortunately, you also see its negative impact in "the mob" mentality where normally good people feel moved to join in damaging behavior.

As children, many are sensitive to the emotions around us. Often, by the time we're adults, we develop filters to ignore other's inner emotional noise and many of our own emotional states.

Anxiety and other strong emotions can permeate the environment. It is possible to be influenced by our culture's emotional signals. Do you need to figure out if anxiety or other strong emotions are your own, someone else's or a general cultural feel? No, not if the intent is to access your intuition. When any emotion keeps you blocked, it's time to move sideways and *change the station*.

Penelope had consciously worked for 30 years to control, as she puts it, her "Mediterranean temper." She normally feels that she has a very calm and direct approach to most challenges. Except for a recent trip to the bank.

"What is going on? I haven't felt anger like this in … I don't know when. I blasted someone at the bank yesterday. Too late, I realized it was a complete overreaction and I apologized."

Penelope said she was embarrassed and simultaneously proud that she was aware enough to not get completely lost in the anger and to shift immediately into an apology. "But today, I have this anxiety. Honestly, it feels alien. Like it's not mine."

"It may or may not be your anxiety. You've picked up others' emotions before," I reminded her. "It doesn't matter. Our intent is to be in a better place *now*."

"Yes. I just want to make this anxiety go away," Penelope said. "Oh crap. I just got more anxious." The language of wanting to *make it go away* caused her reaction.

"Think about healing or transforming the anxiety. See if that helps," I suggested.

"It's a little bit better," Penelope confirmed.

We talked about the importance of saying *I know I'm in a place of anxiety*. Saying *I know where I am* automatically released part of her resistance. The rest was released by not judging herself as wrong to have anxiety. Both realizations kept Penelope from fighting her feelings with denial and self-criticism.

Saying *I know I'm in a space of anxiety* or any difficult emotion gives the real us, not the anxiety, an opening to receive intuitive input and shift our direction. Understanding that the consuming emotion is separate from who we are stops us from fighting it.

"I get it," Penelope said. "So, yesterday at the bank, when I was thinking, 'I'm so angry' like that's who I was, hot anger. I was behaving badly until I stopped and thought, 'This is not my normal self.'"

"Yes, 'this is not my normal self' gave you the space to separate from the anger and see the need for an apology. You weren't the anger," I said. "When we recognize we are lost in emotion, our bigger self has a place to land."

Penelope came up with her own analogy. "It's just like if we're actually lost. We need to see what street we're on to get directions to where we want to be. So, *I know I'm on* Anxiety Street. What do I do now?"

I asked Penelope to describe what her anxiety physically felt like. "Queasy. Alien," she said. "Like a strong hand is squeezing something in the middle of my chest and my heart is fluttering."

"Can you feel a different possibility of sensation next to you?" I asked.

"I have to keep my physical awareness of anxiety to do this, even though I don't like the feeling, right?" she responded.

Penelope had mentally *looked* to see if there was an alternative emotional state or sensation beside her, then realized she disengaged from her senses. She sighed. "Okay, I'm still on Anxiety Street and I don't know how to feel what's next to me."

I told Penelope about the car radio and prompted her to ask for Divine help to turn the knob and change her station. "I didn't even have to ask. I saw a car radio in my mind's eye and felt the knob turn," she said.

"What happened then?"

Penelope spoke carefully as she stayed in the feeling while communicating her experience. "This is incredible … I feel totally different, like I'm me again. Not staticky. I didn't realize I felt static before. I feel clear inside now."

The truth is you don't need to know the origin of your challenging emotions to change the station so your intuition can guide you. When you acknowledge your (or another's) emotion as the station or the street you are on now, you create space between being the emotion and being in a place of emotion. That mental acknowledgment allows room for a physical sensation to refocus the emotional one.

Maeve's stomach clenched. Penelope's chest squeezed. Though uncomfortable, the compression helped them actually feel what was happening in the moment.

Both were able to land in physical sensation.

Both able to know their *now*.

Both changed their station to intuitive direction.

Invitation

Notice what's stationary inside right now.

Is there an emotion present that's undesirable?

Why it's there doesn't have to make sense.

Perhaps low-level anxiety, anger or fear?

Perhaps the feeling is pleasant, like joy, peace or love.
Acknowledge whatever feeling is there as
the station or street you are on now.
Feel if it has a texture, color, smell or vibration.
Now sense the place on the left side of you.
Breathe in what's to the left.
Now sense the space on the right side.
Breathe inward from the right.
Which side has a gentle pull?
Does one have a slightly different sensation,
vibrancy, smell or sound?
Touch into the now.
Ask to intuitively change the station.
Or simply shift your awareness to the left or right a bit.
Try both sides.
Experience all sensation.
Spin the internal dial in the direction you want to land.

25
Shish Kebab Prayers

Elspeth was afraid because she had zero clarity about her life's direction. She *knew* she needed a change but had no idea what needed changing. I asked if she'd ever had her life change for the better when she didn't expect it? She told me about a pivotal incident in her 20s.

Elspeth was visiting her parents for a rare family gathering. She was excited to see Aunt Linda, her father's sister, whose enjoyment of cooking and gardening matched her own.

Their time together was precious. Linda lived a couple of states away and visits were scarce. In the morning, they meandered through the garden together gathering herbs for side dishes and cherry tomatoes for shish kebabs. They spent most of the day lingering in conversation, preparing food and having a wonderful time.

"We'd almost finished with a mound of kebabs, more than thirty, when my father walked in and said we were putting the ingredients on the stick the wrong way," she said. "Instantly my throat closed with a lump. I couldn't move."

Elspeth's childhood was spent trying to please her controlling, unpleasable father. This was just another instance where no matter what she did, he wasn't happy. Still unable to physically move, her mind raced trying to figure out the *right way* to assemble shish kebab fixings. Then, something she couldn't have imagined happened. Her aunt continued to pin kebabs and calmly responded, "Ed, this is the way we're putting the shish kebabs together. You are more than welcome to redo them anyway you want."

Elspeth stood there holding her breath. She had yet to exhale when her father turned and walked out of the room. He didn't fuss or yell to get his way. He didn't say another word. She released the air in her lungs and all of the pressure in her body left.

"I was shocked," Elsbeth told me. "I was still trying to do things his way. I hadn't lived with him in years. I realized I was doing things his way at my home, too!

"That instant intuitive realization reorganized me forever. I had an absolute knowing that I would never live for my father again. I remember smiling as I watched my aunt serenely spear ingredients, like nothing had happened." She paused, "And you know what? I never let him control me again."

Everyone wants intuition to be an epiphany. A moment appears, your life is reordered, you see the situation clearly and are empowered to act. Elspeth's blindness about her father's impact was profound. When she felt her own reaction, compared to her aunt's calm action, the contrast allowed her to finally see another response and unleashed the light of intuition to shine into all levels of her being.

Transformation was unavoidable. Elspeth made different choices from that moment forward. The first was to mimic Aunt Linda's calm demeanor when she established boundaries with her father.

The space you occupy can be an entryway or a closed door to your intuition.

Aunt Linda was anchored in the lovely kitchen atmosphere she and Elspeth had created. When Ed crashed in, he carried a critical, controlling air that swept Elspeth into a conditioned response of fear—body frozen, mind scrambling for the *right* way to please him to avoid rejection and potential abuse.

Aunt Linda was unfazed by her brother's mood. She didn't judge, fix or control Ed. She simply said he could redo the kebabs if he wanted. She remained centered and took action from the enjoyable kitchen ambience. In doing so, she *held a space* for Elspeth, her father and herself.

Ed lost his ground and left. Elspeth easily reentered the space her aunt effortlessly held. Aunt Linda found the place within her to physically, emotionally and mentally relax. The byproduct was an open, calm center for her intuition to reside and transmit a powerful invitation for everyone's intuition to be present.

Aunt Linda occupied the kitchen, her Soul created a portal for transformation. This is highest level of *holding space*. When we are comfortable in our own presence, without judging others, we wordlessly honor someone's choice while presenting them with a different option.

Traditionally, *holding space* for another is the willingness to be with someone without judging their actions, without fixing or trying to control the person's chosen path. It is an open-hearted offer that says, "I'm here to support whatever you choose."

Hospice is the gold standard in teaching others how to *hold a space* for someone who is dying, by supporting them in the way they choose to process death. *Holding space* is a beneficial tool with any transformation.

The term *hold space* implies an outward action. It's not. *Holding space* for yourself is having an inward sense of relaxing down to inhabit this world with your Soul present.

Holding space for someone else is not much different. It is embracing your Soul's presence while consciously including the other person or situation. *Holding space* is to be present in possibility, which unlocks unknown potential.

The space you reside in travels with you and can change depending on how your mental, emotional, physical, and spiritual states are layered in the moment. Your space can influence others.

Our culture has sayings that refer to the space people perpetually carry such as, "He always brightens a room," or "She puts a wet blanket on everything." What you carry can bring people up or down. Unlike Elspeth, Aunt Linda didn't allow her brother's controlling energy to change the peaceful space she was in. She simply maintained a sense of peace for everyone, including herself.

Instant transformation is possible, though not a realistic expectation, when you connect to your intuitive intelligence. Like the shish kebab, many things aligned for Elspeth to be saturated in the knowing that she would never let her father control her again. The main ingredient for her new alignment was that her aunt *held space* for her, even if unconsciously.

Aunt Linda took Soul action from the loving environment she stood in. Her response to her brother's accusation of threading kebabs incorrectly gave Elspeth the other ingredients necessary for her emotions, body and mind to align with an instantaneous foundational change.

The words, *you're welcome to do it anyway you want, Ed*, came directly from Linda's intuition and experience. Elspeth, the spell of fear released, was free to breathe and find herself again.

Witnessing her father leave without a fuss showed her mind what was possible. Elspeth had never seen him back down, and the revelation was backed up with a clear example of how to begin changing the relationship. Most importantly, it was the first time she realized that her father's influence still permeated most of her life, showing her there was work to do.

After Elspeth described her momentous change, I asked her if anything in that story helped to bring attention to what might be blocking her now.

"We don't always know our life's direction. That's normal," I said. "You also told me you knew you needed to make changes, but weren't sure what. Are there any clues from your past that can help you today?"

"Well, that story reminded me of another unhealthy influence from my father," Elspeth said. "To not allow myself to be too happy."

Once, Elspeth was on her way to compete in a sewing contest. She was wearing her entry, a suit she'd made herself. "As I was walking out the door, my father said I looked like a cow. My confidence flailed. I won the contest but couldn't feel any joy and doubted the win."

Elspeth paused. "I've worked on self-confidence, but I'd forgotten how Dad had continually sucked the joy out of me with insults. He trained me to tamp down my own happiness. He's been gone for years and I still do it."

"Can you give me an example of when you do it now?" I asked.

"With people who are unhappy in their life. I have a lot of those around me. It feels like if I show my happiness … I'd be hurting them. When I say that out loud, I realize it's not true, is it?"

"Well, your aunt didn't hide her joy of food prep when your father, who was clearly unhappy, tried to upset everything, including you. She *held space* by anchoring into that enjoyment for herself, without judging anyone's emotional state, and changed everything."

Elspeth agreed. "As a social worker I've been trained to *hold space* for people in many difficult, joyless situations," she said. "I never thought about how my joy for something could be included. In those awful circumstances, I do enjoy being able to help by making things better. I could let myself feel that joy inside."

"Yes, acknowledging that you also carry joy with your ability to help in terrible circumstances is a good step to take," I told her. "Can you also see opportunities to visibly share your joy after gardening or doing other things you love? I get the sense that's the joy you're not showing at home or with friends who are going through hard times."

Again, Elspeth agreed. "Sharing my happiness, whatever my life's direction turns out to be, is a change I want to embrace. To focus on what brings me pleasure and allow that feeling to come out is a BIG change. I'll definitely *hold space* for that possibility."

Repeatedly orienting to your inner spaciousness (holding space) broadens and strengthens your intuitive connection. It's the fitness center for Soul access. From this perspective, it is easier to acknowledge what else you carry on a physical, emotional and mental level. Then you know how to carry yourself differently.

You may need outside help (medical, therapeutic, nutritional) with your pain, attitudes and emotions. And/or you may need to ask for assistance from the Divine. Either way, change happens when you allow yourself to be aware of what's challenging you. Elspeth hadn't registered that she was still repressing her own happiness. Just naming her feeling that she'd repressed her joy instantly gave her ideas on how to proceed in her life's direction.

I said to Elspeth, "You see that *holding space* is an access point to intuition. I believe another way to choose to *hold space* and simultaneously let go into new possibilities would be to pray. Want to come up with a prayer?"

Elspeth laughed and said, "It could be a shish kebab prayer."

Now it's one of her favorite tools of change. The ingredients vary every day, but the structure stays the same.

First, invite the Divine to align with every part of you.

Second, ask for help. This can be one or many prayers strung together.

Third, sit and breathe. You asked for help, now allow a bit of time to receive it.

Fourth, feel gratitude or just say thanks, and move on with the day.

Here's Elsbeth's prayer from that day.

"I ask the Divine to please gather and pierce all of the internal and external ingredients needed to align me to my best self, my Soul, with ease. And please help me know that I'm in perfect timing now for the change I need...Thank you."

I smiled, knowing her prayer was cookin'.

Invitation

Feel the space held now.
Notice if it is fresh or stale.
Ask that the space be cleared.
Notice any differences.
Let analyzing rest.
Release control and the need to feel a particular way.
Let the senses fill with the sensations of now.
Place a hand on the chest to welcome the heart open.
Occupy the chest and relax.

Breathe through the heart space.
Soak in what is.
Immerse in this compassionate open space.
Feel the space you hold, holding you.

26

Know Your "No's"

S ome of my introverted clients had a very difficult time reentering their social lives in 2021 after the pandemic.

Erin was ashamed to admit she enjoyed the extended alone time. She felt guilty finding pleasure in an event that was devastating to so many. I'd talked to others who'd felt similarly. I assured her she wasn't alone and that perhaps it was healthy to embrace any goodness that's found in awful situations.

Erin was quiet a moment, then asked, "Are those clients also feeling anxiety about being with people now?"

"What people?"

"Strangers. The huge thing I realized from the pandemic is that I don't want to waste time being with people I don't enjoy. I won't. Life is too precious," Erin said. "But I'm afraid I've gone too far. I don't like admitting some of the thoughts that go through my head. And ... I missed an opportunity."

Erin then described what happened the night before. She'd been at the counter of her favorite place for a quiet dinner, happy to have a seat where she could watch the chefs do their magic. Suddenly, she felt someone sit down beside her. She turned to look just as the woman said, "Oh, good. You're alone. Now I have someone to chat with."

The restaurant had many tables open, and the counter was empty. Erin cringed and thought, *Oh. No. No. No. You've got to be kidding me. Go away.*

"I was seething mad inside and knew I was being unreasonable," Erin said. She managed to get through the meal without much interaction. As the chatty woman was leaving, she introduced herself as Claire. That's when recognition dawned. They'd seen each other almost daily on the neighborhood walking trail during the worst of the pandemic. Erin and Claire hadn't crossed paths in a few months because of the summer heat. Neither recognized the other without a mask and grubby walking clothes.

"That's when I realized that the belief I'd be wasting time talking to new people might be a problem," Erin admitted.

I asked Erin if she was afraid she'd lost her ability to gracefully get out of a conversation.

"No. Honestly, I forgot I had the skill to do that until this moment. I was only thinking, *I don't want this stranger next to me*," she said.

Erin wasn't nervous about getting the coronavirus; a vaccination was a requirement to eat at that restaurant. She was *afraid* of being drained from trying to come up with what she described as, "mind-numbing, superficial small talk."

Erin *expected* not to be interested in getting to know a stranger. She was wrong. Once she realized who the woman was, she was very interested in getting acquainted. She missed her chance because she was behind a threefold, internal barrier that blocked any opportunity for her intuition to intervene. She'd created a *hard No.*

Fear, assumptions and *expectations* are barriers that lock out intuitive knowing with a single word. No.

Decisions that cause our sentences to start with "I won't, I don't or I must," are signs you are operating behind doors of your own making. The ego is in charge and unwilling to give an inch to other options that your deeper knowing could uncover.

This common trifecta typically kicks in when you don't want something to happen or when you want something to happen in a very specific way. You've made up your mind, taken an oath and don't want to change. There are times when this strategy is efficient and necessary. The great thing is the words *won't, don't* and *must* are easy to detect. Recognizing what mindset you're in is the first step in turning closed doors into open paths.

The second step is to remember you have doors. Keep in mind, you create them when you fear, assume and/or expect. Remember, you have the keys. When you're locked in these judgments, all you need is the key of curiosity.

Notice the word *no* and how you can close doors when you use it. Open even one door and you give some air to the situation. Erin was so focused on wanting the woman to "go away" she forgot she knew how to gracefully extract herself from an unwanted conversation. If she had acknowledged even a slight possibility that she might have enjoyed the person sitting next to her then her curiosity would have automatically surfaced. That would have given her the choice to intuit if this were an opportunity to socialize or not.

Please understand: Boundaries–or guidelines in life that you know work for you–are very important. There are many appropriate *hard no* situations, and you need to have the ability to say *no*. I'm inviting you to *know your no's* so you don't miss opportunities. You need to challenge automatic *no*-ing every once in a while, so your intuitive *knowing* stays involved. Your intuition is patient. It will penetrate inner doors. Opening to your curiosity makes your Soul voice easier to hear.

Joyce called me filled with regrets. She'd turned down a job before fully exploring it. "I know my stupid opinions, assumptions, projections, AND expectations got in the way," she said.

We'd worked on these things before. She was usually astute at navigating these ego obstacles. So I wasn't sure her self-assessment was accurate.

Joyce had owned her own business for more than 20 years. After the pandemic, her business was gone, and she found herself looking for a job.

She had strong ideas about what she wanted that job to be. Joyce admitted that not taking the time to be curious at first and explore what a new career could look like. She hated hunting for a job. Even though she'd hired many people in her business, the other side of the application process felt foreign to her. When she was offered a job that didn't fit her perfect scenario, she didn't check in with herself. She just said no. Now she was filled with regret that she didn't consult her "big intuitive self," just her "small opinionated self."

I asked her why she turned down the job.

Joyce said she wanted a company that she could grow with. "I dismissed the offer so I wouldn't have to look for another job in a few years. The company was a small, family business. I knew I'd never get a promotion. I just said no. It didn't occur to me that I could learn new skills and get valuable experience."

Her automatic *No* killed the curiosity Joyce was so good at engaging. Intuition couldn't get through because she said *No* to even the idea of searching for work again.

Valuable information cannot cross the *No* barrier. She regretted her shortsightedness in not being curious or exploring how the job felt, while acknowledging she might have come to the same conclusion that the job wasn't a fit.

"I want to learn how to elegantly navigate these situations in the future," Joyce said. "How do I process this mistake so I can learn from it without an inner boxing match? I'm tired of being so hard on myself."

I pointed out that she'd already started. Her curiosity was engaged. She'd come up with a list of questions to be sure to ask herself around future job offers. But Joyce was still afraid her ego wouldn't let her align deep within herself so she could feel her knowing.

"I mean, small things undo me. How can I stay aligned and weighted in my body with my livelihood when I still react badly to traffic jams and the toilet seat being left up?"

"Joyce, you're human," I told her. "We all react badly to small things at times. That's not a meter of intuitive success. If you can't find your 'BIG self,' which also happens to everyone, just find where you are saying 'no' and ask questions. Get curious about whether the situation requires a no or not."

"Ok. Wait. What do I ask?"

"Your *No* was around not wanting to have to search for another job in the near future. Ask your insides, 'Is there important information that I'm missing by saying no?' Then pause. Imagine your mind getting on an elevator that sinks down into your heart, your belly or your core. If a different perspective doesn't surface immediately, try going to sleep with the question. Sometimes, time is the space our intuition needs."

About a month later a great job landed in Joyce's lap. She admits it most likely isn't her forever job. But before accepting it she checked inside and felt a calm in her chest, "It's right for now."

When I shared Joyce's story with Erin, she responded, "I think I know what you're talking about. Last week I was trying to decide on the best dates to see some concerts when my body and mind went rigid with *no*."

Erin's part of a small group of fans that travel together to share expenses to see their favorite band. All twelve fans were on a Zoom call the evening the tour schedule was released. Everyone was frantic to buy tickets immediately, fearful that the best seats would be sold. Feeling pressured, Erin quickly decided what dates would work for her. When it got late with no consensus among the group, Erin suggested meeting the next morning.

"Talk about rigid! I was gripped in the tight, hurried urgency of 'I have to do this now.' Something fun became intolerable. Getting into bed I kept thinking, 'Show me the way … make this easy in the morning.'

"You know what? It worked. The whole process felt more open and peaceful. Some dates I had thought worked the night before now felt like the wrong timing. I bought a ticket for a concert I hadn't planned on attending just because it felt right and I discovered later a dear friend was going."

Erin gently challenged her *No's* and *have-to's* with a simple request while falling asleep, "Make this easy." She gave her intuition the keys to open any locked doors and explore. When she woke up, it occurred to her that she didn't need front row tickets. She'd sat in the front many times.

"I actually wanted someone else to have the opportunity. And when I let go of being worried about not getting what I wanted, I finally felt excited and everything fell into place."

Intuition is automatic when we take "No's" off autopilot.

Understandably Joyce didn't want a constant job search and Erin didn't want to get stuck in a meaningless conversation or make snap decisions. Trouble occurred when they both shut out every possibility but *No*.

Entertaining the idea that there's another perspective that you aren't privy to without your intuition is a useful assumption. The results might be exactly the same, but without checking your insides you can feel doubt, regret and any number of uncertainties.

It's smart to understand you only see a partial picture when your intuition isn't involved. Remember that when you challenge your *no's* with curiosity then intuition will chime in automatically.

You may be surprised with a yes or perhaps your *no* will be reinforced. Either way, confidence will permeate your decisions.

Invitation

Find an automatic No inside.

Notice where it is located and pause.

Just be with the No.

Ask the BIG self to give a breath of perspective if it is needed.

Let the mind step into an elevator.

Sink down to the heart and pause.

Take a breath.

Step back in and sink to the belly.

Open the door and pause.

Breathe so the belly rises and expands sideways.

Step back into the elevator and push the button for the deep core self.

Pause.

Know this place.

Relax and be still.

Feel the silent flow of knowing.

27

Dread Is a Messenger

Years ago, I studied with a brilliant woman who used to tell us to, "Drop dread."

Rev. Rosalyn Bruyere would insert this phrase in her teachings in comical ways, but she was quite serious.

Dread prevents you from trying new things. Dread inhibits you from learning. Dread drains your energy to the point of exhaustion. Dread stands in the way of understanding. Dread gives you a skewed view of any situation where it inserts itself.

Releasing dread is great advice. We'd all like to kill that feeling.

I would have loved to follow my teacher's advice. Rosalyn made it sound easy. She never revealed *how* to "drop dread." She was fluid, simply able to shift her thinking and generously thought we all were able to do the same. I was clueless. I had to discover how on my own.

I'm glad I learned that dread *could be* dropped early on in life. It caused me to get to know dread intimately, discovering its value. Now, I don't want to drop it. Instead, I pay attention.

Dropping dread is trying to kill an unkillable messenger delivering a very valuable message. Once the message is delivered, like any messenger, dread leaves on its own. When dread doesn't leave, it's because we've misunderstood the message. Dread hangs out with us until we understand. The problem is we keep misinterpreting the message by believing it's about the topic we are dreading.

Dread's only message is, "You've disconnected from your

intuition. You're not living in the present. Reconnect now."

Amelia came to me because she saw dread taking over her life and thought if she could connect to her intuition, it would go away. She was aware the dread came from being raised by a controlling mother who belittled her every move. As an 8-year-old, she was expected to get straight A's and take on an overwhelming amount of responsibility that included doing laundry, cooking dinner and caring for younger siblings.

She admits that the pressure to do everything well, so her mother couldn't criticize, made her an overachieving perfectionist.

"No matter how well I did something, I dreaded my mother's reaction," she told me. "If she couldn't find fault, she'd ask about something else on my to-do list. I never received praise."

Amelia is very accomplished. Not only does she own a successful business, she's on the board of several others and was the longtime president of a large state organization.

Amelia believed that dread drove her to work harder her entire life. She became a workaholic to outrun the feeling. However, over the past 10 years she'd increasingly found herself frozen by dread, mainly in business.

I asked her what freezing looked like. The enormous pain she carried became evident with her halting confession. "If I don't return a call immediately ... I'm really embarrassed to say this ... I start to dread calling so much that ... that ... I just don't call the client back ... Ever."

Amelia assured me she was calling clients back most of the time. But the frequency of her not calling was increasing, and that scared her. She was beginning to lose business. Worse, dread was robbing her confidence, undermining integrity and marring her reputation. She was aware that dread was starting to consume her life. It had become a snowball. Once rolling, it gathered more things to dread. She was starting to dread the dread.

You most likely experience low-level dread on one or two life issues. Dread is sneaky and often hides just under your awareness. Many times, you don't realize you are dreading. Sometimes you just feel tired.

I remember feeling exhausted and not knowing why. A friend called and asked how I was. "What am I doing today? I'm dreading calling the insurance company. You?" Dread was lurking undetected until the words flew out of my mouth.

The dread of talking to an insurance agent over coverage is not unusual. Long waits on the phone and needs not being met are expected outcomes.

It was still a surprise to me when I said, "I'm dreading" out loud. Dread jumped out of my mouth like it was waiting for me to find it. I marveled that I didn't know dread had hitched a ride on my insurance wagon, though at least three signs of dread were there. One, I had been unreasonably tired for days. Two, I was convinced the insurance call would not go well. Three, I kept forgetting to call.

Unacknowledged, dread is draining, causes you to think you know what's going to happen in the future, and can throw off your timing. Realizing dread's sticky little fingers are clinging to you for a reason is key to stopping energy leaks, false assumptions and avoidance behavior.

Remember, dread will not drop until you get some version of this message:

"You are not here," Dread tells us. "Your head is living in a future that's not real. Your link to present reality is blocked. Reconnect to your physical sensations now. Breathe, feel your inner knowing. It's okay to *know* that you don't know. You're now in a place where you can navigate life effectively. See ya later."

Once I remembered dread's real message wasn't about insurance, I felt better. I acknowledged that I didn't know if there'd be a long wait or an uncaring agent. Possible, sure, but I didn't know.

I asked the bigger invisible part of me for help to settle down into myself. Once embodied, I felt capable of handling the call no matter the outcome. It was a bonus that the insurance agent turned out to be helpful. My intuition helped me ask questions I hadn't thought of beforehand, which enabled the situation to end on a positive note.

After sharing this example with Amelia, she asked, "How did you connect to your intuition after you got the message from dread? I literally can't move."

"Amelia, you do move. You told me you start a different task, one that you're not dreading."

"True. But how do I move forward with the task I am dreading? I know I should be able to, but it's too scary."

I explained to Amelia that sometimes the best thing to do is something physical, like taking a walk, stretching or making a cup of tea. Do this while remembering that dread's real message is that you've disconnected from the moment where the bigger, wiser part of yourself is effective. Small deliberate movements allow you to experience the moment. As you walk to the teapot, feel your feet, heels to toes, touch the floor. Hear the water boil, smell the tea and let the cup warm your palms.

After you move on to a nonthreatening task, take a few soothing breaths and settle into sensation. This awakens the senses automatically and fastens you to your knowing space.

When the task, walk or break is over, continue to be aware. See if you still dread the phone call. If you do, ask yourself why. See if the answer is an iffy conclusion, an imagined scenario or a reaction stemming from past experience that made you afraid.

Invite your bigger self to discern what's true. If there's fear, frustration, anger or other uncomfortable emotions, acknowledge them. Then be with these feelings as you would sit with a child who needs support.

Understand that dread is not an emotion. Dread by definition is anticipating something happening in the future. It is a mental orientation that pulls you out of physical presence. Dread stops your senses from interpreting your current environment accurately. This is important for your mind to understand.

When you bring awareness to your current emotions and engage all of your senses, dread drops.

Remember, dread is reminding you, "Be here now." Where your body and intuition reside.

Amelia and I played with dread for two sessions. At our next appointment the enthusiasm was back in her voice. It was like listening to a high energy HGTV host.

"I got the message! I feel so much lighter. My confidence is back and weirdly, I have a bunch of new clients. I'm not afraid of dread, at least not right now. I may need reminding.

"Especially if I've been with my mother, I never saw it before, but she dreads everything! She even dreads going to the post office. Going anywhere. Doing anything, she starts her sentences with, 'I'm dreading…yada, yada.' I've never noticed it before. I think I inherited being dread-filled from her. No more. Message received."

Dread doesn't always show up holding hands with things you want to avoid.

Judy called me with several things to focus on. When she didn't mention her book, I asked how the writing was going. She seemed surprised by her own response, "I want to get back to writing my book. But … I think I'm also dreading it."

Retired, yet very active in her community and with her family, Judy had been working on her book for years. She usually relished her writing time, so I asked her why she was dreading it now.

"Honestly, I didn't even know I was dreading it until you asked. I think it's because I have so little time. I steep myself in the pages and then get ripped away with other commitments. It's so frustrating. Sometimes I can't get back to it for weeks. Then the flow is gone. I feel like I'm always starting over."

I shared with Judy my belief that dread brings the message that we've disconnected from the present, hampering our intuition. "Do you dread writing?" I asked, "Or being interrupted?"

"Yes. I dread interruptions. No matter what I do to ensure writing privacy, they always happen." She paused, "I think I'm dreading writing … because now when I do write, I can't get into the novel because I'm waiting to be disturbed."

Judy checked her intuition with just about every decision she made, so I asked her, "What happens when you check your intuition about the best times to write?"

"When I think about writing the book, my brain labels it as impossible and my intuition can't even weigh in. Right now, I don't actually feel dread. I just feel it's impossible. How do I deal with the dread if I'm not even aware of it?"

I pointed out to Judy that she was aware of dread now. She was also aware of the potential that dread could hang out around her book decisions. If she felt tired or avoided writing, dread might be present. She was still thinking of dread as a bad thing. I reminded her that dread is the opposite. It is a signal that she needed to consciously be in the moment and connect to the Divine inside, a great place to write from.

I asked her to check inside and see if she dreaded writing. "No. I don't know when I'm going to fit writing into my schedule, so I feel more frustrated."

Frustration, fear and anxiety can lead to dread. They are all signals to dive inside and ask for help.

Judy needed help with a couple aspects of writing. Her top priority was finding time. Next, she wanted to remember how she felt while writing. "I forget how much I love writing when I'm not doing it."

We came up with a plan for dread.

First, if she felt herself avoiding writing, she would take a moment, feel her breath move within the circumference of her ribcage and ask the Divine to help. She wrote down the following request as a reminder.

"Help me find time to write. Help me remember that I have time for what I love. Help me connect to my heart. Help me remember to ask for help. Help me receive the help I'm asking for," she read, then sighed. "I feel better just reading this to you."

Second, she took a few deep breaths to stay open to receiving the help she sought. She'd done this many times before with differing results. Sometimes she'd have the sensation of loving energy flowing down from the crown of her head into her whole body. Other times she'd simply feel her breath move.

This time her breath brought her into a place of secure knowing accompanied by a gentle calm. "I feel like I will know when it's time to write," she said. "Whether I get interrupted or not, if I'm connected, it won't matter. I feel like writing is possible."

Afterwards, I was grateful for the reminder of dread's message. We all have blind spots. I was in one.

A few days before Judy's appointment, our vet told us that the cancer might not be completely gone from our sweet black Labrador, Madison, and recommended a cancer specialist. We'd been bolstered by an earlier laboratory report that appeared promising, so this was an unwelcome shock. This was our third adopted Labrador, in 12 years, that had cancer.

We were scheduled to take Madison to the specialist the following week. I didn't know I was dreading it. I kept saying to my husband, "Everything will be fine," totally avoiding my feelings.

The day of the appointment, I was still in denial. I'd disconnected from myself on this issue. I felt a strong connection to Spirit while working, so it didn't occur to me that I was blocked around Madison's prognosis.

We listened to Dr. MacFadden, as the gentle-hearted oncologist, sat on the floor in soft blue scrubs lightly examining Madison. She carefully explained why we needed to do more tests. It was scary, detailed information that could result in several difficult scenarios. I instantly filled with dread. Or perhaps I finally woke up to its presence.

I remembered Judy's session. As I sat in the clinic's waiting room while Madison was under anesthesia for her testing, I was trying to remember how to reconnect with my knowing while immersed in dread and fear. I couldn't do another task that was physical enough to help me feel my body. I knew looking at my phone would disconnect me even more. My best choice was to spend time asking for help.

I closed my eyes and called on my connection to inner guidance. Slowly breathing, aware of the sensation of air moving through my nostrils, I asked to feel my knowing connection while in this fearful place of not being able to know.

After a few minutes, I felt a calm enter my insides. It was

easier to breathe. The smell of disinfectant, the sounds of clicking canine toenails on the tile floor and the taste of surprisingly good complimentary coffee let me know I was back.

I asked for help to remain present when I received the results of the tests, no matter what they were. I asked to be shown the way forward. I asked for help feeling and receiving the help we sought. It worked. Thankfully, the decisions that needed to be made were clear, and Madison lived twice as long as expected.

What about the dread that comes from something disastrous outside of our control? Such as the global pandemic?

That is the most valuable time to connect in the moment to your deep knowing. That place inside can help navigate personal choices and sift through information to find and feel what's right for you.

It's important to research the facts on crucial decisions, like getting a vaccination. Keeping the data in mind, intuition can help make decisions as to what type of vaccine to get (or not). Remember, intuition shares information for that day. The message might not be to not get vaccinated ever, just not that day. You need to recheck yourself on major decisions.

Intuitive knowing isn't always a concrete or forever answer. Don't look for certainty. Relaxing into curiosity is the best way to remain open to intuitive navigation. Just like the Waze App gives you a choice to redirect your trip route when the traffic in front of you changes, so does your intuition.

Intuition often shares information your mind doesn't agree with. That can be a good way to know it's working. Or, it indicates that you need to tune in at several different times to get clarity.

It's interesting that I find myself working on this chapter

on the anniversary of 9/11. That shattering event shifted much of the world into a culture of dread that remains more than 24 years later. That dread comes from the fear of unpredictable danger. Despite many measures that have enhanced our safety after the attacks many remain in dread of the unknown. This can lead to immobilizing assumptions that limit the full enjoyment of life.

When you act from an assumption instead of from the reality of your current situation, you miss dread's vital message, "Get in your body and act from an intuitive perspective." You don't want to operate from a fear-based conclusion. Life is more complex.

Remember, dread keeps you disconnected from the present, from sensation, from wisdom, and from perspective. It keeps you from navigating the situation from your Soul's view.

Dread is a friend.

Dread lets you know that the bad feelings you are having about a future situation may be wrong. Escalating negative feelings is the way dread gets your attention.

For Amelia, Judy and me, the flashing red light of dread left once we allowed the real message to be delivered: *Stop, you've left the best part of yourself behind. You need it to make the best decisions moving forward.*

Breathe.
Be here.
Dread will drop.

Invitation

Ask dread to help.

What situation is dread dwelling in?

Feel it.

Notice the conclusions drawn.

Know there is a better way.

Ask for help reconnecting to all of the senses.

Breathe.

Take time to experience each one.

Ask for help connecting to Soul wisdom.

Breathe.

Notice the subtle shifts inside.

Breathe.

Relax, a different perspective has begun.

28
Obligation Bind

Any decision you don't recognize as a choice can block your intuition.

A friend was complaining about her monthly neighborhood BUNCO game night, to which she once again *had* to bring her famous shrimp dip. She brought it one time last year, and everyone immediately asked that she make it every month. It's a bit of a pain to make, and it's not cheap, either.

"Plus, I just wanted to curl up and read my new book," she told me. "I didn't feel like BUNCO this month. As a matter of fact, the only reason I went was so I wouldn't hear how everyone missed my dip!"

Sighing, she asked, "Can my intuition help me get out of this obligation without hurting anyone? I'm really tired of being Shrimp Dip Girl every month."

Obligations. Everyone feels their pull, the ways that we are morally or socially expected to behave. We feel obligations toward our friends, our family, our partners and our jobs. To be considered a good partner/parent/employee/child, there are certain duties we think we are bound to perform, duties that just *are*, and don't allow us to choose. It makes sense.

The word obligation stems from the Latin *obligàre*, to tie or bind. And binding implies no choice. If you are bound, therefore you must. However, we have evolved beyond that, especially when you involve your intuition. You may ask, "How can fulfilling my obligations be anything but the right thing to do? Isn't it being a responsible adult?"

Social obligation is one way you fall into the trap of

having to instead of *choosing to*. We can all relate to everyday obligations like feeding the dog, making meals, cleaning, or bringing a snack to an event.

A moral obligation is the duty/compunction to do the *right* thing. What does 'the right thing' even mean? Everyone has a different opinion. At the end of the day, obligations are duties that are laid upon us that can be untruthfully internalized as *this is the only option*.

All of us have heard, "You have to do thus-and-such. You're obligated."

Sometimes that voice can be your own. Consider the idea that this is just a way to manipulate you into doing something that you might not want to do, something that you might not even feel good about doing, harming yourself in the process. Recognizing that *there is always a choice* can prevent the harm of self-betrayal and help to engage your intuitive wisdom.

I know. You're thinking, "No. There are certain situations where there's no choice."

Here's the thing about obligations—they are mental constructs that exist solely to make us behave in what our culture/family/work has defined as correct. Often this defined behavior is the best action to take, which is what tricks you into believing you don't have a choice.

The default response starts with, "I have to," a done deal that automatically shuts down intuitive input. Why? Because I *have to* requires you to be constantly on. This state of output not only prevents you from connecting to your interior wisdom, it leaves you deaf to other helpful options.

It blinds you to the most basic, most obvious choice—to do it or not to do it. Once you see those two choices, there are always more subtle ones that arise. Obligation robs you of seeing that there is *any* choice. This is the problem.

As I've said over and over, everyone has intuition.

Every. Single. Person. And the job of your inner voice, at least in part, is to assist you in making healthy, aligned choices. It's not a voice that says, "This is the right thing to do if you're going to be a good team player/HOA member/deacon, etc." If you are open to your intuition, the wisest choice in any given scenario is always an option. And the wisest way may, or may not, correlate to your obligations.

My friend was not obligated to make shrimp dip every month. She chose to make the dip because she didn't want to disappoint anyone, blinding her to many choices.

She can show up to the BUNCO game without the shrimp dip. She can send a message saying she can't come, make the dip and eat it herself while reading her book. She can bring some chips or something else to the BUNCO game instead, since the agreement is everyone brings a snack. She can stop by the BUNCO game just to say hi and drop off the shrimp dip, then go home and read. She can tell her BUNCO buddies how she feels or quit BUNCO altogether.

Granted, all choices carry consequences, some comfortable and some not. But the point is, *they are choices*. And once you are able to frame obligations as choices, you open the door for your intuition to help you make the wisest one, which may in fact be the same decision as the *I have to* obligation but isn't as draining.

For my friend to get a little *me* time, she needed to be willing to have a few disappointed BUNCO buddies. She said she didn't want to hurt anyone's feelings, yet she was hurting herself by stewing in resentment and pretending that she was happy to be Shrimp Dip Girl. The freeing sensation of having a choice helped her decide what was best for her.

When you choose, you are empowered. And when you feel empowered, resentment disappears and the door to intuition opens. It is much more empowering to say, "I'm making the shrimp dip tonight because it makes me happy to see my friends enjoying something I've created," rather than to say, "I'm making that stupid dip again because *I have to.*"

Sure, the shrimp dip scenario doesn't involve earth-shattering consequences, but the same idea applies to more significant choices.

My client Nancy felt obligated to call her father every Sunday. Any set time was difficult because of her varied schedule. But she said her father "held her hostage to a Sunday call."

If Nancy didn't call on Sunday, her father left a barrage of angry, disappointed voicemails, emails and texts. When she did call, her father always wanted more than just the half hour. It was a no-win situation.

Over the years Nancy started to dread talking to her father and resented making that phone call. We talked about how obligation is not about the other person. It is about the choices we make to use our energy efficiently in a difficult situation so we don't keep ending up drained.

I asked Nancy if she wanted a relationship with her father.

"Yes," she said.

"How does it feel when someone does something for you out of obligation instead of wanting to do it? Good?" I asked.

"No. It feels off ... weird, awful ... Oh."

"So, your father might be feeling something like that from you. By choosing to call because you want a relationship with your father might alter how he responds to you. Is there a possibility you can alert your father beforehand if you can't call Sunday?"

"Maaaaybe ... he'll probably get mad."

"It seems like he gets mad at whatever you do."

Nancy agreed and then talked about how she didn't feel

like her father's needs could ever be met. I suggested she at least meet her own needs. "Why don't you check your intuition and see what works best for you?"

Nancy chose to call her father the next Sunday. Before the call she took a moment to remember her desire to have a connection with him. She told me the conversation was different, not so strained.

Her father was mad that Nancy might want to call on different days, but knowing which day helped. Things continue to be a challenge with her father, but Nancy doesn't dread calling or feel resentful anymore.

"Remembering I do *want* a relationship with my crazy father makes a difference," she said. "I don't know how, but somehow, I'd forgotten that was the point of calling. He lives thousands of miles away and a weekly phone call feels like the best way to maintain a connection."

An obligation *seems* to omit the power to choose, which can feel like a choice dictated to you. Every time you give in to an obligation, every time you deny you have a choice in the matter, you are giving up a little bit of your power and stifling your intuition.

When you feel forced to do something, it is natural to feel resentment towards those to whom you feel obligated. On the other hand, when you make a conscious decision to act, there is little room for resentment. There's freedom and power in saying, "I choose to call my demanding, cantankerous father because I love him and want a relationship."

Let's up the ante a bit and apply this idea to work. This is where I get the most objections, but hear me out and then decide for yourself if it's a better way to look at things.

People who have jobs are not obligated to go to work. It's a choice. Just as you choose to take a day off, you choose to go to work. You might argue, "I signed a contract to provide a service. I'm obligated to show up."

I am not saying you won't suffer the consequences. I am saying you have a choice whether to honor or break the contract. It seems like semantics, but how you look at the world affects your ability to access your intuition. If you believe you don't have the freedom to decide, there is very little opportunity for your intuitive knowing to ever weigh in.

Getting an inexplicable feeling to stay home from work one day may prevent you from getting ill. That vague sense is your intuitive weigh-in recognizing the need for rest. Of course, the consequences of habitually not going to work are generally negative and can lead to a pretty severe change in lifestyle. But physically healthy, mentally stable individuals always have a choice. Recognizing that going to work is a choice reduces stress, opens possibilities and invites the intuitive heads-up to make a healthy decision.

This process can be clumsy. Here's how I initially turned obligations into choices.

My mind notices an obligatory thought and responds, *I just said I'm obligated. Crap. That means I have a choice. But what choice do I have? I have to go to work today. Wait, no. I can go to work or not go to work.* A long, deep sigh ensued, my version of a conscious breath back then. I wait for any directive feeling. I say out loud, "I choose to go to work." I feel my stomach relax and think, *No surprise. Hi ho, it's off to work I go.*

Yes, you might have a job that you don't enjoy, but you aren't *obligated* to go. Here are a few options intuition can help decipher once obligation is untangled.

Option one is to go to work to pay the bills.

Option two is to not go to that job ever again and immediately look for new work.

Option three is to choose to work until finding a different job that's more fulfilling.

Option four is to look at the current benefits that make the unenjoyable job a good choice.

Perhaps your job is close to home, has flexible hours or pays well. Even though it's not fun, it's the best choice for now. It is much more empowering to say, "I choose to go to work today because it provides the means to live the way I want," than to say, "I have to go to work." Try it. See what each statement feels like in your system. Do you feel the same or is there a difference?

I know this might not seem like you are involving your intuition. But you are. You are in the moment when you stop to decide whether to do something or not. You make a choice in the present. The present is where your intuition is turned on. Providing and sorting through a myriad of options is a function of intuition.

When you act out of obligation, you aren't present. You're on autopilot. Autopilot is great in situations like flipping the light switch, making coffee or tying your shoes. But when making decisions, autopilot can be bad news. Autopilot, like obligation, steals your ability to receive intuitive input on more perspectives, options and choices available.

Autopilot situations are usually preceded with *I always* statements. *I always* empty the dishwasher, organize the family gatherings, shovel the snow. etc. All of these things are fine to do unless you are feeling drained or frustrated by them. When you hear yourself say, *I always*, use these words as a signal to invite the right to choose.

Let's talk obligatory social transactions again and the feelings involved. Pretend you are Shrimp Dip Girl. You make the dip because you feel you *have to* and then go to the game. You might end up having a good time. But it is also likely that you end up just going through the motions (autopilot) while you wish you were home.

The other BUNCO players sense that you're not really into the game and may wonder why you even showed up. They could start to feel a bit resentful of you, sitting there all grumpy or pretending to be okay. When something is wrong, others often pick up on how you're feeling, even if they don't say anything. This leads to no one having fun. Think about the ramifications to everyone the next time you find yourself falling into an obligation bind.

Look, there are so many things you don't have a choice to change immediately. But you do have control over your thoughts. Your thoughts can act like a hermetic seal to intuitive input. If you think you have no choice with your obligations, this becomes your reality, leaving no room for options. Taking a breath and offering yourself a choice literally breaks that seal, allowing the wise air of your Soul to permeate your senses.

Whenever obligation—*I have to* or *I always*—appears, see it as a signal to invite choice. Be still. Take a few centering breaths. You can deliberately ask your intuition to aid you in making the wisest choice or not. Either way, the acknowledgment that choice exists opens your intuitive gate.

I'm not saying that intuition will bring neon-lit clarity, shout out an answer or even that intuition's involvement will be felt initially. However, this is a way to make space for your Soul to influence you both consciously and unconsciously.

Remember, we are talking about releasing blocks to intuition. This is tricky because the mind wants quantitative evidence that intuition is working. Don't be tricked into this inner obligation. At first, when you remove barriers, intuitive input arrives sneakily through your unconscious, and life changes are usually recognized in hindsight.

Look to the moment.

Turn autopilot off.

Tune into making a decision.

Acknowledge you made a choice, unbound from obligation. Notice how the freedom to choose feels.

Invitation

Do you feel obligated to read this invitation?
If you do, recognize your choices and feel how to proceed.
If you don't want to continue reading, don't.
Wait for another time or never.
Listen to instinctive impulses, especially in harmless decisions.
Honoring intuition makes it stronger.
Let an obligation surface.
Notice the physical response just thinking about that obligation.
Recognize the simple choice of to do or not do this obligation.
Let your mind list all of the "I have to because..."
Change the word 'have' to 'choose' and notice how your body feels.
Say "I choose to because..." and notice how that wording feels.
Give some time to wrap your brain around this possibility.
Take a deep breath, and smile at the choice made.

Part 4
Connecting With Guidance

29
We Are More

My first memory lives inside with such clarity that I can reexperience it. It is always the same. It has never varied.

I become aware that I am also something else. I am an infant, who while laying belly down, wraps fingers around the thin white rails on one side of the crib.

I look through two openings. The sensation is like gazing through a Zorro mask.

I am infinite space viewing these tiny hands. My awareness is huge. If someone saw me in this state, I'd resemble the entire night sky peering through baby eyes, gently beginning to sense new hands as my own. I have no language for hands or eyes. Just pure awareness.

I feel discovery, interest and realization. There is no thought or judgment, only a spacious sense of Love and a knowing that these hands are the start of what I now have to work with.

When I was almost 4, I remember wanting to be a gypsy for Halloween. I have no idea how I learned about gypsies. My friends were all either ghosts made with old sheets, hobos wearing too-large used clothes with shoe polish beards, witches with pointy nylon black hats or one of the few character costumes Kmart had for purchase.

My Grandma Halls fulfilled my gypsy wish. She put me in one of her bras stuffed with fabric. She found an old cotton dress of my Aunt Kathy's, vertically striped in multiple shades of purple, and belted it with a royal purple satin scarf.

She layered jade-colored beaded necklaces that reached my waist, and wrapped my head in red fabric. She tried to layer my arms with bangles but they slid right off. So, she attached one that pulled apart to my red turban so it would look like a giant earring. Not only did I get to wear her 1960s red lipstick, but she topped off the ensemble with a surprise—a black mask that concealed the top half of my face.

I. Loved. That. Mask.

The instant I put it on I remembered the feeling of looking through my own eyes in my crib. I wasn't able to name the realization at the time, but looking back, I remembered *me*. The real me. The bigger me.

I felt a part of the sky again and didn't want to take the mask off. Ever. I was allowed to play with it until the Halloween box was put away for next year. It is not an exaggeration to say I *pined* for that mask. It made me feel whole.

I didn't remember any of this until adulthood. I put on a black mask to go to a Halloween party and the memories came rushing back. All these years later, I vividly remember both the experience of feeling myself as space and feeling like myself when I looked at the world through that gypsy mask.

I understood from the beginning that there was more to me than what I could see—deep knowing that part of me could be felt here. But I also existed invisibly and vastly beyond here, too.

This unseen part of me sensed a connection to everything. I knew I couldn't be the only one who felt a bigger connection inside and outside of myself. So, when I was introduced to the concept of the Divine and learned we all had guidance that helped us—who also came from the Divine—I finally had words for what I'd always known.

Everyone has to figure out their relationship to the Divine for themselves. We need to reference our personal experiences and come to our own internal relations, which may or may not involve religion or other's opinions.

There are so many ways to perceive your connection to the Divine, and by extension to your Divine helpers. Our minds aren't capable of understanding this type of vast complexity. I know mine isn't. I figure that we have friends in this world, why wouldn't we have friends in Spirit? All I can share is the way I perceive this connection to Guidance—Soul friends who help me explore what I came to explore in this world.

These benevolent Spirit friends only suggest.

They nudge.

They help you perceive a different view of situations. You decide whether to follow the lead of Guidance or not. They cannot perceive everything with perfect clarity here and will never override your free will.

We choose to dance with each other.

Call specifically on your Divine partners, the ones interested in the highest good for you. They may remain invisible. But listen with all of your senses, and eventually you will know help is dancing with you.

Invitation

Think of your close friends and loved ones.
Breathe them in,
allow your focus to shift to heart feelings with that breath.
Let more friends arrive in your consciousness.
Breathe in and feel the love and respect you share.
Remember anyone you loved that has left this world.
Use your imagination to remember them.

Allow specific details to surface in your memory.
Perhaps you see the love in their eyes, their smile.
Ask to feel your memories of them.
Ask them to be with you now.
Notice any subtle shift in awareness.
Note any contrast between how each side of you feels,
In temperature, tension or feelings.
Welcome them, no matter what you sense.
Ask for your Divine friends that you didn't know
in this life to join.
Ask if they will help amplify the experience of their presence and
Help sense your known loved one's presence as well.
Take a few slow settling breaths
noticing any change in perception,
Physical sensations of smell, taste, knowing,
Or not.
Sometimes no sensation or thought is a sign of presence.
Give them permission to help wisely guide you.
Tell them you'd like help in knowing they are there.
Breathe in that possibility
Thank them for coming with love.

30
A Voice

T*he voice* came to me on a mountainside.

Late Spring in the afternoon. The smell of freshly mowed grass mingled with the overlapping blend of conversation, instruments and song from several small stages.

All that sound lifted and blurred around me as I sat alone overlooking the small North Carolina lake where the 1988 Black Mountain Music Festival pulsed, alive with energy.

I had hiked above the fray to mentally organize a to-do list for my drive back to Houston in three days. I was finally committing to Texas and to my guy. All of my belongings were joining me on this trip and it was turning out to be a tricky task to gather everything so quickly.

Abruptly, my mental planning was interrupted. Three words were broadcast inside my head.

"Move to Charlotte."

Unlike a thought, which originates from within my mind, this instruction came directly through my sense of hearing, as if someone had enunciated the words out loud from inside my right ear. I turned, scanning all around, but no one was near. The power of the message reverberated inside. My whole body recognized—this is exactly what I need to do.

Stunned by this new experience, I sat still for at least a minute before my mind intruded, "Who is speaking to me?"

I immediately thought I'd imagined *the voice*. I'd never imagined *a voice* before. I tried to imagine it again and couldn't.

Was it a Spirit? A hidden part of me? I didn't know.

I knew I wasn't crazy. I had definitely heard *a voice*. I just couldn't imagine how I could do what it said.

To move to North Carolina was nuts. I was 63 hours away from moving to Texas. I had a job and a boyfriend there. I knew nothing about Charlotte. The only people I knew from there were here at the festival—Jon, my friend who lovingly insisted I come "listen to great music" had paid for my ticket. And Debbie, a childhood friend of Jon's, who I liked but barely knew.

Thinking of my friends, I wound my way down the mountain, toward the crowd, aware of the gentle auditory blur turning into lively harmonized folk music. Zigzagging around every age and size dancing at the different stages, I navigated my way to the campground on the other side of the lake. Inhaling evening dinner preparations of every grilled variety, I saw our cluster of swimming pool blue and army green tents, scuffed coolers and worn lawn chairs. Jon yelled out from our group, "Did you figure out how to *wrangle* all your stuff together?"

I ignored the Texas cowboy jab, grabbed a beer, plopped down on top of the cooler and laughed while telling our group my you-won't-believe-this crazy *voice* story. I was met with, "Yes! You need to move to Charlotte!"

What? Wait. They should be giving me you're-not-right-in-the-head looks, not enthusiasm.

Then Debbie said, "You can sleep on my couch until you find a job and a place to live."

This was loony. Who offers to share their tiny studio apartment with an almost stranger who hears *voices*? (Later, I discovered my friends thought it was normal that I'd hear voices because I read tarot cards. Go figure?) Being met with incredible support helped me feel the genuineness of the message. The possibility of switching addresses at the last minute started to seem like a great idea.

After an evening of rousing music, seared burgers,

uncontrollable laughter, and drifty sleep, I drove four hours to my mom's house on the outskirts of Atlanta, Georgia. On the drive, logic strapped itself into my passenger seat, ready for a fight. As the miles went by, I couldn't stop the endless questions riding me. "Am I really NOT moving to Houston in two days? You've never wanted to move to Charlotte before, what are you thinking? Is there somewhere else I need to think about moving to?"

On and on my brain churned, yet I continued to return to that *voice*—it felt right. It spoke a truth that literally moved me. The minute I walked in the door, I told my mother about my change in plans.

Without a moment's hesitation, she said, "Charlotte seems like a beautiful place to live. If it feels right, do it. Maybe he'll move with you."

Still, I felt the kind man awaiting my return to Houston might not be so understanding about a *voice* being responsible for a short-notice switch in plans. Long before cell phones, he was the last to hear. I called him from my mom's wall phone. His only question, "Can I come too?"

I can't say whether I'd have been strong enough to listen to that knowing *voice* if I wasn't met with overwhelming support. At barely 23, I didn't think I had much to lose. I do know if I hadn't acted on that sense of genuine truth, I'd have impaired my ability to recognize intuition's illogical wisdom. I didn't recognize it then, but I was beginning to learn one of intuition's jobs.

Intuition moves us toward what we don't understand.

Most people don't hear *voices*. Believe me, I was very aware that people were institutionalized for listening to voices. Instinctively, I tested the message with input from others to notice how I felt about a Charlotte move. I'd been there twice for less than 24 hours, yet I felt excited and relaxed. Which was unusual.

My school years were spent in Pennsylvania, Virginia, West Virginia, and New Jersey. My father's job required multiple transfers. My extroverted mother was masterful at painting my imagination with the adventure of new friends and places to explore. As an extreme introvert I wanted to be excited, but moving filled me with fear and anxiety.

Looking back, I now see that those moves brought me out of my preferred solitude. I had thought the stress of moving was about not having a choice, but attending college in South Carolina had been my choice and it was as stressful as those family moves. And now the move to Texas felt stressful. I'd never felt relaxed about a move before, but I didn't feel afraid to move to Charlotte. My bones resonated yes, even though I had no idea where I'd live or how I was going to support myself.

Things fell into place for my Houston guy and me in Charlotte. I have never regretted listening to that *voice*. Many times over the years I've wished it would return and tell me what to do. But I only heard it once more.

One morning, six or seven years after the music festival, *the voice* said my name—*Jennifer!*—loudly and for no reason I can pinpoint. Not hearing *the voice* again for such a long time helped me learn to drop expectations about how my intuition *should* work.

Intuition rarely works the way you think it will.

There are infinite ways that intuition appears. You only need to recognize a few to get the message. I want to keep you from feeling like a failure if you aren't constantly able to hear or understand your intuition.

To quote the Sufi mystic Hazrat Inayat Khan, "My intuition never fails me, it is I who fail when I do not listen to it."

I think he means well by pointing out that intuition is always there ready to help us. However, he implies there's a problem, that we're broken or failing, when we can't seem to access it. When most of us weren't taught how to listen in the first place, his quote isn't helpful.

It's exceedingly rare to have a *voice* speak inside your head. A story like the one I had on the mountain can make you want a *voice* to tell you specifically what to do.

Your intuition does tell you what to do. Normally, it doesn't shout. It speaks in other ways like the feeling of rightness, inner alignment or relaxation I had after *the voice*. Intuition presents an option to consider. You always have a choice.

Yes, your intuition is always with you. Intuition is subtle. Guides, angels, master teachers in spirit are all a part of your intuition.

Let go of how you think your intuition should work and you'll start to recognize your *voice* has been there all along.

Invitation

Breathe in a slow, soothing breath.
Allow the idea that there are endless ways
our intuition speaks to us.
Breathe in with the intent of opening to those possibilities.
Breathe out expectations of how intuition should work.
Breathe in the invisible ways that intuition communicates now.
Breathe out the expectation that this should be already known.
Breathe in.
Notice that the air that we breathe is invisible and it is felt.
Oxygen sustains us without thinking about it.
Breathe out.

Feel the air release from your body.

Breathe in.

Know that like breath intuition is always there sustaining us.

Feel the sensation of your breath going out.

Allow your doubt to leave with the breath.

Breathe in deeply and feel your body expand.

Remember your inner voice resides in the invisible,

Intuition is felt just like a breath.

31
Help Me Receive Help

Often when we read other people's accounts about receiving Divine help, the stories seem like miracles.

Because those stories are so extraordinary, we allow ourselves to believe and maybe trust that Divine help is possible. Or the opposite happens and we think, "Miracles are for special people. Not me."

Your belief doesn't matter. Asking for help from something bigger than yourself is what's important, even if the request comes wrapped in disbelief and an "I-have-nothing-to-lose-by-asking" attitude. Asking unlocks the door for assistance.

Asking gives permission for help to arrive. The Divine will never override your will. Without permission, the door stays closed from your side.

The problem comes when we expect help to look a certain way. It should be amazing and obvious when it comes from Spirit, right?

Wrong.

We want supernatural help to show up in neon so our minds can't deny it. Unfortunately, it's more subtle. The signs are there, but we're usually looking in the other direction. If you expect help to arrive with blinking arrows pointing the way, you can end up feeling abandoned and believing help from Spirit doesn't exist.

Receiving Divine help can feel simply odd or run-of-the-mill. Often, it's not mind-blowing. Only in sharing the experience afterward can you see a Divine hand.

I've listened to friends and clients say they've never received Divine help. Then they'll tell me a story that's filled with impossible coincidences. When I point out the synchronistic details they've shared, they can't believe they hadn't seen the Divine influence. I understand. The same has happened to me.

You might find it hard to believe that the story I'm about to share didn't feel all that special at the time. The phone call felt like an amazing coincidence, but I couldn't see it as real help. It didn't seem magical like other peoples' stories. My expectations of what I thought the Divine *should* do blocked me from seeing the larger influence of help.

Hindsight has taught me that my imagination is too limited to conceive all of the ways help can show up. More than 20 years ago I created a prayer that covers all bases. It has opened me to fleetingly subtle, weirdly obvious and outrageous assistance. Here's how it goes:

Help me receive the help I'm asking for, especially since I don't know exactly what I need.

My mind has countless opinions about what I need to do, feel or say. Admitting upfront that I don't know exactly what I need allows me to release the expectation of how help *should* arrive. My prayer keeps me curious and alert to assistance I might otherwise be suspicious of or outright disregard.

Six months after I quit my museum job to do intuition consulting full-time, I was diagnosed with the autoimmune disease, Secondary-Progressive Multiple Sclerosis (MS). My fingers, without warning, would suddenly jerk open. A constant electrical energy roamed my legs and feet in a painful frenetic pattern. I was tired, scared and desperate.

I looked to the invisible Divine force for help.

My eyes pivoted to the ceiling as I firmly spoke. "You

wanted me to do this spiritual work and this is what I get? I only have a year left of health insurance. I'm barely paying my bills, and I'm exhausted! How am I supposed to work? Live? I have no backup. I. Need. Help. I need you to help me. I need you to help me receive the help you send. Now. Because I've got to say I'm not feelin' it!"

I figured the Divine knew I was angry and struggling. Why not be honest and let it all out? I said a version of my prayer for a few days seemingly without result.

One morning, as I tearfully finished my prayer/rant, the phone rang. I don't know why I picked up. I had an answering machine to screen calls, yet my hand lifted the receiver. The deep melodious voice of an African man—I'll call him Kwame—greeted me.

"Is this Jennifer? I'm calling because your name has fallen out of my file drawer for three days in a row. I made sure to put it back in the file securely last night and it was on the floor again this morning. Today I got the sense you need help. Do you need help? Are you unwell?"

The sincerity of his voice cracked through my immediate suspicion that he was trying to sell me something. Even though I'd been begging for help, I had a cautious distrust. I couldn't help but ask why my name was in his files.

Kwame was not offended. "Your contact information kept falling out of the file of people who purchased recorded talks from my teacher."

Remembering that I had purchased a cassette tape several years earlier helped me relax enough to finally answer his questions. "Yes, I do need help. I am unwell. I appreciate you calling, but I really don't know how you can help me."

He gently asked what was wrong and encouraged me to share my symptoms and fears. He listened deeply, shared his insights and taught me a Zulu healing practice his teacher had given him. He also asked me to send him a photo of my face because in a week he was headed to Africa to study with his teacher. "I will ask him about you, Jennifer. He is able to look at a photo of anyone in the world and gain helpful information for their healing. He sees and supports the Soul's path."

We were on the phone for about an hour when I remembered he was calling from California. Back then long distance was expensive. I offered to send him money to cover the bill, which I was hoping wasn't more than $20, my weekly food budget. Kwame said to not worry about the bill. He felt an internal pull to help me and wanted to make sure he did everything he could to honor that knowing. He reminded me to send my photo as soon as possible, and he promised to let me know what his teacher said.

I mailed the photo that day. I didn't like that I was skeptical, even after he generously gave me his time, help and kindness. I was vulnerable. A small part of me wondered if I was falling for a long-term con.

Yet after Kwame's call, I gradually felt less tired. Slowly I gained more clarity when navigating my healthcare. I had a nagging knowing I didn't have MS, and when doctors kept saying I did, I sought different medical routes. I found an environmental doctor in his early 80's who agreed that I didn't have MS, saying my whole system was severely out of balance. He even took my insurance.

Around that same time, I received a cassette tape in the mail. Kwame kept his promise to consult his teacher on my behalf, and a recording of their conversation arrived two months after our call. I listened to the voice of a prominent African shaman talking about my health and life from the small photo I'd sent. He spoke of things I'd never shared. He said my health would improve. He said he'd call on spiritual help for me.

My eyes welled with tears when I heard his voice. It carried a compassionate authority that shook my embedded beliefs that this kind of help wasn't possible for me.

I realize now a part of me changed forever in that moment. I felt so grateful to be on someone's radar even though I had no idea *how* I was being helped. Kwame, his teacher and the Divine Source that dropped my name on the floor, helped me in ways far beyond my understanding. I never heard from Kwame again.

It took 11 months until all of the symptoms were gone. This was a miracle of timing as well. My insurance stopped and my new coverage didn't pay for anything preexisting. The last charge I had on my old insurance was a follow-up MRI, which showed that even the lesions on my brain had disappeared. I didn't have MS.

There was more. I was successfully helping others connect to intuitive knowing. But when confronted with constant, painful and scary health issues, I succumbed to fear. If I hadn't received Kwame's phone call, I wouldn't have had the courage to listen to my nagging knowing that something other than MS was the problem. I wouldn't have looked for my wonderful, think-out-of-the-box doctor. Chances are I'd still be treating a disease I never had. I'm certain my ability to help others with their intuition would have stagnated.

My foundation was finally infused with the deep knowing that something bigger really did exist. Help from that source can nudge us towards action when we ask for help. All of these insights registered unconsciously at first and took time for me to see.

I've been fortunate to have help arrive in big, bizarre ways on several occasions. Most are included in this book. Once we witness an undeniably helpful coincidental experience, it reinforces the belief that an interactive benign force exists. Whether the stories of help are our own or from someone we trust, our trust in asking the invisible for help is bolstered.

When you are feeling good your trust expands, and you can easily shift into a receptive mode where help arrives without expectations. Paradoxically, if times are hard these stories can shift you into expectation of what help *should* look like and the painful feeling of "Why isn't help coming to me?"

A good thing to remember is that 95 percent of the time, spiritual help is so subtle we automatically discount it. We expect more, especially after reading stories like mine. When we aren't getting the help we want, or we know people in terrible circumstances who begged for help that never arrived, it's easy to dismiss the fact that help is always available. Or worse, we feel undeserving, that we aren't good enough to be helped.

My client Frances finds it difficult to let go of expectations around asking for help. "Aren't I supposed to expect help will come?" she asked. "I'm having real difficulty here, and I'm getting no help."

Frances has a point. Yes, expect help. But don't expect help to come the way *you* think it should. This distinction can be hard to recognize. In our most challenging times, help from Spirit is hard to receive because expectation, overwhelm and disappointment fill us so completely that we are numb to anything else.

Frances was frustrated by the myriad of complications in her life. She just couldn't understand how to receive help. The help that did come she judged and discarded as not enough.

She said my prayer out loud, "Help me receive the help I'm asking for, especially since I don't know exactly what I need." She paused. "I do feel calmer."

Calm was a state that had been almost impossible for her to achieve, and she acknowledged the Divine was clearly there. Yet when the calm wore off, she became outraged because she thought she wasn't getting what she *needed*—a place to live that didn't compromise her health. Frustration was a completely understandable way to react, and it created an intuitive block.

Frances had been looking for a healthy place to live for six months. She was in constant upheaval during her search, moving more than 15 times because many of the hotels and Airbnb's she stayed in while searching had mold or used harsh cleaning products that caused her health issues to worsen.

Depleted and out of places to look, she heard about some brand-new apartments completed in a town she'd never considered. Used to a market where spaces went quickly, she was pleased to find she had several apartments to choose from. She found one with almost everything on her list: bright open space, hardwood floors that didn't set off her allergies, a sunny balcony with a view of trees, convenient parking, and it was affordable.

Still, her excitement was dampened when she signed the lease—her new home was an hour away from everyone she knew.

Initially, Frances couldn't trust that the calm feeling she received after the prayer was what she needed. She couldn't acknowledge she'd received help in finding a place to live. She felt that if help had been there, she *shouldn't* have had to work so long and hard to find the apartment. Plus, the location *should* have been more ideal.

But after living in her new apartment for two months, Frances felt healthier than she had in more than a year. Her health issues were still present, and she wished her apartment was closer to her friends, but she had a different perspective on Divine help.

"I'm learning when to push and when to let things be," she told me. "I pushed while searching for a place to live and things got worse. I felt like the world was against me. I vacillated between being depressed, frustrated and overwhelmed. It was a crash course in patience that I didn't want but I needed. I'm finally making decisions without resistance."

The intermittent feelings of calm helped Frances understand that the help she actually needed was learning to be patient. She now had a felt sense and positive results from choosing to let things be before she took action.

This was unexpected, since she'd been taught she had to push her way through life. Even though she's a brilliant woman, she didn't realize the extent to which impatience was affecting her. Six months of needing a healthy place to live meant she had to seek other ways to break the exhausting habit of pushing to accomplish everything. Learning to sometimes let things be allowed her to take a moment and receive the help she'd sought.

Some relief, however small, is a key sign that we've received help. Frances received bits of calm that eventually led to more patience and ease recognizing and receiving the rest of the help that came. She slowly released expectations.

There are times when we all feel there's not enough help. Letting go of the expectation of how help arrives from the Divine is so difficult for our evidence-oriented brain to understand. Ultimately, a feeling of comfort or calm after asking for Divine help can give us the sense we're not alone on our journeys.

So that my mind could begin to release expectations of how help should come, I used hindsight to gather evidence of multiple coincidences and synchronicities that I couldn't see in the moment. I also researched other traditions and expectations around asking for help. The two perspectives that had the most impact came from Thich Nhat Hanh and Anne Lamott.

I once heard Zen Master Hanh say there is a mantra that works like magic to help everyone when they aren't well. "I suffer. Please help."

What I recall him saying is that the minute we speak those words there is a modicum of relief. The mantra, *I suffer, please help* brings relief by aligning us to our truth.

Since most people usually don't admit they are suffering, speaking the truth is a relief.

Lamott wrote a book entitled *Help, Thanks, Wow: The Three Essential Prayers*. Notice that *help* is the first prayer. One word. Sometimes that's all you can do and one word is enough. You might not know the kind of help you need. Ask for it anyway.

The diagnosis of MS put me in a position where I had to receive help. I didn't know whether the help would come as acceptance in living a life with MS or as courage to trust in the knowing that I didn't have that disease.

I was by myself, sick, scared, and broke. I had no option but to trust the many strange ways help would come. I needed to learn that help is there even when I'm skeptical. I needed to understand desperation. I needed to have a miracle phone call. I needed to know that Divine help comes from the physical world and that prayer and/or ranting can summon that help. I needed to have the experience of receiving help from Spirit in a desperate situation to truly understand that it's possible. If not, how could I help others do the same?

It was only after telling my story to a friend that I realized I'd lived a miracle.

Why? I hadn't given credit to the Divine at the time. I couldn't because I thought Divine help should be an instant cure.

My mind couldn't see that Kwame fixed anything. My mind undervalued the gift of faith that my prayer had been heard. After a year's worth of exhaustion and doctors' appointments, overwhelmed with symptoms and information, I learned that Divine help is hard to see, especially if you're looking for it through expectant eyes. It was hindsight that saw help was always there.

Remember, asking the Divine for help brings what your Soul needs. That help often looks a lot different than what you think you want, and prayers are answered in ways you'd never imagine.

Even if you don't believe help can come, invite it anyway. Remember, Divine help is hard to recognize at the time. When you ask for help from the Divine, you free your intuition to amplify its message.

Sometimes only hindsight reveals miracles.

Epilogue:

This book was 98 percent finished in December 2023 and was going to be published in early 2024. Then my mother's cancer took a turn. I spent months caring for her while working and doing the minimal needed in my own home. I had no time to care for my own painful physical symptoms that started one week before my mother's decline that December. In February I called a prominent local neurologist and took her first open appointment. It had a four-month wait.

One week after my mother died, the appointment took place. Tests were done and the doctor's conclusion was that I was stressed from my mother's passing. I knew her assessment wasn't accurate. My pain had started one week before my mother's symptoms had worsened. This time my intuition told me to seek further medical evaluation.

I struggled for a few months as to where to turn. I was having trouble focusing on anything but my family and my mom's affairs. Finally, I remembered the prayer: *Help me receive the help I need, even if I don't want that version of help.*

I ended up at the Mayo Clinic in Minnesota in September 2024. The experts there did more testing and came to the conclusion that I had Relapsing-Remitting Multiple Sclerosis (RRMS). The doctor said I'd had it since my first episode 27 years ago. When he looked at my medical history, he could see signs that I'd had MS symptoms surface briefly. But it was disguised as flareups from my eye disease. Otherwise, I'd been fine.

If I had published the book last February, there'd be no need for this epilogue. I wouldn't have known I had MS. Yes, the original diagnosis 27 years ago *was wrong* but only in that I had a milder form of MS than what my first doctor thought.

I had used the prayer, *Help me receive the help I need,* over and over when writing this book. Believe me, this publishing delay and diagnosis was not the help I thought I needed.

I didn't know what to do. I thought of cutting this chapter and not revealing this new diagnosis. But then it occurred to me that 27 years ago *I received the help I needed then*. I did not have the more advanced form of the disease, which would have involved taking a very hard drug for the rest of my life. *I didn't need to receive that drug as help.* I *received* the help of a 27-year break until painful symptoms returned again.

This time, help came with the knowing that the simple diagnosis of stress was a minimal part of what was wrong. Help came by guiding me to apply for assessment with the experts at Mayo. Help *that's needed* can look different in similar circumstances.

By now, admitting that I didn't know exactly what I needed was easy. *Receiving the help* that came was a challenge, even though I'd released my expectations of how help *should* arrive.

Again, only hindsight coupled with intuition revealed that both times I was able to *receive the help I needed*—not what I expected. I don't know what the result of writing this update about my autoimmune disease will be.

I hope it's more miracles.

Invitation

No matter what is going on, say the word help.
Notice the body's response.
If there is any discomfort mentally, physically or emotionally
Ask for help again for those places.
Even if it's only the smallest discomfort.
Breathe in to receive that help.
Notice the sensation of consciously receiving help.
No matter how small.
Breathe out another request for the help
you don't know you need.
Breathe in.
Ask for help receiving the mysterious help asked for.
Notice any sensations, thoughts or emotions.
No matter how subtle.
Ask for help noticing the whisper of help coming in.
Breathe into the belly deeply.
Ask for help releasing expectations about what should happen.
Breathe into the belly slowly.
Breathe out a request for "help" only for you,
no matter how big the problem.
Breathe in.
Ask for help receiving the help asked for
Even if you are skeptical, help is even possible.
Ask to receive help anyway
Even if you feel nothing at all.
Ask anyway.

Help me receive the help I need.
Help me see the results someday, if not today.

32
Paradox of Help

Two huge blocks to our intuition are *not asking for* help and *not receiving* it. Since intuition is designed to provide help, this is a significant problem.

There are many reasons people give as to why they don't seek or accept help. Explanations range from "I don't know how," to "It doesn't occur to me," to "I can't, both make me uncomfortable."

Some upbringings teach us not to ask for help. Some families have a "Do as I say, not as I do," approach. Parents tell you how to ask with "please" and "thank you" but don't provide an example, preferring to give orders. Some of you were taught that to ask for help was weak and a threat to being independent. Others were raised to ask for help but were always told "no." Or were told "yes" but the help never came, leading us to assume receiving help was not allowed. When you recognize where and possibly why this destructive habit starts, solutions naturally appear that start to rewire your connection to your intuition.

Recently, I discovered that my dear friend Anne had been struggling with a major career decision for more than a month. I had assisted her several times before. When I asked why she hadn't called me for help to connect to her intuition, she said, "It didn't occur to me. Honestly, it's never in my conscious mind to ask for help with something like that."

When we don't learn to ask for help it's like having a constant intuitive head cold. When clients call claiming their intuition isn't working, the inability to ask for and receive help is almost always part of the blockage.

Many people tell me they just don't like to ask for help from anyone. Their reasons boil down to six fears:

–Looking weak or stupid.
–Being rejected.
–Appearing lazy, selfish or manipulative.
–If people really wanted to help, they would offer to help.
–Not being able to do enough to pay the helper back.
–Getting bad help that makes their situation worse. The *If you want something done right, do it yourself* syndrome.

Here's the paradox. People who don't know how to ask for help develop a strong connection to intuitive knowledge and a skillful perception to understand what *others* need. But they often don't know what they need and can't receive it. The problem is their intuition is always focused outward, an intuitive survival mode stemming from fear.

Often, highly intuitive people call me for help to connect to intuition for themselves. Most of them started like I did—using intuition at a very young age as a way to navigate complicated family dynamics. My client Lillian, for example, learned to orient her intuition to meet her father's needs.

"I didn't know the word intuition. I just did what I did, I didn't know how. I was expected to know what my father wanted without being told," Lillian said. "An internal part of me was always focused on my dad. It was my job by age four to manage his anger and keep him happy—not to gain praise, but to avoid his constant criticism. Also, if he was taken care of, he was less likely to yell and take out his fury on my mother or punish my brothers and sisters for no reason."

Lillian remembered "concentrating to reach for" her father's mood when she heard his car turn into the driveway. "If I could *feel* him, I could have what he wanted ready when he walked in the door," she told me. "Before he got out of the car, I learned whether he wanted an ice tea, ice water or vodka.

I was rebuked and sent back to the kitchen if I brought the wrong thing."

"Was there anything else you were expected to know?" I asked.

"It was a bunch of little things. Like what channel he wanted the TV on. I was the remote in those days," Lillian laughed. "It's kind of sad. When I was home, no matter what I was doing, a knowing that 'I'd better get to the family room' would pop into my awareness. Often, my Dad greeted me with, 'It's about time.' I wasn't punished for not knowing his whims, just berated."

Lillian stopped a moment then said, "Honestly, I didn't know any different. I was able to manage Dad's moods and it made me feel important knowing what he needed."

When parents or caretakers don't directly ask for help, children don't learn how to ask for help themselves. It didn't occur to Lillian to ask for help with anything until long into adulthood. She thought she was supposed to know how to do everything herself. She reasoned that if she was supposed to know how to meet her father's unspoken needs, it must be bad to ask for help.

"Did you ever directly ask for help?" I asked.

Lillian thought a moment then said, "A few times in first or second grade, I asked my parents for help with my home-work. The response I received was, 'It's not my homework, figure it out for yourself. How will you learn to be independent if you don't?' After that, I never asked. I tried to do everything perfectly myself. The only help I received was when my failures were discovered."

Lillian came to realize that access to her intuition for personal use was stunted by her father's needs. "But he's also the reason my intuition was developed at all. My dad's a rageaholic. My whole family avoided a lot of terrible abuse because my intuition knew how to manipulate his moods," she said. "Now I just need to keep redirecting my intuitive focus for me as well."

Raised in a home where rage roamed unpredictably, Lillian became hypervigilant, constantly scanning for danger. She was always on the lookout for a sibling to set her father off, watching for signs that he was about to blow. She inadvertently carried this state of extreme alertness everywhere she went, long into adulthood.

Autonomy and her ability to effectively help others are gifts that came from developing survival intuition. The curse was hypervigilance.

"My therapist helped me understand why I was so anxious and always 'walking on eggshells.' I couldn't trust anyone," Lillian said. "She taught me valuable tools used for PTSD (Post Traumatic Stress Disorder). It's taken a long time to regulate myself. I don't think hypervigilance is just a state of mind. I think it also came from using my intuition for everyone else but me."

"Absolutely," I said.

"Habitually using intuition to avoid danger, though necessary to protect yourself and your family as a child, turns into constant vigilance when no danger is present. In that state you miss receiving the magical parts of intuition. Enhanced peace, joy, wonder and vitality."

"You know, I found my therapist because the doctors couldn't figure out why I was exhausted and stressed all of the time," Lillian said. "The therapist my doctor referred me to wasn't taking new clients... Oh my goodness, I just realized I did ask for help. I said to the Cosmos, 'I want to live my life without being tired. Help!' And a friend gave me this wonderful therapist's name a few days later."

Now, Lillian balances her focus on others by consciously taking time to include herself. She started by breathing in the beauty of nature on her walk every day. She invites all of her senses to participate in receiving the goodness/help from the trees she passes along the way.

Lillian also learned that being self-sufficient doesn't mean doing everything herself. She asks her intuitive self or "the Cosmos" to help her receive the assistance she seeks. Her decision-making is clearer. More importantly, Lillian is having fun navigating life with her intuition.

Lillian was wise to know she needed to seek a licensed therapist to treat her hypervigilance. If you have lived through a traumatic upbringing, find a therapist. When trauma has an avenue to be released, your worldview changes and intuition thrives.

Part of my intuitive development resulted from being raised by women who never directly asked for help. I was just supposed to know what was needed.

A complicated language of sighs, huffs or gusty exhales reverberated through the house when my mother, aunt or grandmother were preparing meals, cleaning or heading out to do yardwork. Each signaled the type of assistance I or someone else was expected to provide. If I didn't respond appropriately to my mother's puff of need, I'd hear an aggravated spit of air, often followed by a churlish directive or complaint. "Load the dishwasher" or, "Can't you see the counter needs wiping? I shouldn't have to tell you."

The unspoken rules for women in our family were: Do not ask for help if you can do it yourself.

If someone outside the family offered, it was appropriate to first protest in a high-pitched voice, "Oh thank you, I've got it." Followed by, "Well, if you *want* to help, okay."

The unspoken rules taught me that intuition is used to meet the needs of others. I was constantly vigilant. My body was an antenna, wired to scan the environment for signs I was needed. My sensitivity was so developed that I knew a family member wanted help before she exhaled an audible breath.

Being praised for helping without being asked cemented the bad habit that my intuition was only meant to serve others. It took me years to recognize and redirect my focus to include intuition when navigating my own needs. That unintentionally reinforced my belief to not ask anybody for help. I had my intuition to help me, so why bother anyone? Even so, asking my intuitive self for help was a big step towards learning to receive help from others, too.

When we're programed by the non-askers around us to meet their silent demands, we lose the ability to feel our own core needs. Our confidence grows from external praise instead of internal trust. Our inner voice is squelched when we look for approval to be provided by others.

The paradox is that even though we seek outside praise, we don't know how to take it in. If we're focused on others, we don't know our own needs. Just like we can't speak and listen at the same time, constant intuitive output keeps us from discerning what nourishes and inspires us. We genuinely can't receive.

The silent message in my house was you're supposed to know how to do everything you need to do. In third grade I fell hard on my right knee on the asphalt and tore a hole in the light-blue, double-knit polyester pants my mother had sewn for me. I knew I couldn't mend the hole. I didn't know I could *ask* my mother to fix my pants. I only knew to cry and tell her about my accident.

She made a beautiful flower from scrap fabric to patch the hole. Seeing how horrible I felt to have torn my new pants she told me, "Everyone has accidents" and that "The patch made the pants prettier."

She made me feel better. She also unconsciously reinforced the family pattern of answering my need without teaching me how to ask for help. To be fair, she struggled with asking for help her whole life.

By the time I was in junior high, I'd slowly shake my head with a look of disgust when someone couldn't see that I, or someone else, was silently struggling. The kids who asked for help usually got it from the teacher. But I could see the signals that others needed help. If I noticed, I automatically believed it was my responsibility to assist.

Resentment began to seep in as I seemed to be the sole responder to unspoken need. I couldn't say no. I couldn't ask for help. I directed the family language of audible breaths, eye-rolling and pursed lips toward the person ignoring my struggle. I didn't understand that they weren't taught to respond to need without verbally being asked.

Remember my dear friend Anne? She learned not to ask for help when she became her mother's main caregiver. Anne took over her mother's duties as a sophomore in high school. When her mother died of cancer several years later, Anne continued the role of mother for the family. The responsibility she carried at such a young age fueled her independence and natural ability to lead. The cost was the belief that she didn't think to ask for help when she thought she should know how to do something herself.

Anne has a highly developed focus of what everyone needs, which makes her a great CEO. She doesn't have a problem asking, delegating or calling in favors as long as it's for business. She's learned how to effectively receive help at work. Yet, it doesn't enter her mind to ask for help with personal needs.

When I asked Anne if she'd like some help connecting to her intuition, she accepted. In less than a half hour she felt in her bones a clarity and peace to turn down a powerful job opportunity that "wasn't quite right."

Her fierce need to never be dependent on anyone blocked

her from even considering outside help. Anne realized that the thought that she *should* be able to get clarity around a career decision by herself had started to eat away at her confidence. She also saw that the lost sleep and constant stress over the last month were needless.

"I finally understand that asking for help for my personal needs is smart and efficient," Anne confided. "Asking for help puts me at an advantage, both mentally and physically. I don't *have* to take the advice or accept the help I receive. I knew that intellectually, but for some reason a part of me was resisting being told what to do—silly once I realized."

The nature of intuition is to be helpful. Not asking for help clogs your intuition and can prevent you from embracing help when it appears. Not asking for help keeps you afraid of voicing what you actually need. Not asking for help prevents others from receiving the good feelings that come from helping. Not asking for help keeps you in the role of designated giver, which leads to exhaustion and lack of joy when giving. Not asking for help from a friend stunts intimacy from deepening the relationship.

For those who fear being turned down, know that seeking help is empowering for all involved. Asking for help carries the realization that I'm worthy of receiving. It gives the other person the opportunity to say "yes" or "no" or to offer other options. Being told "no" by someone just means to look further, that better help is available from someone else.

Start by asking for little things where there won't be a lot of no's. "Can you hold the door please?" or "Will you give me your opinion on something?" Allow yourself a moment to receive the gestures of help being given. Receiving help is as simple as breathing in and saying, "Thank you."

Remember, not asking for help creates blocks to receiving help from your intuition. Paradoxically, not asking for help forces you to develop your intuition while simultaneously keeping your intuitive wisdom out of reach for your own needs.

Try and understand the origins of your non-asking behavior. Then, regularly do brief check-ins with your senses being present. This is a worthwhile practice of awareness that evolves into inner trust. The feelings of inner approval, knowing you're enough and self-confidence are aided by following your intuitive direction.

Your Soul, your intuitive presence, begins to shift your awareness and dissolve the belief that your self-worth depends on the opinions of others.

If you recognize yourself in the stories about Anne, Lillian and me, claim the parts that mirror your life as your own. Help is waiting.

Invitation

Inhale…
Guide the breath to follow the spine from the neck
down to the tailbone.
Exhale…
Let the breath ride back up the body slightly in front of the spine.
Inhale…
Feel the throat, center of ribcage, abdomen, pelvis.
Let the breath split to ride down the leg bones to heels then toes.
Exhale…
Feel the breath release toes, heels, flowing up the legs,
torso, throat and crown.
Inhale…
From above the crown and all the way down thru the Earth.

Exhale…

Notice the release of tension as the breath
maintains full body awareness.

Inhale…

Ask for help embodying more of the Divine self.

Exhale…

Feel your presence.

The fullness, density and flow inside.

33
Come Passion

Often before a session, I look at the notes I've written about my clients' most recent appointments. This way, I remember to ask them if the skills we worked on have been useful or need tinkering.

This was not the case with Alice. It had been five years since we'd talked. I was more interested in exploring how to help her make beneficial choices for her upcoming surgery, after which she required bed rest for six weeks.

As Alice was describing her situation, my fingers began flipping through notes of our past appointments. I trusted that my hands knew more than my head, and when Alice finished telling me her intent for our session, I looked to see where my fingers had landed. I scanned the short sentence from 20 years earlier, our first session together. I told Alice what my hands had done and she was curious to hear what my notes said.

"It says a compassion master came," I told her.

"Do you remember what that meant?" she asked.

An odd thing happens when I'm in an altered state—with a slight internal shift in awareness I actually do remember the context of the consulting I've done for all these years. When I'm not working, I have little memory of the interactions. It's as if I have alternate backup drive for a client's history in my everyday life.

I switched into the past. The details of our long-ago session returned. "A guide in spirit came. He came to let you know that compassionate help would always be available to you," I said. "Call on that compassion master now and ask what's needed for your current situation."

"Part of why I called you is that I can't feel spiritual guidance anymore," Alice said.

I assured her we'd both tune in, and that I'd help convey possible meanings and/or messages that were just out of her reach. After a minute Alice shared she was "a little more relaxed," but was also frustrated she didn't "experience more."

I relayed a bizarre image I saw and felt. "What's with the curtains in your bedroom. It feels gray and heavy around them," I said. "Do you have bedroom curtains?"

Alice gave a little huff and replied, "Yes, and I hate them. Yes, it feels gray. I hate my bedroom. It's so cluttered. It's literally heavy because it's a dumping ground for whatever anyone in the house doesn't know what to do with."

Knowing she was about to spend weeks in that room recovering from a major surgery, I suggested she at least trash the curtains, even if she couldn't undertake a clean-up. "I'm seeing that you don't even *need* curtains, that your room is private. Is that true?" I asked.

"Yes, we live in the woods with no neighbors. I've hated those curtains for twenty years, and you're right. I really don't even need them."

I asked her to check how her body felt at the thought of throwing the curtains away. "I sort of feel … passionate about it," she said. Her voice sounded stronger.

Then she started to laugh, "Passion! I asked to feel the compassionate help around me and passion came. Come passion. Compassion! I guess my compassion master is back."

Alice texted me later. *I threw the curtains away and cleaned the windows inside and out. Then an old friend randomly sent me this quote by Horace, 'He who has begun his task is half done.' I'm half done. I feel great!*

Asking for help from Divine guidance is asking for help from the space of your intuition. Your part is half done. The second part is to receive it. Sometimes help will come to you in common ways. Humor. Quotes. A play on words. Puns. Lyrics to a song. Bumper stickers. Billboards.

Don't be tempted to think something is too obvious. If you call on the Divine for help it's usually some of the easiest guidance to recognize.

The trick is to follow it.

Invitation

Let your belly be soft.
Breathe into it gently, like a baby breathes.
Ask your inner Divine for help with a current challenge.
Let this request escape on a whisper breath.
Breathe in the idea that you are able to receive help easily.
Now release any doubts on a quick breath out.
Savor a deep breath in,
Knowing you are receiving your request.
Leave your mind open to notice what comes.

34

Intuition & the Labyrinth

At times, your intuition's broad perspective insures you remember *something* that may have little significance in the moment, yet holds a clue to your future.

Only when you bump into that *something* again do you feel the impact. You might not understand the importance revealed, but you feel compelled to investigate.

For me that *something* was the labyrinth.

In July 1986, I found myself in an enormous, gloomy and blessedly cool cathedral in France. I was awarded a full scholarship to study art abroad for my junior summer in college. I usually preferred browsing museums, but religious art intrigued me. Some friends I'd met at The American College in Paris encouraged me to sign up for a weekend tour that included French cathedrals.

July was scald-your-toes-on-the-sidewalk kind of hot. With no air conditioning on our tour bus, Toni, Nicolette, Pitzi and I ran for the huge stone structure with barely a glance at our surroundings. The cool that met us was such a giddy relief we couldn't maintain inside voices. Knowing our behavior was disrespectful, yet unable to contain chatter, we chose to explore alone.

We spread out—my friends meandered toward the dark wings in the back of the cathedral. I found myself drawn into a large unoccupied space towards the front. I sat down on a woven-rush-seated ladderback chair, part of a row of 10 chairs bolted together. An inexpensive way to make pews, I guessed.

as there were at least forty rows of 10 connected chairs in that section facing an altar. It wasn't comfortable but it *felt* like the right place to stay, so I pulled out my art journal.

Within three minutes a group of five or six loud, middle-aged American women came and stood near me, then bustled around the rows of chairs, pointing at the floor, swearing under their breath. They bitterly complained, "Why on earth would the labyrinth be covered?"

I gathered from their grumblings that they wanted to walk a design on the floor called a labyrinth, but "these damn chairs" blocked it. I looked at the stone floor. There were curved lines about a foot wide, made by dark mahogany stone, next to lines of golden stone that covered most of the cathedral. Still, I had no idea what they were talking about. I wrote the words *labyrinth walk* in my journal with a question mark, along with the date and location—Chartres Cathedral, France.

Months later, I looked up labyrinth at my school's library. Research was more challenging then with no Internet, computerized book searches or cell phones. The dictionary definition wasn't satisfying. There was no mention of a labyrinth in the information I found about Chartres Cathedral.

An additional search led to a Greek myth—Ariadne helping her lover, Theseus, escape a labyrinth with jeweled thread, after he slew the Minotaur. But that's all I could find. I couldn't figure out why the labyrinth intrigued me so much. My curiosity wasn't quenched, but with little time and a dead end at the library, I let the labyrinth go with an, "Oh well."

Seventeen years later in 2003, I was curled up on my comfy oversized couch as my friend Marie cozied-up on the other end. We'd been catching up for over an hour. She'd just carefully placed a second mug of herbal tea to cool on a coaster when suddenly her hands jumped from her lap, "I almost forgot! Have you ever walked a labyrinth?"

Memories of the French cathedral instantly returned.

In the middle of recounting my frustration over the lack of information I was able to uncover, it dawned on me what Marie had said. "Wait. You *know* how to walk a labyrinth?" I asked. "I couldn't find anything about that—I figured, like the myth, it was about solving a maze."

"Noooo. It's not a game like a maze. You don't have to think at all. Just walk. You can't get lost."

"Why walk it then?"

"You need to experience it to understand."

"Okay. When and where?"

"My intuition is on today!" Marie laughed and pointed at me. "I can't believe you of all people haven't walked a labyrinth. It will change your life *aaand* I'm walking with you."

When Marie made a decision, there was no stopping her. We made a date to meet at a large outdoor labyrinth in our community that anyone could walk. In three weeks we'd walk together. We shared a long hug goodbye. She waved from her car window shouting, "Three weeks!"

The next time I saw her was at her wake. Her passing wasn't completely unexpected. She'd been fighting cancer for years, though no one anticipated such a rapid decline. She had felt great until one week before she died. I walked out of her funeral two days before our scheduled walk, determined to keep our date.

I arrived at the labyrinth 10 minutes early, mentally reminding myself that the time really didn't matter. I looked around for signs of a labyrinth and saw a cross-shaped wooden marker. It read, The Labyrinth Prayer Garden. I got out of my car and followed an uneven line of octagonal, cement stepping stones for about 50 feet. A simple wooden archway opened to a clearing with a large circle about the size of a tennis court. The labyrinth.

How to walk the labyrinth was obvious. The single entry point was conveniently located about 15 feet in front of me. The circular path curved around but unlike a spiral, it turned back on itself many times until ending in a round center.

I moved to the entrance and lingered as a wave of grief rolled over me. Only three weeks ago Marie and I were laughing as we made today's plans. The blessing of knowing her suffering had been short didn't prevent my grief as I started our walk alone.

The soft crunching sound of silver-grey gravel under the weight of my slow pace gave me a focus. I could be present and grieve. My heart felt lighter with that thought. I rounded to an outer circuit of the labyrinth. A warm breeze caressed my face, and I caught the unmistakable lemony scent of a Southern magnolia flower. I stopped, looked around, but there was no sign of the huge, white-cupped blossoms.

Wait. Magnolias don't bloom in September.

I paused, closed my eyes and breathed in deeply. My mind let go of locating the intoxicating aroma. I stood still and enjoyed the scent. My grief dissipated. I felt Marie standing beside me.

I didn't expect to feel her. It felt like standing next to a loved one, not facing one another, and knowing they are smiling. Or the feeling of meeting up with a dear friend—we feel their physical presence before seeing them. It felt like that.

I started walking again and whispered, "Hey, Marie." A wave of joy surrounded me, and her presence became more palpable. She continued to be my companion just like we planned, staying next to me as I wound my way around. The path was only 2 feet wide. Realizing that in-person, one of us would have to follow the other, I felt the blessing of walking side-by-side. It was a perfect, sunny, 70-degree September day in South Carolina, and I was walking beside my friend.

Marie was right. This labyrinth walk changed my life.

I had felt loved ones who died, but none this physically for almost 20 minutes.

I didn't see or hear her. If I remained focused on the details of my walk, the bird songs, the warm sun, and the colors of nature around me, I felt her. If I got preoccupied with my absorbed thinking-self, her presence started to dissipate. Refocusing on the sensory details of my turtle pace, Marie and I walked to the center where I paused, said a prayer of thanks, and turned to retrace my steps to the entrance, now an exit.

Departing the labyrinth, I carefully spun to gaze over this magical circle. This time I didn't whisper, I simply said, "Thank you, Marie, you were right."

A sense of disconnection occurred, like hanging up the phone still smiling from the conversation. Marie was gone. Yet, I felt steeped in gratitude for the experience, and for honoring my desire to keep our labyrinth date.

Reading this you might be thinking, "If your intuition is so great, why didn't you know she was going to die when she did?"

I struggle with that question, but I've learned intuition doesn't alert you to *every* important thing. The short answer is—don't mistake intuition for omnipotence. You can't know it all. You're not supposed to. Your intuition helps you focus on *your* knowing—what you need to know for your Soul's journey. Sometimes that includes knowing people are about to leave the planet. Sometimes it doesn't.

After my walk with Marie, I researched labyrinths again. The walk had activated a space inside me where my intuitive perception was heightened. By walking different labyrinths, I noticed my intuitive perceptions were amplified even without Marie's presence. A variety of intuitive insights came to me during and after each walk. I began to wonder if labyrinths were originally designed to access our intuitive/Divine self.

Most labyrinths are circular and with different walking patterns. The circle is universally recognized as a symbol for wholeness and unity. We may never know who created labyrinths or why. Those facts aren't necessary to understand the countless benefits a labyrinth experience gives. I know walking the circuits of a circular labyrinth helps me feel whole, my body aligned and unified to my intuition. I've heard many people describe a labyrinth walk as, "a way to help you find yourself."

A maze tricks you into getting lost or *losing yourself.*

When you enter a labyrinth you don't have to think about where you're going. It has only one entry/exit point, with one path to follow into the center and out. Likewise, you only have one path to walk in life, your own. When you find yourself, your intuition is waiting for you and you feel oriented to the path you've chosen.

My hypothesis that a labyrinth is a tool to connect to intuition was confirmed when I came across the book, *Walking a Sacred Path.* In it, Reverend Dr. Lauren Artress writes, the labyrinth "… enlivens the intuitive part of our nature and stirs within the human heart the longing for connectedness and the remembrance of our purpose for living."

She further affirmed the labyrinth, "does not engage our thinking minds. It invites our intuitive, pattern-seeking, symbolic mind to come forth. It presents us with only one, but profound, choice. To enter a labyrinth is to choose to walk a spiritual path."

The labyrinth movement has grown exponentially since I first read that book in 2006. They are popping up everywhere, and LabyrinthLocator.com makes them easy to find. Many churches have built them as a spiritual tool. Hospitals and hospices in the United States have constructed walking labyrinths for healing purposes. Research shows that walking a labyrinth has long-term health benefits including lowering blood pressure and heart rate, reducing anxiety and insomnia, alleviating chronic pain, improving fertility, and much more.

Not every walk on the labyrinth is an epiphany or peak experience. I've learned not to expect epiphanies. Of course I welcome them, but the health benefits are enough. Some of my walks have a "meh" quality to them. I find that releasing expectations of what you think *should be happening* and be present to *what IS happening* is the best frame of mind for a walk.

Whether walking a large labyrinth or tracing a hand-held labyrinth with your finger, using this ancient tool brings us to exactly where we are in the moment. Catherine Anderson in her book *Meeting Your Soul on the Labyrinth* says, "The labyrinth is a tool to hear our Soul language."

Soul language is a beautiful term for intuition. The present is the forever birthplace of Soul language. Staying in the moment allowed me to feel Marie next to me.

Labyrinths mirror life. Life's endings are all the same. Both labyrinths and life are about the journey and experience rather than the destination. The labyrinth can help you on your journey. What you observe or experience during a walk is often your intuition communicating. If you are present, your intuition draws your attention to solutions for your current life situation through metaphor.

For instance, on my second labyrinth walk I noticed countless stones littering the 2-inch-wide raised concrete lines that defined the circuits of the circular path. I spent my entire walk to the center bent over brushing the stones back onto the gravel path. I mind-grumbled the entire time imagining people carelessly kicking the stones, cluttering the linear symmetry.

Once in the center, I looked all around and felt satisfaction at the order I had made, though I was exhausted and my lower back was unhappy. I stood in the center and realized that the rocks symbolically represented all of the cluttered thoughts I needed to release to be able to receive clarity. My mind felt clearer as I began to walk my way out. I didn't think about what type of thoughts I needed to let go of. I was pleased I received a clear metaphorical message—focusing my mind will avoid mental clutter and exhaustion.

I had walked about a quarter of the way out when a short slim woman wearing sensible church attire entered the labyrinth. She took a few steps, bent down, picked up a rock and gently placed it on the path marker I'd just cleared. I tried not to stare. She walked a bit more, bent down, picked up a rock, stood and walked a few steps, head bowed down, holding it prayerfully in her hand. She bent down again and placed it on the ledge. We passed each other silently with a nod and continued our journey. Exiting the labyrinth, I turned and paused to look back at the labyrinth. She was placing more stones.

I couldn't believe my synchronistic luck. The woman placing rocks clarified my metaphorical message. The cluttered thoughts I needed to get rid of were assumptions, shoulds and expectations. I had assumed people were being careless. I assumed the lines defining the route *should* all be clear. I expected other walkers to behave, not kick rocks around. It never occurred to me that those rocks were placed with prayerful purpose.

Focusing on endless small stuff left me ignorant to my life's big picture, keeping me off-balance and exhausted. I could finally see the myriad of distractions operating throughout my life. Those small disgruntled thoughts were hampering me, impeding my perspective. Just like I was blind to the beauty of the whole labyrinth until those stones were cleared, I needed to stop chasing all of the little things and take action from a larger perspective.

There are no rules for journeying through a labyrinth, whether on foot or with your finger. There are many helpful ways to focus your walk. My favorite way is to think about the three parts of the path (entering, experiencing the middle and exiting) involves three R's: Release. Receive. Return.

Release. Focus on your steps, pace and breath while walking to the center. With every out-breath imagine that whatever you need to let go of, known or unknown, releases.

Receive. At the center, on your in-breath, invite whatever you need, known or unknown, to fill you.

Return. While walking back, engage your senses. Invite whatever needs to be noticed or understood in the moment on your in-breath and clear the way for more on the out-breath.

I sometimes add two more R's. Before the walk I *Reflect* on what's important to me and ask that the walk address it. For example, the second walk I took I knew I needed insight as to why I was exhausted. That walk alerted me to shift my focus to the bigger picture. After my walks I frequently *Record* my experience. Writing them down often leads to more insights.

Sitting in Chartres Cathedral at 21, I had no idea I would return 25 years later in 2011 to walk its famous labyrinth.

At night.

Candlelit.

With Lauren Artress (the author who wrote that the labyrinth enlivens our intuition).

The rows of wedded chairs still clutter the labyrinth's surface but are moved on Fridays so pilgrims from all over the world can walk. Just like our intuition, the hidden power of the walk was there waiting.

My intuition opened and embedded into my conscious-ness the knowledge that a labyrinth had value before I knew what a labyrinth was. Our intuition sees a bigger picture than we can imagine.

My initiation to the labyrinth was accidental, brief and forgettable, yet it burned into my memory. That long-ago introduction from disgruntled strangers held a power that moved me to keep a date with my deceased friend.

Your intuitive self knows what is meaningful to your life, even when your conscious mind is unaware. Intuition amplifies what you *need* to remember so that when you arrive, in hindsight, you find meaning.

<u>Invitation</u>

Enjoy this finger/stylus labyrinth.
Place your finger or stylus for a moment
on the opening at the bottom.
Feel the paper.
Breathe in the scents of your current space.
Begin to trace the line to the center.
Let your mind rest in the movement.
Allow your breath to help merge with the pattern.
Find your pace.
Breathe.
Keep bringing your mind back to focus on the line.
Rest in knowing you can't do this the wrong way,
Even if you don't finish.
Breathe and invite this invisible wisdom to guide you.

Chartres Labyrinth Design

35
Spirit Babies

When I left the museum, the local newspaper published a front-page story about how I was answering a "calling" to give intuitive readings.

A woman I'll call Estelle saw the article and scheduled an appointment. Since the article mentioned I did readings, she thought I only focused on the future. She asked for insight on health and family issues. Her expression, like her body, was stiff as if bracing for bad news.

Neither of us expected her secret past to show up.

As we worked together, I asked her to invite her helpers in spirit. She looked at me quizzically, "You mean like dead relatives?"

"Yes. We can have family members that watch over us. Also, you can simply call on God's helpers." I was careful to use the words that resonated with her faith.

Estelle agreed, closing her eyes to invite Spirit. Once finished, her eyes softened as she acknowledged that the room felt warmer and cozier. I closed my eyes to begin her reading.

I followed my breath to a feeling of inner spaciousness. This is the place that intersects with Divine intelligence and where I internally asked how to approach Estelle's family issues.

I felt a very strong, comforting presence, and a diaphanous young man showed me the circle of Estelle's family. He gave me the sense that *he* was family and stood just outside the circle to watch.

Everyone I saw in my mind's eye, except Estelle, was a featureless vague blur. When the young man saw that I'd registered his position as outside the circle of family, he fully infused me with the feeling of protection. Then number 34 appeared to float around him, so I assumed it was his age. All of this information came forth in less than a minute. I asked if any men in her family had died at age 34.

"No. None that I know of."

I told Estelle about the Spirit I felt/saw as I continued to interact with the young man. More information trickled into my awareness and I relayed it as it came.

"I asked him for his name or initials and got the sense he didn't have any. He keeps showing me he's part of the family, but just outside. Like he protects you all. Also, the number 34 continues to rotate counterclockwise above his head. Did something happen 34 years ago maybe?"

Estelle thought for a moment, "Let's see ... I'd have been 19. A sophomore in ..."

She stared down, froze, her face went blank and her eyes filled to the brink of release. I carefully told Estelle the words that came to me. "Please tell her to forgive herself. I knew what she had to do. I'm grateful I got to start again."

Estelle's tears began as her features reddened then contorted into an impossible expression of pain. I carefully nudged a box of tissues close to her as she fought for composure. She whispered to herself through intermittent sobs, "This is impossible... impossible... I've never told... impossible."

It turns out she'd had an abortion. It was illegal then and a huge risk but Estelle *knew* she couldn't have a baby. She never knew the fetus' sex and carried the weight of feeling like a murderer silently all these years. She never told anyone. Even her husband had no idea.

When they married, she was quietly terrified that she wouldn't be able to have children. Each pregnancy brought a renewed fear that something would be wrong with the baby because of what she'd done as a teen. She had four healthy babies, now young adults. She'd judged her decision as unforgivable and stuffed the pain down, a dormant secret for God to judge.

Estelle asked me many questions at once. "How is this possible? How can he forgive me? What does it mean he got to start again? I just don't understand how you could know this."

"I don't know how it's possible either. I'm unsure what 'starting again' means except that he's been a guardian for you and your family. All I feel is love from him."

She slowly nodded. "What do I do?"

"Forgive yourself." My words were infused with the feeling of love her son was emanating.

"Maybe the fact that there is no way I could have known this… is the irrefutable evidence you need… to feel you deserve forgiveness. Proof you did what was right for you *and* for him. Remember he said he knew what you'd have to do. That implies he had a choice too."

After a while Estelle's face looked calmer. "I do feel lighter. But I don't know if I can forgive myself."

"That's okay," I reassured her. "You don't need to today. Maybe knowing his spirit wants that for you is enough to begin."

By the end of the reading her demeanor became more open and easier. I assured her I'd never share her secret. Her bearing further softened as she thanked me. I never saw Estelle again and though I've shared the heart of her story, her identity and secret remain safe.

Not long after my encounter with Estelle, my childhood friend Bella kept entering my mind. Since this was before everyone had cell phones I waited until evening to make the long-distance call.

She was happy to hear from me but her cheerful tone held a note of grief. I waited until we'd each caught up on life and said, "Okay, tell me what's wrong and don't say 'nothing.'"

She let out a deep breath, "It's the anniversary of the abortion I had two years ago. I know, I should have told you, but Phillip and I decided not to tell anyone. I'm just sad."

I told her that the spirit of a terminated pregnancy came to a client of mine at the age he would have been now. I then asked if she wanted me to check if there was a 2-year-old spirit around her.

She was quiet for a moment before she answered, "Yes."

After letting Bella know that the same thing might not happen, I turned inward, asking my guides in spirit to help.

What I felt/saw was a joyful, happy, cloud-like presence. Silvery blue and magenta highlights gracefully swirled teasingly in transparent billows. I felt undulations of love laced with words, "Tell them I'm still their *first* child. I'm happy waiting for next time."

The words came and held a promise. It was such a quick bright transmission of information I laughed with the joy I felt then quickly shared the details, "This cheerful, loving little spirit is waiting for you both to be ready. She's coming back."

I didn't know until the word *she* came out of my mouth that they would have a girl. I asked Bella if she could feel the truth of what I was saying. "Yes," she quietly cried. "Most of me feels relief. My mind is scared it's not true, but my heart doesn't hurt so much."

I don't remember much of the rest of our conversation other than my friend felt hope. She, that joy-filled little Spirit, was born two years later and a few years after that a sibling joined her. Which helped me understand more fully what her message about being the first born meant.

In the first chapter, *Blind Calling*, I refer to a profound session I had with Susan Hough that changed both of our lives. At that time, we didn't know each other. Neither of us had an agenda for our first appointment together, but *Spirit* did.

Susan and I quietly sat cross-legged on the floor in a cozy little room with soft teal carpet and low lighting. If she had a focus for her session, she didn't reveal it. She simply said, "I'm open to anything."

I sank deep inside asking for a wise direction for our appointment to take. When I opened my eyes I saw an outline, like wavering heat coming from hot pavement, of two androgynous children with her. Experienced now, because of the other times this had happened, it felt okay to gently say, "I'm seeing two children with you. Have you ever had an abortion?"

"No ... but I had a miscarriage and an ectopic pregnancy. Why?"

"I'm seeing children with the numbers nine and seven standing on either side of you. They feel like part of a team of spirits that help you."

Susan confirmed that the pregnancies she'd lost would have been those ages now and that sometimes she'd wondered if they were with her. "Sometimes I feel a sense of sweetness surround me for no reason. I think 'that's my baby' but I didn't know. I thought I was projecting."

Susan told me years later that our first session together finally gave her closure to those painful losses.

"That session was validating. I felt a sense of relief. Of course, I was sad I'd lost them, but you confirmed my feelings that I didn't *really* lose them.

"Also, it gave those pregnancies meaning—*we* started working together. Because of them so many people have been helped."

The rippling effects of Susan's Spirit babies were substantial. As I said before, that session prompted Susan to schedule clients for me once a month. Going into business together allowed me to stay in business. It enabled Susan to quit her night job and stay home with her 8-year-old and 9-month-old baby.

Every month, I stayed a week or more in Susan and her husband's home. That gave me an opportunity to help raise children, which I loved. I didn't know it then but I wasn't able to have kids of my own. Being involved in the lives of her children continues to be a priceless gift.

I didn't see Spirit babies again for several years, until Candice tearfully told me she wanted to have a family.

"I'm running out of time. If I meet a man today it will take months to make sure we're right for each other, then time for engagement, wedding, house… by then I'll be 38. It could be too late."

I closed my eyes and begged the Divine to give me something real to say, to help lift Candice out of her hopelessness. I saw two beings of translucent light similar to the spirit I saw with Bella, but with more of a rainbow color spectrum. They felt far away. Again, I sensed overwhelming love coupled with this message. "Don't worry. We'll be there when it's time."

My job is to help people feel intuitive information in their own bodies. The other women I'd helped were in a receptive state because their loss was in the past. Candice, however, was lost in the future with no inner-spaciousness to feel anything but want and fear.

In her present state, it would have been irresponsible to share that I'd seen two light spirits in the distance. I didn't want to pin her hopes on a prediction. The future is more flexible than we realize, and when we get fixated on the way something *should* look, it makes it difficult for our path to be seen.

When I considered sharing the rainbow-lit message

with Candice, my chest tightened. This wasn't the right time to tell her. So I didn't. I said I had a sense she was going to have children. A platitude perhaps, but along with taking some slow breaths, these words helped release her anxiety.

A few years later Candice called. She was married to a good man who wanted children as much as she did. She'd had several miscarriages and was afraid she'd never be able to carry a baby to term. I asked her to close her eyes. "Ask your Divine guides to connect so you can feel their support."

I closed my eyes and did the same. I felt one of those bright beings that I'd seen years before happily floating closer to her. I asked Candice what she felt.

"I feel some warmth on my shoulders. It's really peaceful."

Carefully, I suggested she ask to feel the spirit of the child that would come to her. This wording left room for more possibilities than giving birth herself. Candice was apprehensive at first, afraid to ask for fear she'd feel nothing.

Eventually we found a way for her to release her fear and ask, "If I'm meant to feel my child's Spirit now, please help me."

A few seconds later she exclaimed, "I feel a really bright happy energy… I feel some excitement, which I haven't felt in a while. I hope I'm not making this up."

"Have you ever made up a feeling like this before?" I asked.

"No." Candice laughed. "Even if I tried, I wouldn't be able to make this wonderful feeling up. Am I crazy?"

"Do you feel crazy? Or just a sense of knowing?"

"Knowing. A whole body knowing."

At this point, it finally felt right to tell Candice what I'd seen years before especially since she was in a space where she could receive and discern the accuracy of the message herself.

I told her about the rainbowed swirl of energy and then asked her to feel if the *don't-worry-we'll-be-there-message* felt aligned to her.

"Definitely," she said. "I feel relieved, relaxed and solid. I've been so scared and tense. My mind makes up horrible stories, but my body knows. This feels true."

Then I described what I sensed earlier in the appointment. "Today what I received came from one Spirit and was more like a zap of electricity that instantly imprinted, 'Don't give up. It will be okay.'"

I searched for the words to convey the rest of the experience. "I'm not saying this will happen, but I have the sense it might take some time to get pregnant. Keep inviting the spiritual support you feel now to release any fear that comes up."

Candice sighed, checked the information I shared in her core, then sighed again. "I can't get clear now. Probably because I was wanting this to mean we didn't have to wait any longer. Does one Spirit mean I'll only be able to have one child?"

"I don't know," I said.

An incredibly difficult year followed with two more miscarriages before Candice conceived and carried to term a healthy energetic son. After he was born, she told me, "I don't know if I can go through any more loss and our doctor is cautious. We'd like to give Paul a sibling but ... we'll see."

A couple of years passed before I spoke to Candice again. "We have a little girl! A few months after we last spoke, we signed up to adopt, knowing it could take a while. But it didn't! It was a miracle how quickly this little one came to us. Everything went smoothly with none of the endless red tape and endless waiting I saw other couples experience. She's already a year old and a whirlwind like her brother."

Was the second spirit I saw around Candice long ago this little girl? I can't say for sure, but in my heart it feels true.

They are 6 and 4 now.

It may seem like these stories are about my ability to connect to Spirit. They aren't. I share them for two reasons.

First, to add another perspective to the conflicting views of difficult or unwanted pregnancies. My hope is one of the stories will awaken an intuitive truth for those who have lived through these difficult experiences. Many of my clients have lost children prematurely and their Spirits didn't show up in a session. Perhaps they were already born into their family, to someone else or like Bella's second child, didn't show himself to me. Or their brief experience of incarnation allowed them to start over, like Estelle's son, but in a different way. I don't know.

Second, is that these stories demonstrate how to enter the unknown and how to begin interpreting layered messages from Spirit. Intuition is the space where Spirit can merge to communicate with you. Your body is the place where the subtle communication of Spirit is translated.

Intuition is how I felt those incredible baby spirits. My essence met their essence in an inner space of possibility, the unknown. I never have an inkling of what will happen in any session. The first thing I do is to invite Divine help, which automatically takes me to the spaciousness of I-don't-know.

I don't know, the Divine does. Experiencing my divinity merged with the mystery of a vast benevolent space is when *knowing* becomes possible.

Your senses/body translates Divine messages. You will forever be learning to decipher the multilayered nature of intuitive language. That's why I asked Candice to check what I saw and felt "with her core."

If I receive an intuitive hit for my clients, or if they receive one, I ask them to feel the message in their bodies by breathing the words down inside. A physical response of expansion *(yes this makes sense)* or constriction *(no that's not quite right)* is invaluable. It's the body's inner signal of direct knowing.

Estelle didn't have any male relatives who died at 34. Instead of embracing the unknown, many people stop here, afraid they aren't really connected or aren't able to interpret the information presented. When a message doesn't land for you or someone else, an easy way to reenter that spaciousness is by inviting the unknown. I did and the number 34 remained moving, which led me to ask my body to translate again. Then I felt 34 moving counterclockwise, which prompted me to ask about the past, and this engaged Estelle's memory.

The rarity of these encounters suggests they came for a *Soul* reason, not a sole reason. Susan and I are grateful to those babies of Spirit that changed the trajectory of our lives. It's impossible to count the numerous gifts that unfolded over the years because of them.

Connecting with Spirit is not a test of your abilities. If it's a test at all, it's how comfortable you are hanging out in the unknown, the mystery. The place of Spirit, of Soul, is space. The reasons are hidden as to why people feel Spirit in different ways or why one Spirit shows up and another doesn't. This applies to all Spirits, not just babies.

Intuition is that vibrating color and love you had before this body and will continue to have after it. Tapping into your inner spaciousness is a way to connect to your purpose, your calling, your Soul.

Engaging your intuition is caressing your own indestructible, infinite, Divinity. This connection in*forms* this funny, fragile, miraculous human form you were born to be.

Invitation

Allow vision to soften.
Let the mind follow the breath to the spine.
Feel the ribs expand sideways, back and forward.
Release.
Now follow the breath to the spaciousness of the belly.
Let the mind meander around inside
as the space extends in all directions.
Release.
Feel the whole body's reaction to releasing air.
Feel the constriction of release.
Feel the spaciousness of following inhalation deep inside.
Feel this as a way to enter the space of the unknown,
The space of intuition,
The space with and without borders.
Feel the simplicity of the body's response to the breath.
Let go of how and why.
Acknowledge this is a location of endless expansion inside.
Feel how the sensation permeates and extends
beyond the boundaries of skin.
Or doesn't.
This is the space of mystery.
This is the space of the unknown.
The mind might argue or ask how.
Respond by following the breath inside.
Experience not-knowing and ask for help
being comfortable there.
This is where knowing arises.
Visit, without agenda, often.

36

Approaching the Invisible

Sound cannot penetrate my husband Michael's attention when he uses the weed whacker to edge our sidewalk. The grinding arrhythmic buzz, flying dirt, confettied grass, combined with his artful concentration, blind him to anything but a straight line.

I've tried over the years to get through the racket to deliver a timely message or remind him of other commitments. Yelling, whistling, arm waving at a safe distance, and a light touch on the arm elicit no response. Either I wait for him to turn the trimmer off or walk up behind him and place my hand firmly on his shoulder. I don't want to startle him, but inevitably I do.

My guess is that our guides in Spirit must go through something similar when they try to get our attention.

It might not seem like you weed-whack your way through life, yet in a way you do. It's normal to focus your senses on whatever job is in front of you. When you learn it's possible to feel the invisible world of Spirit, you focus your considerable attention the same way you have always focused on a task. You *try* to do. Or in this case you *try* to feel. *Trying* in the invisible realm usually ends in frustration. You need to approach life in a new way to engage the invisible.

Having witnessed countless people experience connections to Spirit, I've learned that encounters with the unseeable are different for everyone. Initially, many people get a sense of peace and relaxation. Some see colors with their eyes closed, smell scents or taste tastes that aren't physically there. They hear an old song in the back of their mind, feel warm or cool on one shoulder, arm or hand.

Initially, most don't recognize these examples as a Spirit connection. Often, I need to ask multiple questions to help clients discover the subtle sensory cues Spirit is offering.

But not with Henry. He approached life differently.

At 81, Henry asked for my help to connect with his mother. Though we'd become friends 10 years earlier at a soiree of my exotic poet-neighbor, I did not know his mother had died from cancer when he was only 6.

I also didn't know other parts of his past, including his extraordinary accomplishments: Yale grad, activist, professor, journalist, therapist, mythology student under Joseph Campbell, to name a few. Our conversations revolved around the healing arts, favorite restaurants, poetry, and night-time dreams.

Henry told me a month or two after we'd met that he'd dreamed of our meeting the night before the party. In the dream he saw a woman he knew but didn't recognize, with long curly red hair, wearing a large embroidered artsy-type wrap in a foyer with a grand stairway. Dream Henry walked up and greeted the woman warmly with a hug.

In reality, Henry said he was startled when we actually met. Every detail he had dreamed came to life in front of him. He realized that for the first time he had experienced precognition, seeing an event before it happened. He knew our meeting was important. One detail from his dream changed: He did not hug me. Instead, he introduced himself with a handshake.

Later Henry explained, he'd kept the dream about me to himself at first because he didn't want to "scare me or sound creepy" when we met. Even though, "It was like we'd known each other forever."

I agreed that when we met it felt like I'd known him forever. I shared that I was struck by his appearance as well. He looked like a younger version of my grandfather, same hairline, height and build.

Henry was 72 and I was 33. We began emailing and talking on the phone sporadically. We'd have concentrated back-and-forths emails for a few weeks, then a few months with no contact, to an occasional call with a flurry of exchanged ideas.

Sprinkled in between were in-person meetings. The only scheduled event we shared was a yearly "Dutch treat" lunch with our mutual friend, my poet/neighbor Susan. Our three birthdays were separated by two calendar days.

So when Henry invited me to lunch by saying, "I'll buy. I have a favor to ask," I paid attention.

We met at his favorite Mexican restaurant after the lunch rush so we'd have some privacy. Sitting in a quiet corner booth, Henry told me he'd been unconsciously searching for his mother his whole life. He was finally ready to do something about it and wanted to know if I could help him communicate with her. He gave me no other details.

I explained that sometimes we have the hardest time feeling the loved ones we most want to reach. I wanted to minimize his expectations and not get his hopes up. He understood and asked if I'd try.

"Of course," I replied, "but it doesn't matter what *I* feel or who comes. I want *you* to feel a connection and learn how to do this for yourself at home. Okay?"

Henry said that was exactly what he was looking for. I sat in the booth and inwardly asked how to help Henry connect to his mother.

I started by opening a protected circle of energy between us. "I ask that the divinity inside ourselves connects with whomever in Spirit you *need* to reach. I invite our master teachers in

Spirit and the light of the Divine so that all the work we do will be blessed. Does this invitation work for you?"

"Yes. I'd also like to invite my mother, Lucile, even if she's unable to come."

I nodded in acknowledgment then closed my eyes and felt a calm surround us. I was about to ask for the next step when a red-haired woman appeared to me. Her image came into the part of my brain where I remember how someone I know looks—but I didn't know her. I'd never seen this woman before. She had blue eyes, as did Henry. She didn't look like Henry. Her face was rounder, her eyes were big and looked a little sad. I *saw* her in my mind but felt her standing behind Henry.

"A woman with auburn hair, maybe 40ish with 1920s or 1930s-style clothing is standing behind you. Does that resemble your mom?"

Henry's eyes glistened. He gave a slow nod.

"Henry, close your eyes and let your mind follow your breath down into your heart. Yep. Nice and slow. Now ask your mother if she'll put a hand on one of your shoulders. Breathe into your heart and gently allow your awareness to feel if there is a difference between one shoulder and the other."

"There is," Henry said. "I feel warmth and softness not only in my shoulder but on my right ear and face. I'm asking if she'll hold my hand."

Henry took his time. His face showed awe as he slowly noticed every detail of sensation. "The warmth plus a kind of buzz has moved to my hand," he told me.

We asked Lucile to increase her connection with Henry.

"The buzz in my hand is stronger," he said.

Henry sat quietly reverent. I was silent until I sensed a heavy seriousness come over him. I told him that his relationship with his mother didn't have to be a serious matter.

"It's easier to deepen the connection if your approach is more playful."

Henry told me that his childhood relationship with his mother almost always felt serious because of her illness.

"Well, it doesn't have to be that way now," I said. "Let's strengthen your connection in a fun way. Ask her to stand in front of you instead of in back and tell me what happens."

We spent about 10 minutes asking his mother to stand in different places around him. Henry carefully tracked his inner changes: carefully testing the different sensations on either side of his body; expressing when he didn't feel much or when tiny changes occurred. Finally, I asked him where he'd like his mother to stand when she visited. He was a bit surprised that he had a choice. "Behind me on my right side is most comfortable, holding my hand."

Henry had many questions, the most important being: "Did she love me?"

"By saying that to me out loud, you just asked her," I said. "What are you experiencing now?"

"A sense of peace expanding."

"An expansive response usually affirms the question asked. It's a way for her to say, 'Yes. I loved you,' without words," I said.

Henry nodded with the barest smile.

"Now that you know you can feel your mother's presence, I suggest that you set aside some time to visit. Invite the Divine like we did today and write down questions for her Or just simply talk. Tell her everything you've wanted to tell her. You may not get a verbal response. Or you might.

"It's possible your hand might write a sentence that your mind isn't consciously aware of which answers a question or responds to something you share," I said. "Perhaps write down any thoughts or feelings that come to you. The most important thing is to drop your awareness into your heart, belly and hips so you can feel her presence. It may feel different than it does now. More subtle. If you need help I'm always here for you."

Henry liked the idea of writing and talking to his mother, and asked if having photos of Lucile around him would help. I told him to try different things, photos or items that belonged to her to see what felt good.

"Remember to close the session with her. Like ending a phone call, except thank the other Divine help that came as well. It can be as simple as saying, 'Thanks everyone. Great talking to you. Let's get together again soon,' before you say goodbye."

He closed his eyes, and I watched him sink down inside, silently ending the communication. When he opened his eyes, he smiled. "Well, that was something," he said.

For the next year I received many beautiful emails from Henry. He loved to help and affirm people. Over and over, he shared that not only did he feel a healing connection to his mother, he felt he knew more about himself.

Our correspondence stopped when Henry became too ill. He left this world a little over a month after his 83rd birthday. I know he would want me to share the following emails. The description of how he communicated with his mother might help others find connection with their loved ones.

Greetings,

I sat this morning in my favorite chair and spoke to my mother. I held out my hands and asked her to take my left hand in hers. Soon a buzz came into my hand. I said "Thank you; would you also take my right hand?" And the same reaction in my right hand, but stronger. I continued talking with her for quite a while. I told her I loved her and thanked her for bringing me into life and for being here today. I could feel energy maintained in both hands for half an hour or so.

I thought this would interest you.

Thanks for being with me on this journey. And for your help.

Henry

He sent this note a few months later:

Jennifer, I had a thought this morning. WOW! What a concept! But I did and that is *the reason for poetry is that it searches for the Divine,* and it occurs to me that the Divine is what is often exiled in our busy lives... Sharing this poem I wrote.

-- Blessings, Henry

When Mother returns

After decades ---- seven of them ----
In a black-and-white silent movie,
the marvel is that she is laughing:
something I never saw her do in life.

Now circumstance has given me this happy side
And I am getting to know the mother
I haven't known except in emptiness;
I feel I have a mother now:

Something new and wonderful:
We have developed a mode of communication,
And we are finding out a lot about each other.
Magic? Perhaps, but with its own reality.
HB 3 28 08

For Henry, the regular conversations with his mother, writing poetry and painting were his connections to the Divine. He told me once that poetry was his teacher and painting his meditation.

The few times we saw each other after the Mexican restaurant, I noticed a joy in him I hadn't seen before. Some members of his family, he said, thought his experiences with his deceased parent to be a sign of old age coupled with symptoms of his cancer. He was old enough not to care what they thought and continued to have long conversations with his mother. He told me she always answered through sensations, never words.

Henry was a great teacher to me by example. He had stopped weed-whacking his way through life and didn't discount subtle sensation. In doing so, he established a strong connection to the Divine part of himself. A friend told me that right before Henry died, he talked about joining his mother, his friends and poets. He told his minister, "There's no excuse for not knowing yourself. This (death) is a big change—there's nothing casual about It."

I'd tried for months to write this chapter. The day I was finally able to complete a first draft, I invited Henry to join me. I don't know why I didn't think to ask him before.

The idea came after I felt a strong desire to write outside on my porch. I always write inside and sit in the same chair. It was only after sitting on the porch that I remembered Henry's love of trees and the outdoors. I thanked him for getting my attention and asked for his help.

I didn't feel him over my shoulder or as a buzz. His help came from impulses I didn't initiate but was present for. The weed whacker analogy popped into my head like magic. Memories of him surfaced with clear sensory details. I jumped up at one point when I remembered that my old computer in the back of my closet might still have Henry's emails. It did.

I know Henry is still with me today helping me edit. The writing sessions for this chapter have the joy and melancholy of reconnecting with an old friend. Memories and ideas subtly surface. I never thought my fingers could move this quickly over the keys, catching nuances and anchoring them with words on the screen.

Months ago, when I tried to write about Henry, I'd been whacking hypothetical weeds. I was trying to bring up memories instead of letting them arise. I was focused on the straight line of getting Henry's story out and not on the possibility of receiving his help.

Thank you, Henry, for pointing me to the porch, where nature quieted me enough to feel your presence. Thank you also for reminding me to invite you every time I write. May your story inspire others to continue a relationship with their loved ones.

Invitation

Let the eyes rest.
Rest the mind.
Let the muscles rest.
Rest any part that wants to grab for an experience.
Let yourself remember a loved one
who is no longer here physically.
Notice where your body remembers them
by sight, smell, voice, touch…
Notice where the desire to feel their presence is
and ask to get curious.
Let curiosity of the subtlest change inside be the focus.
Ask that the divinity inside connect

to whomever in Spirit you need.
Invite your master teachers in Spirit and the light of the Divine.
Ask that the person you miss be with you now.
Ask that the connection be blessed.
Notice any difference in sensation around or inside.
Rest in the knowing that the smallest change is a response.
Feel an inner leaning back into your spine.
Notice any relaxation or opening sensation.
Ask for help letting go of expectations.
Linger a bit in the senses.
Say thanks to Spirit and body for the experience.
Know that connections always build.

An Invitation to Experience Your Guide(s)

"We are all leaves of one tree.
We are all waves of one sea."

~Thich Nhat Hanh

Now that you've read this book, you know that intuition is the infinite, the eternal Divine part of you.

I want to make sure it's clear that guides are not something outside of you. The part of you that is spirit is a part of all Spirit. Guidance is a part of you and separate from you all at once.

There are guides on this earth that help you every day. They are the friends you instinctively know to call upon that have information, a natural ability to help, guide, listen or simply be with you through anything.

Guides are friends, relatives, teachers, doctors, etc.— that we have on earth and we also have in Spirit. The difference is guides in Spirit are part of the invisible realms you have been exploring in this book. That is why if you awaken your senses and embody intuition you can experience help and guidance of many kinds.

Your own Soul is a guide to you.

Just like all people are different souls, there are souls in Spirit that have lived on earth before and can help guide and protect you. Some are relations or friends that have passed. Usually, you have Spirit teachers that you've known before in the energetic realm/heaven. Different guides come help you at different points in life, but there is a core group that remains with you always.

Yes, angels exist.

It is absolutely possible that an angel might show up for you. I used to think angels were total woo-woo, but since I've had personal experiences with them, I feel differently. Angels are powerful when they come to help, not airy-fairy at all. Believe it or not, Angels and all Divine guidance give practical help.

I'm all about practicality. Inviting a connection to have a direct experience with your guides using this invitation is practical. Divine guidance can't prevent you from what you need to learn in this life, but guides can help you navigate it as safely and as fully as possible.

When calling on the Divine that's what you are getting— God's help. If you feel afraid or unsure that you might be dealing with something not good, then skip this invitation. Your guides have no interest in scaring you. They only want to bring healing, help and comfort. That is why everyone doesn't feel this kind of help; their foundational beliefs don't permit it.

If you believe in a Divine guidance, you might also believe guides should communicate with you in a particular way.

They don't.

This invitation will help you begin to discover their unique way of communicating through physical sensation because it's difficult for your mind to disregard. It's also the fastest way to build trust. Let yourself be curious about the mystery of guides, drop your expectations, and see what happens.

You may want to sit up if you're laying down. (Though "lying down" grammatically correct, I was taught not to use the word "lying" because it signals a lie to our unconscious.)

Half of this invitation is to your body and the other half

is to your Spirit. Directed breath is a great way to open you to the optimal state to receive the subtle sensations required to communicate with your Guidance. The expanded state, created by breath and by slowing down, is more conducive for experiencing physical sensation.

If you start to get impatient and rush, don't worry about it. The mind wants what it wants. It gets in the way of receiving what it desires by rushing and having expectations about what should be going on. This can even happen to veterans of this work.

Be kind to yourself by recognizing what's happening in the moment. If expectations start to slide in or if you find yourself reading quickly to "just get to it," stop, close your eyes and see if you can pace yourself again. If not, come back to this invitation another time. No big deal.

This invitation is written so you don't have to stop and do anything. You may want to pause and close your eyes at certain points so you can focus on what you're feeling. Or you can just follow along as you read. Lingering in subtle sensation from the very beginning is the key to visceral experience. You may need some extra time or a different day. Or you might want to connect to your guide now. Your choice. You are always in control. Your guidance will never try to control you.

If you ever get the sense you are not in control, it usually means your mind is interfering. Guides suggest. They don't get offended if you get frustrated, lose focus or don't follow their advice. They are infinitely patient and are happy you are consciously connecting with them.

Also, please know that whether it's the first time you've read this invitation or the ninth time, each experience will be different. Your guidance likes to give you different experiences to help you release your expectations while developing a stronger long-term connection.

Remember, these helpers came because they love you. They are your friends. Enjoy your reunion.

Invitation

Notice how your body feels right now.
Now move that feeling into your memory so
you'll have something to compare later.
Slow your reading pace
to more easily experience
what you're reading, when you're reading it.
Invite your constant guide,
the one who has been with you since birth,
your guide of protection.
Simply say,
"I ask my divine guide,
that's been with me my whole life,
to come and be with me now."
Take slow deep breaths.
Feel your belly expand and contract when
the breath enters your belly, side ribs, chest, and jaw.
Notice how your awareness expands
from concentrating on reading this in your head
to being aware of expanding into your body.
Let your gaze soften while reading.
Allow the words to slowly float into your eyes.
Notice your breath's gentle movement in your back.
Keep your eyes soft on the words

and extend a softer inner gaze to your lower back.
Acknowledge the feeling you find there.
If there's any discomfort in any part of your body,
ask that spaciousness and healing ride
in on your breath for those areas.
Now take your time and include the rest of your back
with your breath.
Move up the spine from the low back,
value how your breath moves the back ribs and shoulder blades
with your soft inner gaze.
Allow your breathing and inner gaze to join your back to
the awakened parts of your front body.
With a long filling inhale,
slowly expand your mental awareness throughout your body
to connect your torso to your thighs, calves and feet.
Exhale gradually from your chest down your arms,
feeling every muscle gliding down into your hands.
Notice the delicate pulse of your heart in your fingertips,
follow its rhythm into your whole body.
Acknowledge one or two subtle differences
in how your body feels now
versus when you started the invitation.
Smile and ask the guide you invited to,
"Please stand directly behind me."
Take a sweeping breath through your nose
and down your back to awaken to more sensation.
Notice if there is any difference in the way the air feels
around your back with your guide standing there.

Ask your skin to feel any change in temperature.
Notice any image in your mind's eye,
a faint smell or a new sound that arrives.
You might get a feeling
somewhat like when a friend walks into a room behind you.
Take a moment and recognize
that this Divine being is your friend
who has given you the best protection they could
from when you were conceived.
Keep your gaze soft,
let your mind drop down into your heart,
like an elevator.
Ask your guide to put their hands on your shoulder,
just one shoulder.
Release a breath down, sensing both shoulders.
Notice if your right shoulder feels different
from your left shoulder.
Relax.
You have nothing to do other than reading and being curious.
Take your time exploring both shoulders with your breath.
Lead with your curiosity and ask your guide,
"Please increase the pressure on one shoulder."
See if there's any change.
Take your time,
clues to the invisible world can be minute.
Return to savoring the feeling
of your whole body being in sync
by breathing all the way to your toes.

Release your breath with a deep sigh through your mouth,
rest into the weight in your bottom.
Be sensitive to any differences
in the way your right and left sides feel now.
Briefly shift focus to your shoulders,
then extend that awareness into your sides.
Check to see if there is an effect on either
or both sides of the body.
If you have been feeling clear sensations from the beginning,
savor this time.
Create a conscious connection with your guide by
simply relaxing with awareness
of the change in sensation your guide brings.
Breathe in through your nose.
Bring your whole body awake to full sensation.
Release your breath.
Notice the movement
from the back of your ankles
to the web of your fingers.
Ask your guide to,
"Please let go of my shoulder and stand firmly behind me."
Notice any changes in temperature,
weight and awareness.
Take a breath from the top of your head to your tailbone to
re-enliven your spine.
Ask your guide to,
"Please step 20 feet behind me."
Know that physical space restraints are not an issue

in an energetic realm.
Notice if something behind you changed.
Breathe in any differences...
a pull, a stretch, a change in temperature...
Ask your guide to, "Step close behind me again."
Investigate any subtle difference
in physical sensation, the air, emotions, or texture.
Linger here with your guide.
Ask, "Please touch both of my shoulders."
Bring your awareness to your shoulders
and sense for any change.
Ask, "Please make the connection stronger between us."
Be alert to what happens.
Now call on your body to
remember the feeling you put to memory
when you began.
Honor any differences, big or small.
Know that your work guidance will continue
anywhere or anytime.
Acknowledge that this is Soul work
therefore blessed.

In Closing

I hope this closing will be a continued opening to deepen your relationship with intuition.

I invite you to stay curious. Honestly, my intuition shows up a bit differently all of the time. Building this relationship is a constant process of getting to know each other step-by-step, in the moment.

Yes, your Soul is getting to know you, too. Getting to know who you are in this physical form. Helping you stretch and explore more of who you can be.

I invite you to use discernment and have fun when getting intuitive information *for yourself*. It took a long time for me to be discerning about who I shared my own intuitive messages with, as you read in the *Gaslighting* chapter. I longed for a trusted friend who also explored their intuitive insights.

Ask a friend if they are interested in intuition. If they are, ask if they are interested in exploring with you: sharing synchronicities, places they find in their body where intuition hums, and experiences with guides to encourage and question each other. This is a fast and fun way to build your confidence and skill.

A fast way to get frustrated is to share your personal insights with just anyone. I hate to say this but you'll often look like a crazy person. Most people lose ground in relating to their intuition when this occurs.

The reason much of the mystical arts can't be talked about is because an experience is needed to understand the concepts. Words don't convey the whole meaning. Only experience does. When sharing experiences with willing friends, your intuitive relationship will thrive.

So why write a book if words are incapable of conveying a supernatural experience? Our minds like examples of what's possible before we experience the mystical ourselves. That's why the invitations came after the stories so you can have your own experience. I hope my words have given you a way to keep the aperture of your intuitive focus, heart and mind wide open.

I also invite you to use caution and discernment when sharing intuitive information you receive *for others*. I know people who say they want intuitive input and in actuality are frightened by it. You don't want anyone to be afraid. Besides, you understand by now that sometimes intuition is literal, sometimes it's symbolic, and often it is hard to tell the difference.

There are other tricky things about using your intuition with others. I call this phenomenon "intuitive dyslexia." For example, I've never once been accurate (in person) with whether a friend's baby will be a girl or a boy. Those are incredible odds. When you figure out the things you are usually wrong on, you begin to establish a more complex relationship with your intuition. Here's another example.

As you may recall, at the beginning of my career I didn't empower people to use their intuition. I did tarot readings to give clients something to look at and to give me further insight on my intuitive information about them.

A new client came in wanting a reading. She sat sideways across from me, never looking at me or the cards. Very quickly I received one of the clearest messages I'd ever received from Spirit. I told her verbatim what I had heard and seen. She abruptly stood up, finally looked at me with disgust and said, "You are shit. That is the exact opposite of what I need to do," and stormed out.

I was confused and upset. I spent the rest of the time I'd allotted for the client with my friend Susan trying to figure out what had gone wrong. Neither of us had any idea why a clear message would glean this result. A few days later the answer came.

One of my regular clients came in who didn't like tarot cards, so I just used my intuition to tell her what I saw. Again, I quickly received a very clear message, which I shared. She gave me a funny look and said, "That's so weird. You got the topic I wanted to focus on correct, but it's the exact opposite of what I've been thinking about doing."

At first, I thought I was broken. Then I asked my deep insides, "What's going on?"

What I heard was, "Ask her if she is clearer on the decision she already made?"

I was astonished when she answered, "Yes."

I asked her how that happened when I was so far off the mark. She said, "You weren't completely off the mark. You got the topic right and we've never discussed that before. Plus, when you said the opposite, I knew what to do. Because you were so wrong, I could *feel* what was *right*."

My intuition gave my client exactly what she required to empower her. She needed to make that decision by herself. The reading wasn't about me being right. It wasn't about me giving her the answer. It was about me providing her with the means to find direction herself. Hearing the exact opposite of what she felt was right allowed her to feel the inner "No" that pointed her to "Yes."

Like I said, a relationship with your intuition is complex. That reading redirected me from a career to a vocation. You never know where your intuition may send you.

In closing, here's an inspiring way to nourish a deeper relationship with your Soul.

The grandmother of my late friend and mentor, Sobonfu Somé, had a ritual for the children when they woke up in their African village. First, they had to go out to greet the world. Then they welcomed their Soul *and* each other back every morning with a big jump up.

Sobonfu exuberantly demonstrated. Her arms were wide as she jumped up then landed with her arms tightly wrapped around her. With a wide smile she yelled: "Welcome me! Welcome Sobonfu back to this body, this tribe and this world." She turned and gave me a tremendous hug and sang, "Welcome Jennifer! I welcome you back to this house, this family and me!" She was taught that our spirits journeyed at night and to call her Soul back to her body each day.

I was not taught how to embody my Soul, let alone every morning. Most of us weren't. This is why we need to invite and nourish a relationship with our whole selves daily. Sobonfu told her students that if she didn't welcome her own Spirit, it was hard to welcome anyone else, or to be honest and genuine with those around her.

Remember: You know. And You know when you don't know. Intuitive living is circular, enlivening, messy, and fun. Intuitive living pokes our curiosity and prods exploration. Intuitive living is easiest with a playful attitude. Intuitive living is wide, Soul-infused and we can all live it.

Get to know your Soul, your intuition.
Invite it.
Nourish it.
Build a relationship together.
See where it leads you.

With Gratitude

*"Cultivate the habit of being grateful for every good thing
that comes to you, and to give thanks continuously.
And because all things have contributed to your advancement,
you should include all things in your gratitude."*
~Ralph Waldo Emerson

There are so many people to thank for their help with this book and my career which led to writing it. I've attempted to name everyone, even those who have passed away and those I haven't had contact with for a very long time. To those not named, I'm sure I will fly awake in the middle of the night remembering my oversight—please forgive me.

To all of the marvelous people I am blessed to work with, thank you for sharing your stories. I know you will help and inspire many to connect to their intuition. You have helped me have the best job in the world. I love you dearly.

To Sobonfu Somé, thank you for your love, guidance, rituals, and bossiness. Without you I might never have listened to the call to write. I miss you my friend.

This book was made infinitely better by:

The forewords written by Kathie Collins and George Tanber. Thank you for your time, candor, generosity and stories—they touch me deeply. I know your words will echo inside others as well.

My dear friend Kathleen Miritello. Thank you for your eagle eye, knowledge, care, time, and love put into copyediting this book.

My talented book designer Elsa Safir. Thank you for your loving patience. And for taking such time and care to tune into your intuition when creating what this book needed to look and feel like, I couldn't be happier with the result.

My friend and the extremely talented photographer, Amy Hart, who took my author's photo. I am typically not photogenic. Thank you for capturing my essence through your eyes.

Everyone enrolled in and who taught the 2019 Charlotte Lit Authors Lab. Thank you especially to Kathie Collins, Sarah Creech, Paul Reali, and Kim Wright. Also, to Patrice Gopo for teaching me about the possibilities of essay before the Lab started.

My AWE Circle writing cohort, Nancy Zupanic, Rebecca Wallace, Daphne Thompson *(Cold War Crossing, Jordan Williams)*, Meredith Richie *(Poster Girls)*, and Rebecca Jones. Thank for your love, incredible skills, holding me to deadlines, cheering me on, believing in this book and teaching me to write with your insightful feedback.

My dear friend Joanne Brunn. Thank you for enthusiastically reading *everything* that I've written (even when it was really bad), offering gentle corrections and not letting me off the hook of this book for the last 20 years.

My Beta Readers. They read the first draft and pointed out errors, concepts that didn't make sense, and wording that could be misconstrued. This is a time-consuming job in which they only receive a thank you. I was incredibly fortunate to have several talented writers, a minister, a client, and a friend of 45 years volunteer. I am incapable of expressing the depth of gratitude I have for each of your perspectives and feedback. Thank you Joanne Brunn, Kathie Collins, Nadine Ellsworth Moran,

Mary Wiedmuller Knierim, Tara Nauful, Paul Reali and George Tanber.

Thank you to Katharine Sands who wrote a spot-on book description that I'm sure will inspire readers to access their own intuition.

I am deeply grateful for:

Phyllis Rollins for introducing me to energy work, inviting me to hold classes in her studio and *not* allowing me to quit when I was faltering. And for being my longtime yoga teacher, neighbor and friend.

Susan Hough, Ashley Poliak Hammad, Branner and Chuck Grimsley, for inviting me into your family every month for 13 years. I can't imagine my life without all of the bathtimes, comforting meals, reading bedtime stories, haircuts, popcorn dinners, snow shovelings, Christmas parades, running hugs, sharing dreams in the morning, gatherings of people, so much love and so much more. Without you, Susan, I wouldn't be doing this work. Thank you.

Jane & Bill Armstrong for the many times they offered (and I accepted) staying at their waterside home. Being there helped me to focus and write the beginnings of this book while taking beach walks, eating wonderful food and watching dolphins from the top porch.

Beverly Marlow, Lee, Bruce & Addi Davis for the month-long writer's residency in Falmouth, MA. I completed the last 9 chapters of this book on their porch looking out at a beautiful bay, basking in friendship, card readings, and great food.

My mother's friends (and mine), Elizabeth Frederick, Jane & Jim Billingsley, Lewis & Angela Fowler, Char King, Kathy Miritello, Ann Miller, Karol Mackey, Laura Davidson and Mollie Cardell for checking on her, bringing food, alerting me to problems when I couldn't be there, and helping her with so many little things I'll never know about. And to

Shante Pearson for caring for my mother's dog, Murphey, so my mother wouldn't worry while she was in the hospital for six weeks. Also, for promising to adopt Murphey after she died which gave my mom so much peace. Thank you all for loving my mom, I know she dearly loved you all.

Jon Shannon for taking me to the Black Mountain Music Festival and for introducing me to Deborah Munroe, who gave me a home in Charlotte and continues to be my Tracy-Chapman-playing friend. And for allowing me to use your names in the book.

Kristen Forno for generously giving me advice on what and how to do things on my website and with social media that I didn't even know were possible. Over the many years we've worked together, you've never once made me feel stupid even though I can be a *very* slow learner.

My 3-G friends Paula Smith and Catherine Rains. I couldn't ask for more compassionate, talented, generous, loving support over good food, conversation and laughter.

My Coker girls Donna Craig, Gaye Hopkins Graham and Kim Nesbitt Wilberger. I appreciate your friendship, riotously fun memories, and allowing me to use your real names.

My EP Gals, Kathleen Schneider, Rebecca Haworth and Karon Luddy, for years of meeting at Wingmaker, beach-time readings, creative talks, shared food and space, and consistent encouragement.

My Kool Group family, Mary Elizabeth DeAngelis, Ed, Vincent & Allison Williams; Tim Funk; Kathy Haight, Jim, Max & Will Morrill; Carol Leonnig, John, Elise & Molly Reeder, for SJR questions, great food, mind blowing playlists, dancing, wicked humor and full hearts.

St. Francis Springs Prayer Center in Stoneville, N.C., for being a supportive place of solitude, kindness and generosity, especially Kay Barnett, Ann Bauer, Father Louis Canino, Father David Hyman, Tony Nitz, Bob Pearson, and Steve Swayne.

My accomplished reviewers, Catherine Anderson, Jenni Field, Susan Hough, Catherine Rains, and Patrick Scott, for working with a tight deadline to read the book and write a review before it was published. I know that technically I'm not supposed to thank reviewers but—thank you all so very much!

My Healing Family, Jane Appleby, Gail Brenz, Rosalyn Bruyere, Laura Davidson, Gerry Hartmeyer, Elaine Kain, Dinah Kitchens, Jen McLamb, Karol Mackey, Ann Miller, and Kathy Miritello, for making life more meaningful with eclipse blessings, Covid grace, incredible birthday wishes, labyrinth magic, connection and prayers.

I'm grateful for all of the friendship, support, and remarkable kindness I received over the years from: Gary & Alison Albert; Paul Anderson; Heidi Bellairs; Henry Berne; Dean Best; Beckwith Bolle; Marie Bott; Carolina Brown; Caroline C Brown; Chip Brown; Charlie Burt & Karen Kinsley; Jessica Cardimon; Lin Hiley Carey; Betsy Carpentier; Mary Chamberland; Laura Chapman; Scott Chapman & Carol DeFranca; Cynthia Cloud; Wanda & Gene Cosnahan; Catherine Craig; Dan Crawford; Jason, Maryeli & Dylan Culbreth; Nancy Cullen; Nancy & Marilyn Curtis; Harry & Becca Dalton; Glenn Danzler; Lee, Bruce, Matt & Elizabeth Davis; Dottie Deans; Carol De Santo; Dona Dickenson; Charlotte Doerner; Lynne, Dewey, Hank & Molly Dunne; Scott Ely & Susan Ludvigson; Alix Felsing & Tommy Tomlinson; Martha Ferrante; Kathryn Ferner; Brian & Cynthia Fillman; Connie Fogle; Shelley Forrester; Mitch Francis; Eileen & Scott Friars; Beverly Frye; Lou Gallagher; Fran Gardner; Karen Garloch; Irene Giessl & Barb Hensley; Jason, Susan, Abigail & Ben Gilliam; Harriet & Martin Goode; Debbie & Stan Gregor; Akasha Halsey, Bill Hannah; Terri Harris; Heidi Thompson-Henyon; Marcia & Paul Hersey; Stuart & Heidi Darr-Hope; Shannon & Gretchen Hope; Carly Howard; Scott & Julie Hubbard; Dan Huntley; Kim Blum-Hyclak; Kathy Izard; Karen Jackley; Pam Jamison; Jenifer Janovy;

Mickey Jenkins; Paul Jordan, Libby & Zeke Neely; Aimee Kehoe; Kevin Kennedy; Judith Kent; Jim Kepner; Sharon Kershner; Michelle & Michael King; Stacey Klein; Carol Kost; Kathleen Kost & John Walker; Margaret Kupferle; Bob Lawson & Joe Tate; Jeri Leach; Dani Lewis; Lois Liggett; Rachel Linnett; Valerie Louis; Jane Luce; Cheryl Lyerly; Sue McClam; Elaine McDonough; Dusty McGinty; Beth Mack; Debbie Maravetz; Paul Matheny; Mary Beth Mayhall; David Menear; Jessica Miller; Kent Miller; Lisa Miller; Jeanna Mills; Jeff & Grainne Miser; Dianne Moore; Dottie Moore; Erin & Steve Marino; Cheryl Morway; Elissa Nauful; Terry Nicholetti; Dan Nichols; Mary Lynn Norton; Dale O'Brien; Terri Ober; Kim & Michael O'Donnell; Susan O'Malley; Thom Overton & Jodi Tompros; Michael Pane; Suzi Peetros; Lori Phannenstiel; Cathy Pickens; Kathy Policaro; Jack Pringle; Dannye & Lew Powell; Barbara Richards; Jeff Riehm; Beth Rollinson; Catherine Romelfanger; Regina Rubeo; Faith Russell; Carol Saunders; Bren & Helen Schell; Sue Schweikart; Susan, Jenna (Jack & Charlie Ruhle) & Michaela Scott; Deborah Semple; Connie & Jessica Shade; Ruchi Shah; Annie Shaw; Terry Shaw; Ann Shengold; Gaye Shelley; Sally Sibley; Debbie Siday; Jan Iris Smith; Heather Snyder; Brenda & Larry Sorkin; Christina Summer; Ben Taylor; Brittany Taylor; Gwen Thompson; Stacy Thompson; Karla Tropea; Carol Trull; Lou Veltri; Alf & Caroline Rust Ward; Joana Wardell; Maureen Watson; Janet Wayland; Molly, William, Griffin & Chandler West; Shirley White; Beate Wolf; Mei Ping Yang; and Betty Zane.

There are many more phenomenally kind people in my life—thank you all.

I am especially grateful for my family:

My dad, Larry Halls, for always trying to understand what it is I actually do for a living. And to Jackie Halls and her mom Eula Smith for loving him and me. I love y'all so much.

I was blessed to have my mom, Jean Halls Hollister, who used intuition every day, usually without knowing it. She believed in me and cheered me on in whatever I chose to do. She wanted to see this book published. Instead, she listened intently as I read it to her before she died. I love and miss you, Mom.

My grandparents Harold & Milouise Halls and Harold & Bernice Rauschert.

My brother Jay Halls and his children and grandchildren, Kaj, Lianne, James and Brian Halls; Jay, Courtney, Ivy & Ava Halls; Amanda, (Nick Wines) & Mila Halls

My entire family: Milo, Sandy (Jodi Broll), Bill, Kathy Wallingsford, Jim & Melonee (Christine, Charlie, Tyler, Dillon, Hunter Crawford) Jimmy, Amy & Ava Halls; Tom, David, Claire, Martha (Roy Welburn), Peter & Stephanie Gordon; Cathy & Pete Hasbrouck; Susan Hough, Ashley, Amir & Paolo Hammad, Branner Grimsley & Sarah Rowan; Jennifer, Olivia, Winston, David, Holly, Graham, Reid, Korra & Nia Hollister; Cal Kennedy; Marilyn Kirshner; Amy Lassiter; Jorie, Steve, Susan, Pete, Jack, Tommie, Frankie & Penny O'Malley; Sonrisa Reed & Emmett Trippe; Andrew, Rob, John, Evelyn, Matt, Kim & Katy Stetson, Elvera & Astrid (Jacob-Jan, Niek & Roosmarijn Appelman) van Diepen, Tao & Jessica Ventre.

And my ancestors: The Beards, Emersons, Gosnells, Halls', Hamiltons, Hazels, Huntingtons, Kelleys, Rauscherts, Roots, Tishers, & Tubaughs.

I am grateful to the generous teachers that I have learned from in person: Sobonfu Somé, Rev. Dr. Lauren Artress, Catherine Anderson, Rev. Rosalyn Bruyére, Erin Butterworth, Kim Chalmers, Arn Chorn-Pond, Phil Cousineau, David Davis, Dr Malcolm Doubles, Joy Drake, Chris Faulkner, Jessica Fleming, Chip Fortney, Elaine Geouge, Jean Grosser,

Mary Branch Grove, Shelby Hammitt, Susan Harper, Claudine Kurtz, Rebecca Lawson, George Lellis, Pat Lincoln, Jen McLamb, Maggie McMahon, Conner Middelmann, Don Riggs, Phyllis Rollins, Tosha Silver, Brenda Sorkin, Hyemeyohsts & Swan Storm, Mary VanDeWiel, Helen Yamada, and the 33rd leader of the Bon-Po, His Holiness the Gyalwa Menriwa.

I am fortunate to live in a time where wise teachings are available at the push of a button. I am thankful for and inspired by these written and audio teachings from: Nadia Bolz-Weber, Gregory Boyle, Brené Brown, Stephen Harrod Buhner, Pema Chödrön, Wayne Dyer, Clarissa Pinkola Estes, Mathew Fox, Khalilil Gibran, Elizabeth Gilbert, Adam Grant, Hafiz, Thich Nhat Hanh, His Holiness the Dalai Lama, Benjamin Hoff, Stephen King, Anne Lamott, Eileen McKusick, Cesar Millan, Vusamazulu Mutwa, Mark Nepo, John O'Donoghue, Mary Oliver, Rachel Naomi Remen, Rumi ... to name a few.

Thanks to our sweet black Labradors: Louise, Ann and Madison. Each laid by my side—one following the other—over the past 15 years while I wrote. All shared their love and support to calm me, make me play or stop me at the perfect time.

Finally, to my husband, Michael Gordon. Many of our friends assumed that you (being a professional writer) were writing this book for me. You quickly corrected them and praised my writing ability. Thank you for helping me *hard* edit eight of the chapters and do the final edits of the whole book. You made this book better. You make me better. I love you dearly and am beyond grateful that you found me.

"Gratitude is a celebration of love."
~Br. David Steindl-Rast

About the Author

Jennifer Halls is an intuition consultant, trance medium, author, artist, speaker and educator. She has led more than 25,000 sessions to help clients experience, understand and nurture a relationship with their intuition. She values intuitive methods that are straightforward, practical, fun, and timesaving.

Her first book, *The Runes Workshop: A You know.® Intuition*

Workbook, helps you gain insight and perspective on any situation.

Runes are ancient symbols of wisdom that guide us to our intuition. They are easy to learn, create and understand.

On her website, Youknow.net, Jennifer offers more than 175 TuneInward audio teachings that engage, open and nourish different aspects of intuition.

Jennifer shares a three-porch, butter-yellow home in South Carolina with her husband, Michael Gordon. There, between sessions with clients, she writes, draws, and takes daily walks along the Catawba River, marveling at the subtle changes in nature throughout the seasons.